OUT IN THE PULPIT

The Lived Experiences
of Lesbian Clergy in
Four Protestant Mainline
Denominations

PAMELA PATER-ENNIS, PHD

LifeRich Publishing is a registered trademark of The Reader's Digest Association, Inc.

LifeRich Publishing books may be ordered through booksellers or by contacting:

LifeRich Publishing
1663 Liberty Drive
Bloomington, IN 47403
www.liferichpublishing.com
1 (888) 238-8637

ISBN: 978-1-4897-2601-8 (sc)
ISBN: 978-1-4897-2602-5 (hc)
ISBN: 978-1-4897-2603-2 (e)

Library of Congress Control Number: 2019917158

Print information available on the last page.

LifeRich Publishing rev. date: 10/25/2019

To the brave women, out in the pulpit, who unabashedly told their stories so that the women who come after them will not have to struggle so much in the church that they love.

CONTENTS

ACKNOWLEDGMENTS

Over this decade-plus of working on my dissertation, there are many people I want to acknowledge for getting me through the project. First, I want to thank the women who courageously agreed to be interviewed for this project. Without the women's poignant stories of pain, healing, and tenacity, this dissertation would not have reached its completion. Secondly, I want to thank my dissertation committee members for taking time away from their personal lives to guide me through this work: Dr. Robert L. Miller Jr., adviser; Dr. Katharine Briar-Larson; and Dr. Zulema E. Suarez. Next, I want to thank my research assistants for their tedious work in transcribing the interviews: Sarah Pater, my niece; Meghan Aileen Hayes, MSW; Caroline Sarayai, MA; Leah Dunlap-Ennis, my daughter, who completed the transcriptions. I also want to extend my gratitude to my third "daughter," Alexandria Tava, who assisted me in some preliminary editing processes. In addition, I extend the sincerest gratitude to my first professional editor, Jacob Miller, who began the editing process. My second professional editor, Evelyn Kintner, got this project completed, and I am deeply indebted to her and her heaven-sent skills.

Last but not least, I want to thank my family for always believing in me and in this project. First, my two daughters, who became adults in the time I completed my degree. Second, of course, my husband and never-failing partner in ministry, Rev. Mark William Ennis, for supporting me in wherever my career has taken me. Thank you, Mark, for personally letting me bounce ideas off of you again and again and for being very, very patient while I completed this project.

LIST OF TABLES

ABSTRACT

This study explores the multiplicity of challenging issues that lesbian clergy face today from a social work perspective, utilizing the intersecting concepts found in social work and theology as an interpretive framework. From the social work perspective, the theoretical constructs of social identity theory, ecological theory, and anti-oppressive theory inform the qualitative questions of this study. Answers flow from the data extracted from interviews with the sample, utilizing modified *grounded theory* and *listening guide* methodologies to give voice to the lesbian clergy and the challenges that they faced due to their religious, spiritual, and sexual identities. Specifically, this is a qualitative study offering new insights into the current debate about the inclusion or exclusion of lesbian clergy in four Protestant mainline denominations: the Reformed Church in America (RCA), the Evangelical Lutheran Church in America (ELCA), the Presbyterian Church in the USA (PCUSA), and the United Church of Christ (UCC). While lesbian clergy remain marginalized in each of these denominations, nonetheless, this study reveals the many positive contributions made to the church and society by these lesbian clergy, who remain active in their denominations and utilize their abilities to benefit their congregations.

CHAPTER 1

INTRODUCTION TO
THE STUDY

BACKGROUND

In the last fifty years or so, female clergy have in general made great strides in moving into leadership positions in their mainline denominations. However, they still lag behind their male counterparts in terms of the types of positions they can get. According to a phenomenon called the "stained glass ceiling" (Purvis 1995), female clergy are more likely to have less prestigious positions for less pay and often serve outside a parish setting (RCA Commission on Women 2011). In general, female clergy still are not accepted as widely as male clergy in most mainline Protestant denominations. And if one considers the lesbian subset of female clergy, the problems of unequal treatment and marginalization expand exponentially. A survey (Hartford Institute for Religion Research 1994) of most major denominations in the United States revealed that female clergy make only 91 percent of the salary that male clergy make, when adjusted for denomination, size of the congregations, and title. For lesbian clergy, this trend is compounded by the increased problems they find when competing with straight female colleagues for jobs.

The influence of theology, biblical translations, psychology, and behavioral science on lesbian clergy is explored in the literature review. Specifically, through a theological perspective, the concepts of sin and purity are examined in terms of homosexuality (Via and Gagnon 2003; Gagnon 2001; Helminiak 2000; Rogers 2006; Miner and Connoley 2008; Scanzoni and Mollenkott 1994; Scroggs 1983; McNeil J. 1998; Heyward 1984; Heyward 1989; Heyward 2000; Douglas 1999; McNeill 1993) by employing biblical interpretation to explain the various stances toward homosexuality. Furthermore, the theoretical constructs of social identity theory (Tajfel and Turner 1979), ecological theory (Gitterman and Germain 2008), and anti-oppressive theory (Dominelli 2002) are utilized to guide the questions and the analyses for this study. The study consists of data extracted from extensive interviews utilizing both grounded theory and the listening guide to glean the often ignored voices of the lesbian clergy, with particular attention to their religious, spiritual, and sexual identities.

DISCRIMINATION OF LESBIANS IN SOCIETY

Before discussing the discrimination of lesbian clergy specifically, it is important to explore the broader context in which lesbians experience employment discrimination in the general population. Compared to straight women, lesbians are more likely to face discrimination in the job market (Cowan 2011). Thus, lesbians are more likely to experience employment discrimination, report less job satisfaction, and have higher poverty rates than heterosexual women.

EMPLOYMENT DISCRIMINATION

There is a dearth of studies on sexual orientation and labor outcomes, and for those few studies that do exist, measurements tend to vary from country to country on employment statistics. The findings on labor studies regarding lesbians appear to be ambiguous in Western countries. In the United States, during the period between 1980 and 1991, 44 percent of lesbian, gay, bisexual, and transgender (LGBT) persons reported discrimination in employment (National LGBTQ Task Force 2015). Whereas gay men generally earn less than heterosexual males, in some countries lesbians

2

actually earn the same or more than heterosexual women (Drydakis 2015). Interestingly, in the United States, lesbians earn 20 percent (Sears and Mallory 2011) more than heterosexual women when controlling for education, skills, and experience. Comparatively, research has shown that lesbians do earn less than heterosexual women. For instance, a survey in the United Kingdom revealed that the average salary is 1.4 percent less for LGBT persons than for heterosexuals and that LGBT persons are 5 percent less likely to be offered jobs than their heterosexual counterparts (Drydakis 2015). Within the same study, there were sixty-three heterosexual women who were offered jobs in the human services sector, but there were no examples of only lesbian candidates being offered even an interview.

In the United States, lesbians earning more than their heterosexual counterparts may appear to contradict perceptions that employers discriminate based on sexual orientation (Badgett and Frank 2007). However, this may be a self-selecting function of lesbians early on investing in more education and tracking earlier into high-powered careers that require longer hours rather than entering traditional household patterns generally held by their heterosexual counterparts (Badgett and Frank 2007). As noted by Badgett and Frank (2007), they may also have been less likely to adopt traditional gender-biased careers for women (Badgett and Frank 2007). Despite the higher levels of earning power reported for lesbians living in the United States, it is unclear how much variation there is from region to region. In addition, Cowan (2011) argues that those persons who have a minority sexual orientation still experience more obstacles to getting a job, express lower job satisfaction, and report higher levels of bullying and harassment at work.

JOB SATISFACTION

According to a meta-analysis on LGBT employment studies conducted by Sears and Mallory (2011), all the qualitative studies examined suggest that gay and lesbian employees are more likely to be harassed by work colleagues than their heterosexual counterparts. Half of gay and lesbian employees do not reveal their sexual orientation in the labor market for fear of discrimination (Sear and Mallory 2011; Badgett 2007). In contrast, gay and lesbian workers who do reveal their sexual orientation report higher levels of job satisfaction and more ability to be creative (Sears and Mallory 2011; Blodgett 2007). Keeping one's sexual orientation a secret leads to anxiety and stress, which can undermine work productivity and job satisfaction (Sear and Mallory 2011; Badgett 2007).

POVERTY RATES

Research has shown that lesbians earn less than heterosexual women. Poverty among LGBT persons is as high as, or higher than, among the heterosexual population (Sears and Mallory 2011). However, according to the University at California, Los Angeles (UCLA) Williams Institute (2009), studies have found that 24 percent of lesbians and 15 percent of gay and bisexual men are at the poverty level, compared to 19 percent and 13 percent of heterosexual women and men, respectively, in the United States (Sears and Mallory 2011; Badgett 2007).

MEDICAL COVERAGE

Reflective of the LGBT poverty rates, this population has corresponding poor medical coverage. According to the National Gay and Lesbian Task Force Policy Institute (2015), LGBT people are twice as likely to be uninsured as the general population. According to a recent report, 22 percent of gay and lesbian respondents reported having no insurance, compared to 12 percent of heterosexual adults (National LGBTQ Task Force 2015).

THE STORY OF HOMOSEXUAL CLERGY

The issue of homosexuality in mainline Protestant churches is currently considered the most divisive and debated issue (Olson and Cadge 2002). In 1997–1998, and again in 2002, Hartford Theological Seminary conducted a study that sampled membership in many mainline Protestant denominations in the United States regarding their views of homosexual inclusion, which still is relevant today (the Hartford Institute for Religion Research 2002, 2007).

History of Lesbian Clergy

Female clergy still are not accepted as widely as male clergy in most mainline Protestant denominations. Although there is no literature to support the assertion that the employability of lesbian clergy is even more limited than that of their straight female colleagues, anecdotally there appear to be existing attitudes within congregations that prevent the hiring of lesbian clergy (Hartford 1998), despite the recent passage of denominational policies allowing LGBT ordination (ELCA 2009; PCUSA 2011). By extrapolation, lesbian clergy, who are not yet recognized as legitimate through denominational legislation, would appear to have virtually no opportunities for ministry. With few exceptions, lesbian clergy can serve in ministries within the Reformed Church in America, but their geographic movement is limited. In the Presbyterian Church (USA) and Evangelical Lutheran Church in America, there remain regional pockets of significant discrimination against employability, despite legislation allowing their employment, of lesbian clergy (Kaleem 2011). In the United Church of Christ, lesbian clergy are more employable than the other three denominations; the first male homosexual minister was ordained in 1972 in the United Church of Christ (UCC.org). In the Evangelical Lutheran Church, LGBT persons have been able to be ordained since 2009 (ELCA. org), and in the Presbyterian Church (USA), LGBT persons have been able to be ordained since 2011 (PCUSA.org). In the Reformed Church in America, there are openly LGBT clergy, but at the time of this writing, there is no legislation protecting them (RCA.org). See table 1 for evidence of these trends.

Table 1. Views on homosexuality in Protestant mainline denominations[1]

Denomination	Percent of Those Who See Gay Issues as a Concern	Of Those Who See Gay Issues as Important, the Percent Who …		
		Support Inclusion	Oppose Inclusion	Have Mixed Opinions
All Mainline Protestants (191)	50%	26%	31%	43%
United Church of Christ	24%	22%	44%	33%
Presbyterian Church (USA)	81%	35%	12%	53%
Evangelical Lutheran Church	33%	--	20%	80%
Reformed Church in America	36%	20%	--	80%

However, even for those in denominations that have legislation allowing LGBTQs to be ordained, in some of the regions of the church, lesbian clergy face the fear that their ordinations will be stripped. Lesbian seminarians who are out have limited opportunities for employment and, therefore, for ordination.

Homosexuality continues to be a controversial issue in many mainline Protestant denominations in an era when the denominations continue to struggle with racial parity and multiculturalism (McNeil, Richardson, and Perkins 2004). Lesbian clergy, in particular, remain more marginalized in the church than their heterosexual female clergy colleagues. As stated earlier, although female clergy in general have made great strides in moving into leadership positions in their mainline denominations, the stained glass ceiling phenomenon keeps female clergy from being as widely accepted as male clergy in their denominations (Purvis 2011; RCA Commission on Women 2011).

In many mainline Protestant denominations, because lesbian clergy are typically disallowed from seeking positions within their own denominations,

---

[1] The Hartford Institute for Religion Research (2007).

some have sought ordination outside of their own denominations—despite being trained within their home denominational seminaries. In other cases, lesbians have found that there are regional differences within their denominations where they have the ability to be ordained or have received calls to serve in churches. Despite these differences in parts of each of the denominations, many of the clergy who sexually identify as lesbians still found that they need to remain closeted to maintain their employment and their ordination statuses. The degree to which discrimination impacts the lesbian is unknown, however. It is not fully clear about the manner in which lay or clergy lesbians are treated in the life of the ELCA, PCUSA, RCA, or UCC, on either a local level or on a denominational level since the author could find no literature that specifically addresses the lived experiences of lesbian clergy within their denominations.

In theological circles, women have promoted the idea of social justice for lesbian lay and clergywomen who remain caught in a purity theological vortex but believe they are called to do ministry despite the discrimination. Many feminist theologians who speak about the possibility of transforming relationships have helped raise the church's conscience about not only the place of women in the church but also the place of LBGTQ persons in the church (Douglas 1999; Heyward 1984; Heyward 2000). However, just what the place in the church is or will be for lesbian clergy still, at the time of this writing, remains unclear.

The proposition that the church can expand its vision of social justice does not lack precedent. Canda and Furman (2010) cite three historical phases of religiously related social justice in the United States that further supported this phenomenon of theological purity (Ellwood 2000) that many mainline Protestant churches experienced in the 1950s, in supporting homogeneous thinking in terms of its biblical views on social issues (e.g., civil rights, women's rights, abortion, gay rights, etc.). First, during the two world wars, there were religious rationales for the rise of a pacifist movement. Second, after World War Two, the civil rights movement, and the Vietnam War, ethical debates came to the forefront in many denominations. However, since the 1960s, there have been two parallel trends in the church—one toward homogenous/purity thinking and one toward heterogeneous thinking that supported social justice movements of activism. In other words, there has been a trend of rising Christian conservatism with organized political action, coupled with an opposing liberal trend for ecumenical and interfaith cooperation, which has led to increased use of feminist approaches to explain the incongruities now seen between spiritual goals of the church and the discrimination evidenced toward gays and lesbians the mainline denominations. Ironically, as Christian conservatism grew, perhaps in response to oppressive practices being sanctioned by faith communities, the profession of social work adopted the Judeo-Christian principles of justice into its original 1960 code of ethics (NASW Code of Ethics 1960).

According to Canda and Furman (2010), spiritually sensitive social workers "are committed to a whole person in environment perspective, [and] need to take a bio-psycho-social-spiritual view" (p. 5). As such, social work has a place in the debate on the issue of lesbian clergy and seeing that social justice goals are achieved for this oppressed population. Indeed, their involvement is required if we examine their ethical creed, which requires them to promote social justice and social change with and on the behalf of clients.[2]

PROPOSED THEORETICAL CONSTRUCTS

Specifically, the transcripts of the interviews of the PMC lesbian clergy are examined through the lenses of a synthesis of ecological, anti-oppression, and social identity theories. Utilizing a social-psychological perspective to synthesize, the study incorporates ecological theory (Bronfenbrenner 1979; Gitterman and Germain 2008), anti-oppressive theory (Dominelli 2008), and social identity theory (Tajfel and Turner 1979). Use of ecological theory (ET) allowed for the lesbian clergy participants to identify their sense of environmental/person fit (Bronfenbrenner 1979; Gitterman and Germain 2008) in their various subsystems of family, congregation, and denomination. At the same time, social identity theory offers an explanation of the discrimination or oppression by denominations of the sampled clergy. Finally, the social identity and subcultural identity (Wellman 1999) theories further offer an understanding of the participants' development of

---

[2] The term "clients" is used inclusively to refer to individuals, families, groups, organizations, and communities.

their religious, spiritual, and sexual identities. While this study offers new understanding via the general perceptions of the sampled lesbian clergy, anti-oppressive theory (AOT) also provides a framework for exploring how the experience of the oppression of lesbian clergy either disempowers or empowers them (Dominelli 2002).

Within the literature review, through a theological perspective, sin and purity were explored as they relate to homosexuality in the various views of biblical interpretation, as it impacts upon denominational stances. These developments were then compared to the historical development of biblical translations and theological trends as related to the concept of homosexual orientation. Lastly, through a behavioral science perspective, the development of homosexual orientation as a construct is explored historically, behaviorally, and theologically.

And finally, the NASW Code of Ethics has taken a proactive stance with regard to the diversity of homosexual orientation, as well as other aspects of human diversity and oppression (National Association of Social Work 2008). However, many gaps in understanding the issues at play remain to be addressed. This study, written from a social work perspective, incorporates a social justice perspective in drawing its conclusions and findings.[3]

---

[3] By virtue of their ethical standards, social workers should be sensitive to cultural and ethnic diversity and strive to end discrimination, oppression, poverty, and other forms of social injustice (National Association of Social Work 2008).

---◈---

CHAPTER 2

LITERATURE REVIEW

HISTORY OF LESBIANS IN SOCIETY

HOMOSEXUALITY FROM A SOCIAL WORK PERSPECTIVE

Early social work in the late nineteenth century and early twentieth century grew out of church influences[4] (Knight 2003; Holmes 2000). The social work profession implemented initially was based on Judeo-Christian ideals of charity, caring for the poor, mercy, and justice. In other words, these early concepts were translated into secular social justice principles, specifically regarding the reform of individuals living in insane asylums and slums. Long before women could be ordained as clergy or function as governing leaders of their local churches, they were instrumental in running domestic and international missions (Coakley 1999) in the Protestant mainline denominations.[5]

Yet, despite their contributions, women typically could not be ordained

---

[4] Jane Addams, founder of Hull House in Chicago, was baptized as a Presbyterian in 1886, and Dorothea Dix, who was a pioneer for improving the rights of the chronically mentally ill, started teaching Sunday school in a prison in the 1840s.

[5] In the RCA, women staffed the Women's Board of Foreign Missions as early as 1875, and women were also in the foreign mission field in places like Borneo, India, and Arabia as early as the midnineteenth century.

10

as ministers until late in the twentieth century. Rather, they ran their own organizations (often as under the purview of their Protestant mainline denomination), focusing on local charities, world missions, and social justice issues (Miller P. 1985; Coakley 1999; Schmidt 1994; Schmidt 1994).[6]

From a social science perspective, the social construct of lesbianism is a twentieth-century invention (Kitzinger 1987). Homosexuality is defined as a romantic or sexual attraction or behavior among members of the same sex (American Psychological Association Help Center 2011). Homosexuality is one of the three behaviors along the homosexual-heterosexual orientation continuum that includes homosexuality, bisexuality, and heterosexuality, without clear demarcations between each of the classifications (American Psychological Association Help Center 2011). However, homosexual orientation versus homosexual behavior is differentiated within the psychological literature. Homosexual behavior is an activity that someone engages in, but an orientation is a statement of one's identity. "Sexual behavior" refers to the types of sexual activities in which a person engages and the gender with whom one chooses to have sex. A sexual encounter between two men, for example, is a sexual behavior that is homosexual in nature regardless of either of the participants' sexual identity (HIV Counselor Perspectives 2001).

In contrast to homosexual behavior, homosexual orientation refers to "an enduring pattern of or disposition to experience sexual, affectional, or romantic attractions primarily to people of the same sex; it also refers to an individual's sense of personal and social identity based on those attractions, behaviors expressing them, and membership in a community of others who share them" (American Psychiatric Association Help Center 2011).

In sum, vast incongruities remain between the social science and theological, biblical, and denominational literatures. Whereas the behavioral science literatures present increasingly new understandings on the biological and psychological aspects of sexual orientation,

---

[6] According to Coakley and Prelinger, the mission-oriented "parallel church" provided nineteen- and twentieth-century women opportunities to acquire roles of leadership in the institutional church, but they were a part of separate organizations within the church structures. Examples here are drawn from Reformed Church in America, Episcopal Church in America, United Methodist Church, and Presbyterian Church, USA sources.

many of the theological and denominational literatures lag behind the secular literatures' understandings of LGBTQ issues. In contrast, some theological, biblical, and denominational literatures continue to present older understandings of homosexual behaviors. Of great concern is that these latter literatures are often used as tools to promote homophobic policies in various denominational organizations.

UNDERSTANDING LESBIANISM FROM A BIBLICAL AND THEOLOGICAL PERSPECTIVE

The term "lesbian" is derived from the name of the island of Lesbos that the Greek poet Sappho (630–560 BCE) wrote about, in which the concept of infatuation with women has been originally dated (Beige 2015). In ancient Greece and in Rome, the practice of lesbianism was accepted. Ancient pre-Christian, pagan literature offers a wealth of examples of the existence and acceptance of lesbianism. In Greek literature, examples include Ovid's inclusion of a lesbian character, Iphis, in his book *Metamorphoses*. Another ancient example of lesbianism is that in the female Roman public baths, married women relied on female servants for same-sex encounters (Brooten 1996, 1).

With the spread of Christianity in Europe, the public practice of lesbianism declined. St. John Chrysostom in the fourth century stated it was shameful. Historian John Boswell (2007), in his essay "The Church and the Homosexual," attributes Christianity's denunciations of homosexuality to a rising intolerance in Europe throughout the twelfth century toward anything different from what the church prescribed. In the thirteenth century, St. Thomas Aquinas condemned homosexuality as being in opposition to "natural law" (*Summa Theologica*) and by the late Middle Ages (1300–1500), same-sex encounters had become illegal as a result of the influence of the Holy Roman Empire and the Spanish Inquisition (Crompton 2014, 11–25). For example, in 1477, a woman was executed in Germany, which was part of the Holy Roman Empire, for "lesbian love." During the Protestant Reformation period, Luther actively condemned homosexuality. In 1522, Luther wrote:

The heinous conduct of the people of Sodom was extraordinary, inasmuch as they departed from the natural passion and longing of the male for the female, which is implanted into nature by God, and desired what is altogether contrary to nature. Whence comes this perversity? Undoubtedly from Satan, who after people have once turned away from the fear of God, so powerfully suppresses nature that he blots out the natural desire and stirs up a desire that is contrary to nature. (*Luther's Works* 1522, vol. 3, 255).

During the same time frame in Europe, however, French author de Bourdeill noted that lesbianism was fashionable for noble women in Italy and France during the sixteenth through eighteenth centuries (Latin Networks Limited Corporation 2010).

In the New World, the same ambiguity was evidenced. Homosexuality continued to be condemned by religious groups. For example, in 1636, Puritan minister John Cotton proposed a capital offense law for anyone caught in acts of homosexual behavior (May D. 2004). But in 1650, Sarah White Norman and Mary Vincent Hammon became the only known prosecuted lesbians in the seventeenth century who were charged with "lewd behavior with each other upon a bed" (Borris 2003). And by 1779, one of the founding fathers of the nation, Thomas Jefferson, proposed a law to outlaw homosexuality (Abramson 1980). Incongruities continued into the nineteenth century in the USA, with the term "Boston marriage" being used to talk about two unmarried women living in a committed relationship in the same house. As argued by Faderman (1981), it was somewhat accepted, so long as it was hidden. If lesbians were open about their relationships, however, they were thought to be mentally ill and were oftentimes committed to asylums, where it was acceptable practice for male physicians to rape them for the purpose of "curing" them.

The founder of modern-day social work, Jane Addams, is purported to have been a lesbian. She and her partner, Ellen Gates Starr, cofounded Hull House, the first settlement house in the United States, in Chicago in 1889 (Schoenber 2007; Simonette 2008). It is with Jane Addams that we see the intersection of social work and religion within the "social Christian movement" (Morrow and Messinger 2005). Not only an active Presbyterian and therefore a member of a PMC, Addams was also a seminary graduate and an interfaith attendee at both a local Unitarian church and Reformed synagogue.

As one steps forward into the twentieth century, slow movements toward lesbians coming out of the closet may be observed. Once again, however, oppression was still the norm in society at that time. While several lesbian novels appeared in the 1950s (MariJane Meaker, a.k.a. Vin Packer, 1952, wrote *Spring Fire*, and Patricia Highsmith, 1952, wrote *Price of Salt*), they were written against the backdrop of the Comstock Act, a federal law that deemed such publications "obscene."

Toward the middle of the twentieth century, however, Kinsey published his *Sexual Behavior in the Human Female*, asserting that 13 percent of women interviewed in his study had experienced a homosexual orgasm (Kinsey, A., Pomeroy, W.B., Martin, C. E. 1953). Then in 1955, four lesbian couples founded the Daughters of Bilitis (who lived on the isle of Lesbos, alongside Sappho), which was the first national lesbian political and social organization in the United States (Gallo 2007). And finally, moving into the latter part of the twentieth century, in 1969, Ivy Boltin, an out lesbian of the New York chapter of the National Organization of Women (NOW) held the forum, "Is Lesbianism a Feminist Issue?" Although Betty Freidan (1953), the feminist author of *The Feminist Mystique*, referred to the NOW lesbians as the "lavender menace" in 1970, lesbian rights became a part of the NOW agenda, and one of the NOW lesbians, Barbara Gittings, was a strong advocate for the removal of the term homosexuality as a mental illness from the DSM-II in 1973 (Polikoff 2008).

SHAPING OF THE DEBATE ON IDENTITY

While the church, its leadership, and its members have traditionally considered homosexuals and clergy to be mutually exclusive identities, this historically held assumption is currently being hotly debated in the twenty-first century at local and national levels. This study specifically seeks to add to the discourse that is transpiring, using the lived experiences of lesbian clergy to humanize and give depth and dimension to our understanding of the adverse impact that such philosophies, practices, and policies have imposed on this population.

Probably no other group has been so prolifically singled out as "candidates for hell" as homosexual people (Scanzoni and Mollenkott 1994). Repeatedly, homosexuality has been touted as an exemplar of sin by much of the church community. Usually such condemnations are backed up with the so-called six or seven biblical clobber passages that speak about same-sex acts in the context of prostitution and temple worship (Miner and Connoley 2008, 1–26). In truth, the term homosexuality is never used in scripture, as the term was coined in secular literature in the nineteenth century (Myers and Scanzoni 2005).

While homosexuality has historically been classified as a sin, it is worth taking a moment to look closely at the general leading theological views regarding sin as a concept. From a Judeo-Christian perspective, sin has generally been thought of as any action, attitude, or thought that is against God's will for humankind. Biblically, sin is defined as a transgression of the law of God (1 John 3:4 New Revised Standard Version) and as a rebellion against God (Deuteronomy 9:7; Joshua 1:18). It is generally broken down into two categories—either sins of omission or sins of commission. Sins of omission are things that one should have done but did not, and sins of commission are things that one should not have done but did (Spranca, Minsk, and Baron 2003). The Roman Catholic Church has traditionally viewed sin as either mortal[7] (committed with deliberate consent and full knowledge) or venial[8] (committed without full knowledge and without both deliberate and complete consent) (Hardon 2000). The prevailing Protestant view is one of original sin, beginning with Adam's disobedience in eating from the Tree of Knowledge of Good and Evil, which in turn has affected the human race for all eternity. This original sin affects human

---

[7] Mortal sins (Latin, *peccata mortalia*) in Catholic theology are wrongful acts that condemn a person to hell after death if unforgiven. These sins are considered mortal because they constitute a rupture in a person's link to God's saving grace: the person's soul becomes dead, not merely weakened. A mortal sin is not necessarily a sin that cannot be repented, unlike an eternal sin. Thus, even after a mortal sin has been committed, there is a chance for repentance.

[8] "Venial sin does not deprive the sinner of sanctifying grace, friendship with God, charity, and consequently eternal happiness."

nature and the ability of humans to stand before God; even infants are affected, although they are not old enough to commit conscious sin. The Calvinistic doctrine states that humans are unable to overcome sin, apart from the power of the Holy Spirit and reliance on Christ and His atoning sacrifice for human sin upon the cross (Japinga 1999). Essentially, the Protestant Reformer Calvin struggled against the Roman Catholic Church and wrote extensively about concepts such as being saved by God's grace and not human works and about God predestining humans for salvation, as well as prolific writings on new liturgies and forms of government. Among his many works, his *Institutes of Christian Religion* laid out his theology (Calvin 1536).

As this is a social work study, the author is offering this information as a way of introducing to the social worker that the antilesbian clergy debate has been weighted in biblical and theological interpretations for the better part of forty years. The rise of feminism in the United States had a tremendous impact on bringing this issue of LGBTQ inclusion in the church, and specifically the issue of ordaining lesbian clergy, to the fore.

THE ROLE OF FEMINISM

Approximately forty years ago, feminist theologians began to challenge conventional Christian thought by hypothetically examining why women's voices have historically not been heard and how Christian tradition might have been shaped differently if women had played a more decisive role in its theological development (Japinga 1999). It is clear that the Judeo-Christian tradition "is decidedly patriarchal," as it has been largely shaped, formed, and written by men (Harmon and Rhodes 2008, 31). Due to the male privilege that continues to exist in the church, female clergy repeatedly have to prove themselves in some ecclesiastical settings. Harmon and Rhodes (2006) write, "Women are challenged to prove themselves worthy of the calling of God. Often [they] have quoted Acts 2:17 to someone who openly opposes women in the ministry, 'I will pour out my Spirit upon all flesh, and your sons and your daughters shall prophesy'" (p. 48).

Feminist theologians posit that theology is not free of bias but is, rather, socially constructed. For instance, feminist theologians have written how historically the church's understandings of scripture have constructed patriarchal interpretations of church leadership and family life. These understandings consequently led to oppression of women in general, and lesbians in particular, in the leadership of the church. According to Douglas (1999), when scrutinized in light of preexisting prejudice, the "Bible then becomes a tool of oppression and is taken up as a weapon to censor the behavior and restrict the life possibilities of others" (pp. 90–91). This occurs in congregations and in denominations when the emphasis is on a purity of religious beliefs and a sameness of thoughts and beliefs. Douglas (1999) continues to assert that censoring by the church serves to maintain a traditional view of the Bible in terms of issues of race, women, and homosexuality. Specifically regarding the homosexuality issue, she writes, "It is probably safe to say that homophobic prejudice has driven our reading of the Bible, as opposed to the Bible shaping homophobia" (p. 90).

Heyward writes, "Let no one convince us that 'women's rights' do not belong in the church, or that 'women's rights' are less urgent and less critical than other human rights" (Heyward 1984, 4). It is Heyward (1984, 1989) who clarifies the debate about lesbian clergy. For her, lesbians, unlike gay men, bear the burden of not only being homosexual in the church but also being women in the church. As noted previously, the traditional churchwomen in leadership, particularly those serving as clergy, have experienced discrimination. For Heyward (1984), "lesbianism is an implicit and bold NO to the God that is limited, by definition, within the categories of light, Logos, and the Father" (p. 39). In her lesbian, feminist, theologian voice, she speaks to ways in which lesbian women have learned within the church to share power as creative and relational, rather than coercive, individuals. She writes, "To speak this truth is also a matter of authority and revelation—of giving embodied sensual, audible, and visible power to the real presence of lesbian feminist women in the churches, synagogues, and elsewhere" (Heyward 1989, 11).

From a purity-themed perspective, there is a theologically conservative voice in the church that promotes the idea of being sexually pure until marriage. This theological thinking precludes premarital sex for heterosexuals and mandates that homosexual persons refrain from sexual behaviors and remain celibate. Thus, from a decidedly purity-themed perspective, Gagnon (2001) challenges the role of female and male homosexuals in the life of the church. According to Gagnon (2001), "the greatest crisis facing the church today is the dispute about homosexual practice" (p. 40). He continues, "No other issue has so consumed mainline denominations for the past thirty years or holds a greater potential for splitting these denominations" (p. 40). Liberal theologian Jack Rogers (2006), who is professor of theology emeritus at San Francisco Theological Seminary and moderator of the 213th General Assembly of the Presbyterian Church (USA), states that homosexuality is a "defining issue of our time" (p. ix). He talks about how the conflict historically has related to issues of societal order, social justice, and equal rights; to him, it is a matter of morality, spirituality, and biblical scholarship.

> For some, it is an issue of maintaining tradition and customs that have given order to our society. For others, it is an issue of justice—all citizens should be entitled to equal rights under the law. For this author and a growing number of others, it is a moral and spiritual issue. How can the church live up to the highest ideals of Jesus Christ? How can we most faithfully act according to the central principles of the Bible? How can we most honestly and equitably share the love of God with all people? (Rogers 2008, ix)

Homosexuality and Church Doctrine and Belief

According to a 2011 study, with data drawn from the longitudinal National Congregations Study, 52.6 percent of mainline Protestant congregations allow gay men and lesbians into leadership positions (Chaves 2008), as opposed to a 2012 report that only 4 percent of theologically conservative churches allow LGBT persons to be in leadership positions (Chaves 2012). Further, the LGBT leadership issue in black churches is complex, as there has long been anecdotally a "don't ask, don't tell" kind of policy regarding LGBT leadership. In other words, black preachers speak from the pulpit about homosexuality being a sin, but it is the best-kept secret that gay men are in the choir. There are no statistics regarding this issue of LGBT leadership in black Protestant churches. However, Sharon J. Lettman-Hicks's statement on this issue is poignant. Lettman-Hicks is the executive director of the National Black Justice Coalition, which is a LGBT advocacy group (National Public Radio, 5/22/12). She stated, "They would rather suppress their identity than denounce their church."

In the backdrop of these studies, debates continue to rage in denominations across North America about the extent to which homosexual individuals should be received with full inclusion (Ostling 1989). These debates on homosexuality have been so contentious that it has caused many denominational loyalists to worry about whether the Protestant mainline denominations will survive as ecclesiastical organizations. For instance, Tony Campolo, who is a well-known and respected theologian (2004), has written extensively on difficult issues, such as homosexuality, that often get sidestepped in churches and in entire denominations, for fear of polarizing Christian communities. Campolo and his wife, Peggy, are known on the Christian speaking circuit because they present on opposite sides of the homosexuality issue intentionally as a means of encouraging entire denominations to have the discussion about LGBTQ inclusion. Tony Campolo holds a conservative view, believing that same-gender eroticism cannot be reconciled with scripture, whereas his wife believes that the church should legitimize gay marriage. Here are Dr. Campolo's reflections on preventing the homosexuality debate from splitting entire denominations and local congregations:

> What makes matters worse is that on each side of the argument, people demonize those on the other side. For many evangelicals, this is a defining issue, and they say that to approve of homosexual marriages is to throw out the Bible. They even question whether they can stay in a church or a denomination that does not agree with their stand ... While I believe that this is an important issue, I don't think it is a defining one. We must not allow ourselves to think that those who differ with us on the matter of homosexuality are less Christian or even less committed to Scripture than we are. Differences over this issue should not be the cause of church schism. My wife and I are evidence that it is possible to have opposing

opinions on this subject with getting a divorce. (Campolo 2004, 55–56).

Many denominations have taken a position that avoids condemning homosexual orientation but at the same time refuses to condone any homosexual lifestyle other than celibacy. Hence, they do not condemn people for having the orientation, but they view practicing homosexuality as living outside of biblically prescribed behavior (Campolo 2004). In fact, denominational leaders so fear that the homosexual issue will split their denominations that they minimize the actual tensions that exist at times. In their interviews with sixty-two mainline Protestant clergy across the United States, Olson and Cadge (2002) report that very few clergy respondents discussed homosexuality in a prophetic (i.e., theologically visionary manner) way but instead in a pragmatic way, with expressed concern about the survival and unity of their denominations. Further, the respondents spoke about homosexuality in terms of an abstract notion rather than talking about gay men and lesbians as human beings in society and the church (Olson and Cadge 2002).

The contentious nature of the debate has had an impact on LBGTQs in the church. In a 2013, Public Religion Research Institute survey researchers found that approximately 37 percent of LGBTQs reported having left the church because of the negative stances and teachings toward them (Kaleem 2014). The survey also reveals that gay, lesbian, bisexual, and transgender Americans are also far more likely than other Americans to report leaving their childhood religion. Like Americans overall, few LGBT Americans were raised outside a formal religious tradition (8 percent versus 7 percent). However, nearly four out of ten (37 percent) LGBT Americans are now unaffiliated with a church, as compared to 21 percent of Americans. Overall, roughly three out of ten (31 percent) LGBT Americans left their childhood religion to become religiously unaffiliated (Kaleem 2014).

From a clergy experiential perspective, Heskins (2005) utilized a "critical conversation" methodology in his qualitative study of male and female homosexual clergy couples in the Anglican Church. Heskins details his in-depth interviews with gay and lesbian clergy couples throughout England utilizing a practical theology methodology called critical conversation (Pattison 2000), in order to elicit the stories of the gay and lesbian couples who participated in the study. Some of Heskins's (2005) findings were the following: when many couples emerged from the complicity of imposed celibacy or fearful loneliness, they felt liberated; the interviewed couples had hope for the future in the "virtues and qualities that underpinned life in a Church context" (p. 176); the couples believed that through their act of living in committed partnerships, God was creatively changing the church; and the couples felt that it was important to live in understanding that they are part of the healing process that God began in them and exemplifies in the broader church. In contrast to their own internal liberation that they experienced in coming out as gay clergy, the clergy couples that were sampled expressed that, despite their own discovery of their capacity to share intimately and faithfully, they were still unable within the denominational structures of the church to live in an open and intimate way as gay and lesbian couples because of their fear of discrimination (e.g., being terminated, not getting positions in the future, being underemployed in congregations where no one else would work). Heskins's work is informative in its practical and humanizing perspective of the experiences of gay and lesbian clergy. This pro-LGBT look into the needs of the gay and lesbian clergy enables the reader to better understand the ongoing and painful theological debates in most Protestant mainline denominations.

IMPACT OF TRADITIONAL AND NONTRADITIONAL BIBLICAL PERSPECTIVES

Together, Gagnon and Via (2002), who are from different sides of the theological sides of this debate, wrote a book on the scriptural understandings of the LGBT issue in the contemporary church. Gagnon, a conservative theologian, supports this traditional view and states that the church's support of homosexuality represents a radical devaluation of the "Scripture's moral imperative—of the place of holiness, obedience, and repentance" (Via and Gagnon 2003, 41). According to Gagnon (2003), the contemporary church's push for the endorsement of homosexual practice represents an assault on human sexuality within its ranks. Further, they assert that those who engage in homosexual behaviors are at risk of losing their salvation. In contrast, Via (2003) observes that the nontraditional view seeks a more accepting position of homosexual acts. In other words, homosexual acts are not, in themselves, immoral or sinful, and like heterosexual acts, they are good or bad depending on the context that defines and gives meaning to them. For a better understanding of this debate on LGBT inclusion in the Protestant mainline church, see table 2.

Table 2: Theological references to homosexuality
(Via and Gagnon 2003)

Via	Gagnon
The biblical texts that deal with homosexual practice condemn it unconditionally.	The biblical texts that deal with homosexual practice condemn it unconditionally.
Experiential or existential view that the Bible is authoritative only in those parts that are existentially engaging and compelling and that give grounding and meaning to existence.	A priori view that the Bible is authoritative in all of its parts and is so prior to interpretation.
Three factors override the Bible's condemnation of homosexuality: (1) the biblical understanding of creation and redemption and of the bodily sexual definition of human existence along with the Bible's belief that acts must be understood and evaluated in the light of character; (2) the reality of a destiny created by homosexual orientation; and (3) the experience of gay Christians.	God intended sexual intercourse to be for the remerging of two sexual halves into "one flesh."

While both Via and Gagnon agree that homosexual practice is condemned in the scriptures, they diverge on the use of the scripture in the contemporary church. Thus, Gagnon's view that homosexual practice is wrong diverges from Via's view that homosexual practice must be viewed within the experiential context of gay men and women in the church. According to Via, "the experimental or existential view [of biblical authority] says that the Bible is authoritative only in those parts that are existentially engaging and compelling—that give grounding and meaning to existence" (Via and Gagnon 2003, 2). Via's emphasis on experiential hermeneutics parallels the feminist view of the Bible that sees the scriptures in the context of the experience of power and relationships (Japinga 1999) and as the sacred feminine (Harmon and Rhodes 2008), in addition to the patriarchal view of scriptures. Finally, Via's view allows for a biblical emphasis on justice, in addition to purity.

In contrast, the writings of feminist theologians like Heyward (2000) and Douglas (1999), who have helped to raise the consciousness of the church in stressing a nontraditional view of the Bible as it relates to homosexual acts, have tended to emphasize justice, rather than purity, in their writing. For Heyward (2000), justice is "the actualization of love among us, [it] is the making of right, or mutual, relation" (p. 17). While Douglas hesitates to use the Bible in support of a position of homosexuality, given its lack of clarity on the subject, she is at the same time very concerned that the Bible has been used as the "cornerstone of homophobia in the Black community" (Douglas 1999, 90) and presumably in other church communities. Douglas states, "Homophobic prejudice has driven our reading of the Bible, as opposed to the Bible shaping homophobia" (Douglas 1999, 12). These bitter debates over homosexuality in most Protestant mainline denominations have become particularly heated in regard to the debate about homosexuals becoming ordained as ministers.

THE INFLUENCE OF THE VARIOUS BIBLE TRANSLATIONS ON PROBLEM DEFINITION

Prior to 1952, the Protestant mainline denominations used the King James Version (KJV), which was published in 1609. The 1937 KJV translated two critical Greek words (explored in detail below) as "effeminate" and as "abusers of themselves with mankind." In 1952, the American Bible Society released a new translation of the Bible, the Revised Standard Version, which has become very popular in the mainline Protestant denominations. This new biblical translation appears to have tolerated homophobia and heterosexism in the North American church.

Homosexuality had already been conceptualized as inconsistent with most religious traditions. As noted above, many clergy indicate their rejection of homosexuality and acceptance of heterosexism, based on scriptures from the Bible. Of the sixty-six books of the Bible, six often-cited verses (Genesis 1–2, 19:1–9; Leviticus 18:22, 20:13; 1 Corinthians

6:9; Romans 1:26–27; and 1 Timothy 1:10) are most often used as evidence that heterosexism is scripturally normative—and subsequently allows for homophobic disdain for same-sex relationships. Religious denominations actively use these verses to repudiate same-sex romantic relationships, to devalue homosexual genital experience, and to refuse ordination opportunities for gay aspirants (Miller 2007).

The Revised Standard Version of the Bible introduced new terminology, replacing the earlier "effeminate" and "abusers of themselves with mankind" translations with the word "homosexual" (Helminiak 2000). He posits that it is important to note that in biblical times, there was no understanding of homosexuality as an orientation, but instead it was simply reduced to same-sex contacts or same-sex acts. The word *homosexuality* was never used in scripture. Homosexual orientation, as understood through modern science, is not mentioned in the scriptures, nor is anything said about the loving relationship of two same-sex persons who have covenanted to be life partners, as it is understood in contemporary times (Myers and Scanzoni 2005). Nor do the Judeo-Christian scriptures mention the term *lesbian*. Male homosexuals were considered more punishable by law in ancient Israel due to the evolutionary need for male seed to promote the human race; therefore, male sperm could not be wasted (Guest, Goss, West, and Bohache 2006).

Within the ancient culture, male-female sexuality was hierarchal. Whereas Western gender and sexuality systems are constructed around a series of binaries—female/male, homosexual/heterosexual—Genesis comes from and reflects a world in which gender and sexuality are constructed as a hierarchical continuum. This hierarchy is based on penetration. Men are the ones who penetrated, and they stand at the top of the hierarchy. Below them are women, and below women are eunuchs, female virgins, and hermaphrodites. At the bottom are the monstrous—penetrated men and penetrating women (Carden in Queer Bible Commentary 2006, 23–24).

Table 3: Variations among Bible translations*

Bible Version	Translation of the Two Greek Words
New English Bible, 1961	"guilty of homosexual perversion" (combining the two Greek words)
Revised Standard Version, 1963	"sexual perverts" (combining the two Greek words)
Jerusalem Bible (Roman Catholic), 1966	"catamites" and "sodomites"
New International Version, 1973, 1974	"male prostitutes" and "homosexual offenders"
Today's English Version (Good New Bible), 1976	"homosexual perverts" (combining two Greek words)
New Jerusalem Bible, 1985	"the self-indulgent" and "sodomites"
New Revised Standard Version, 1989	"male prostitutes" and "sodomites"
Revised English Bible, 1989	"sexual pervert" (combining the two Greek words)
Contemporary English Version, 1995	"pervert" and "behaves like a homosexual"
Oxford New Testament Inclusive Version, 1995	"male prostitutes" (combining the two Greek words)
New Living Translation, 1996	"male prostitutes" and "homosexuals"
Today's International Version, 2001	"male prostitutes" and "practicing homosexuals"
New English Translation, 2003	"passive homosexual partners" and "practicing homosexuals"

*Adapted from (Myers and Scanzoni 2005, 96)

Again, individuals who view homosexuality as being inconsistent with the scriptures view homosexuality as a sin. As previously mentioned, although these biblical citations have been interpreted to be evidence that homosexuality is a sin, there are also dissenting opinions among some biblical scholars in their study of the original biblical languages of Hebrew, Greek, and Aramaic (Scroggs 1983; Scanzoni and Mollenkott 1994; McNeil 1976; Helminiak 2000). Out of 31,103 Bible verses, only seven frequently quoted verses, none of which Jesus spoke, speak directly of same-sex behavior. Mostly these verses are written in the context of idolatry, temple prostitution, adultery, child exploitation, or violence (Myers 2008).

A thorough New Testament Greek exegesis is not necessary for this social work treatise, but suffice it to say that the meaning of two Greek words, *malakoi* (Rogers 2006, 74) and *arsenokoitai* (Rogers 2006, 74; Miner and Connoley 2008, 21), are not well known, and their translation is highly debated by biblical scholars. Malakoi has no specific reference to homosexuality and instead appears to mean "the effeminate," "boy prostitutes," (Helminiak 2000, 108), and as a "pederastic" or abusive relationship between an older man and a boy (Scroggs 1983, 33). Arsenokoitai has been rendered in multiple ways as "homosexuals," "sodomites," "child molesters," "perverts," "homosexual perverts," "sexual perverts," or "people of infamous habits," to mention a few derisive terms (Helminiak 2000, 106).

Unfortunately, the 1952 translation, which combined these two obscure Greek words and rendered them into the simple translation of "homosexuals," has often been utilized by the opponents within the church in asserting that homosexual clergy do not possess the spiritual fitness to hold office. Once these two Greek words were translated as "homosexual," the door was open to such reductive pronouncements as the following:

> Do not be deceived; neither the immoral, nor idolater, nor adulterers, nor homosexual (*oute malakoi oute arsenokoitai*), nor thieves, nor the greedy, nor drunkards, nor revilers, nor robbers will inherit the kingdom of God. (1 Corinthians 6:9–10, Bible, Revised Standard Version, American Bible Society 1952)

Table 4: Clobber texts (Miner and Connoley 2008; Rogers 2006)

Bible Verses/ Story	Original Intent	King James Version, 1604	Revised Standard Version, 1946/1952	New English Bible, 1961	New International Version, 1983	New Revised Standard Version, 1989	Contemporary English Version, 1995	Queer Bible Commentary, 2006
Genesis 19 Sexual abuse and gang rape in Sodom and Gomorrah	Sacred obligation of hospitality for travelers and the ways in which sinful people violated this obligation (Rogers 2006, 70)							An account of mass genocide that was interpreted by Christians as a divine judgment against women and homosexuals (Carden in Guest, Goss, West, and Bohache 2006, 38)

Leviticus 18:22 and 20:13 Cultic prostitution in Israel	Holiness code prevents male same-sex acts for religious reasons, not sexual reasons, because it is associated with Gentile activity (Helminiak 2000, 54) with individuals from Canaan and Egypt (Miner and Connoley 2008, 10–11)	"Thou shalt not lie with mankind, as with womankind; it is abomination." "If a man also lie with mankind, as he lieth with a woman, both of them have committed an abomination."	"You shall not lie with a male as with a woman; it is an abomination." "If a man lie with a male as with a woman, both of them have committed an abomination."	"Do not lie with a man as one lies with a woman; that is detestable." "If a man lies with a man as one lies with a woman, both them have done what is detestable. They must be put to death; their blood will be on their own heads."	"You shall not lie with a male as with a woman; it is an abomination." "If a man lie with a male as with a woman, both of them have committed an abomination."	"It is disgusting for a man to have sex with another man." "It's disgusting for men to have sex with one another."	Even if these two verses in Leviticus condemn male homosexuality, which is not the focus of chapters 18 and 20 (Stewart in Guest, Goss, West, and Bohache 2006, 83), these verses do not condemn sexual relations between the unmarried, nor lesbian relations, nor nonincestuous relations between men (Stewart in Guest, Goss, West, and Bohache 2006, 82).

Romans 1:26–27 Immorality in Rome	Unconventional and something out of the ordinary (Rogers 2006, 77). The model of homosexual behavior that Paul is addressing is associated with temple prostitution (Miner and Connoley 2008, 14).	"natural relations for unnatural ones"	"natural relations for unnatural"	"natural intercourse for unnatural"	"natural relations for unnatural ones"	"natural intercourse for unnatural"	"sex in a natural way" and "things with each other that were not natural"	It is not Paul's intent here to zero in on homosexual sex and to create a new "ethical absolute" against homosexuality but to focus on the 'sin of oppression and the sin of injustice" (Hanks in Guest, Goss, West, and Bohache 2006, 589),

1 Corinthians 6:9 Secular prostitution and sin in Corinth	"Soft" people will not inherit the kingdom of God. Paul was condemning moral weakness here (Miner and Connoley 2008, 16).	"male prostitutes"	"homo-sexuals"	"homosexual perversion"	"male prostitutes" or "homosexual offenders"	"male prostitutes" or "sodomites"	"a pervert" or "behaves like a homosexual"	Malakoi is "decadence," and arsenokotai is "pimping." Thus, the entire list of vices listed here can be seen to revolve around behaviors that involve excess and exploitation (Hearon in Guest, Goss, West, and Bohache 2006, 614).

1 Timothy 1:10 Those whom the law condemns	"perverts"	"sodomites"	"perverts"	"perverts"	"sodomites"	"perverts" or "those who live as homosexuals"
	Paul was condemning moral weakness here (Miner and Connoley 2008, 16).					In his determination to avoid sinning and deviations from the norm, Paul's vision of the church. that is "inviolable to difference," may not be able to withstand the diversity of men from women, straights from gays, and so on (Goss and Krauss in Guest, Goss, West, and Bohache 2006, 688).

Jude 7 Fallen angels going after strange or different flesh	"perversion"	"unnatural lust"	"unnatural lusts"	"perversion"	"unnatural lust"	"sexual sins"
	Heterosexual sex between male angels and human women (Miner and Connoley 2008, 7)					Jude's primary concern here is not sex but religious or spiritual elitism. Jude particularly objects to the creation of a new form of Christian practice that is open only to the spiritually advanced, epitomized in human followers of Jesus having sexual intercourse with angels, who are messengers from God (Countryman in Goss and Krauss in Guest, Goss, West, and Bohache 2006, 752).

Interestingly, the 1977 Revised Standard Version (RSV) translates those two words together as "sexual perverts," and the 1989 RSV translates the two words separately again as "male prostitutes and sodomites." It appears that as societal attitudes have changed, so have the translation constructs. For more understanding of the origin of the Hebrew and Greek words that are referenced, see table 5 below.

Table 5: A chronological comparison of secular and sacred texts

Term	Sacred Texts	Secular Text	Linguistic Origin/ Meaning of Word
Toevah			[Hebrew] abomination; ritually unclean (Rogers 2006, 72)
Malakoi	1604 King James Version (KJV); 1937 King James Version (KJV)		[Greek] soft; lack of self-control and yielding to pleasures were both signs of effeminacy (Rogers 2006, 74)
Arsenokoitai	1604 King James Version (KJV); 1937 King James Version (KJV)		[Greek] sexual exploiters (Rogers 2006, 74); those who force themselves on others (Miner and Connoley 2008, 21); "Abusers of themselves"
Para Physis	1604 King James Version (KJV)	181 BC, Aristotle	[Greek] acts "against nature" (Rogers 2006, 77; Gagnon 2001, 384)
Homosexual	1946 Revised Standard Version (RSV) Translation	1892, introduced from German into English, derived from Latin (homo), meaning man, and from Greek (*homoios*), meaning like or same (Via 2003, 1)	

Homosexual Perversion	1961 New English (NEB)	1962 translation inserted into Q. 87 of the (1562) Heidelberg Catechism	
		1989 translation; Q. 87 footnoted that the phrase was not in 1562 version	

THE CONCEPTUAL FRAMEWORK FOR UNDERSTANDING IDENTITY

In his essay, Wellman (1999) argues that the *cultural war* explanation for the contentious debate among and within North American Protestant mainline denominations regarding the issue of homosexual ordination is too polarized and, therefore, fails to grasp the positioning of debaters within the various denominations. Instead, he posits that the *subcultural identity* theory offers better explanation, arguing that religious groups actually thrive in a pluralist and open religious market because "they need to be in tension with, though not separate from, the common cultural milieu. Moreover, there is need to create outgroups against which group and religious identity is further solidified" (p. 187). According to Coser (Coser in Wellman 1999, 188), "the construction of enemies, imaginary or real, is integral to group solidarity." Wellman (1999) concluded that the construction of outgroups is critical to understanding how religious and group identities are maintained and mobilized.

According to the 2006–2007 National Congregations Study, 52.6 percent of mainline Protestant congregations allow gay men and lesbians into leadership positions, as opposed to black or Evangelical Protestants (Whitehead 2011). Wellman (1999) synthesizes Kniss's (1997) taxonomy that dichotomizes the orthodox and progressive rhetoric that divides religious and ideological leadership and Williams's (1997) model of cultural differences between personal morality and public justice. Interestingly, Luidens and Nemeth (1987) found in their research that much of the fight over controversial issues, such as homosexual ordination, is a competition between these traditional and progressive factions within denominations to win over the minds of the "loyalist middle," which make up an estimated 60 percent of church membership in the PCUSA (Wellman 1999, 190). Luidens (2009) also describes the "loyalists" in the RCA, who have a strong denominational identity and who have sought to bridge the differences between the liberal and conservative factions that divide the church regarding social issues.

Hiltner (1972) and Olson and Cadge (2008) provide context against which to understand Protestant mainline clergy attitudes on the issue of homosexuality in the church. As early as 1970, Princeton Theological Seminary professor Seward Hiltner presented a lecture at Indiana University titled "Kinsey and the Church—After Twenty Years," which was later published in the (1972) *Journal of Sex and Research*. He described the attention of church leaders toward Kinsey's books as being one of shock— interestingly, the exception being the supervising clinical pastoral education professors. Overall, however, the church leaders of that era reacted strongly against Kinsey's conclusions and his research methodologies. Practicing homosexual clergy were among the issues discussed in the article.

THEOLOGICAL IDENTITY DEBATE: PURITY OR JUSTICE?

There have been two historical parallel streams in biblical theology: purity and justice. The purity versus justice tension runs throughout the Old and New Testaments of the Christian scriptures. The purity stream emphasizes the importance of homogeneous thinking or unity on an issue, whereas a justice stream stresses a priority on social problems and causes over the sameness of thoughts. It is the purity emphasis that appears to have dominated the denominational debates on homosexuality.

The assumption of being a pure individual, or church, is to be without sin or "transgression" (Buttrick 1962, 361) or "error," "miss," "fail," "revolt," or "rebel" (Buttrick 1962, 361). Within the Judeo-Christian scriptures, the concept of being pure is to be without sin; however, sin has a long and complex development that complicates the simplicity of this connotation. The very first time the word "sin" appears in the scriptures is in the Cain and Abel story (Genesis 4:7), when God says to Cain, "But if you do not do what is right, sin is crouching at your door; it desires to have you, but you must master it." The early Hebraic writers view sin as not obeying God's laws and the importance of maintaining the purity laws (Leviticus 12–15), whereas the Old Testament prophets view sin as not doing justice (Hosea 14:1; Micah 6:8).

In the New Testament, the Gospels reflect Jesus's view that sin is shared by all humanity, and he stressed his concern that the extrinsically religious tend to focus more on ritual and purity laws, rather than focusing on doing acts of kindness and mercy. Jesus taught that it is more important to practice one's piety in secret rather than make a public display, as the Jewish leaders of the day were doing (Matthew 6:1, 6). However, Paul reflects in the Epistles more of a purity-based perspective on sin (Galatians 5:19–21; Hebrews 1:3). At last, the final book of the New Testament cites sin (Revelation 1:5) one time, with this same emphasis on hope in Jesus's atonement for human sin.

Following a social work justice-like theme, multiple theological writers (Helminiak 2006; Heyward 1984, 1995, 1999, 2000; Douglas 1999; Ellwood 2000) have written about justice in the last twenty years or so. Their observation is that purity themes outweigh justice themes in many Protestant mainline denominations. Therefore, while justice is central to the foundations of Judeo-Christian principles, the current emphasis on purity tends to define the homosexual ordination debate within many mainline Protestant denominations and has resulted in homosexual oppression becoming equated with maintaining the purity of the denomination. If justice means care for all, that includes homosexuals; but if purity means to be without sin or transgression, then it essentially legitimates homosexual oppression, which is viewed as defiling purity (Buttrick 1962, 361; Strong 1990, 966). Succinctly stated, it seems in the scriptures that justice is equated with inclusivity for all persons at the same time that purity results in an exclusivity of those same individuals who do not uphold the ritual normative standards.

From a theological perspective, this purity theme depends on the ritual purity that maintained the Jewish culture in their belief as a "people set apart for God" (Scanzoni and Mollenkott 1978, 64). This concept of ritual purity in the Hebrew culture is related to the value of honoring regulations for everyday aspects of life, such as sex, menstruation, eating, clothing, and so on. Among the ritual purity regulations is a prohibition regarding two males participating in sexual activity (Leviticus 12–15). Interestingly, however, in the body of the purity laws, there is not a specific prohibition for women having sex with women.

The perspective of Christians is that the purity requirements of the Jewish law were no longer significant with the coming of Jesus. Helminiak, a Roman Catholic priest, offers that Christianity brought a new understanding of purity; he interprets the "pure in heart that Jesus spoke about (Matthew 5:8), as those who will see God, not those who are merely pure or clean" (Helminiak 2000, 71). Liberal feminist theologians, such as Douglas (1999) and Heyward (1984, 1989, 2000), further extended the concept of justice beyond love to include reconciliation among groups of people that are divided on significant social issues. Along the continuum from liberal to moderate to conservative are theologians Heyward to Via to Gagnon, in that order, with views on homosexuality that similarly match the milestone along a justice-to-purity continuum. For instance, conservative theologian Gagnon (2001) believes that there is a scriptural imperative to maintain purity standards when it pertains to the issue of homosexuality. However, Heyward (2000) asserts, "Justice cannot be achieved unless we take our differences seriously" (p. X). Via (2003) offers a moderating voice between the polarized stances of Heyward and Gagnon. He states that homosexual acts are not in themselves immoral or sinful and, like heterosexual acts, are good or bad depending on the context that defines and gives meaning to them.

DOMINANCE OF PURITY THEMES IN THE FOUR SAMPLED DENOMINATIONS

As the above suggests, the current debate about homosexuality in general, and lesbian clergy in particular, while leaning heavily on biblical and theological sources, appears to really boil down to whether the denomination endorses the purity perspective over that of justice to frame the question of homosexuality. This appears to have occurred in three of the four historical Protestant mainline denominations in the United States (i.e., the Evangelical Lutheran Church in America, the Presbyterian Church, USA, the Reformed Church in American.). Thus, this ongoing Protestant mainline debate about homosexuality is, in reality, a theological debate about the construct of sin (Helminiak 2000; Rogers 2006; Miner and Connoley 2008; Scanzoni and Mollenkott 1994; Scroggs 1983; McNeill 1993), which has only become more exacerbated in the expansion of the debate in most Protestant mainline denominations to the issue of whether homosexual persons should be ordained as clergy. It is interesting to note that both the pro-gay and antigay sides of this debate feel justified by their polarized views. This reliance on a purity theological framework to pose the question of homosexuality within the church, which serves as the basis for bringing clergy to ecclesiastical trial, continues to be the language used in the constitutions of the mainline Protestant denominations (Reformed Church in America 2007) from which the lesbian clergy in this study were sampled.

DENOMINATIONAL STANCES ON HOMOSEXUAL ORDINATION

There are multiple examples of the perceived bipolar division (Wellman 1999, 184) between movements that support the full inclusion of gay individuals into the life of the church and those opposed to same. These debates have often been to linked to sociology and the cultural war's theoretical approach (Hunter 1991). For example, the RCA has continued to uphold its 1978 stance that homosexuality is a sin (RCA 1978), but this rule was tested at the 2005 General Synod when one of its seminary presidents was put on ecclesiastical trial for officiating at the marriage of his lesbian clergy daughter and her lesbian clergy partner (RCA 2005, 2008). As recently as 2009, at its biennial assembly, the Evangelical Lutheran Church in America (ELCA) voted to allow homosexuals the possibility of ordination (Evangelical Lutheran Church in America 2009). However, the more theologically liberal United Church of Christ (UCC) has allowed the ordination of homosexuals for forty years, since 1972 (United Church of Christ 2009).

Understanding the denominational positions on the homosexuality issue in general, and the ordination of lesbian clergy specifically, is crucial to understanding the "lived experiences" (Van Manen 1990) of the lesbian clergy sampled in this study—as well as their understanding of how they "fit" (Gitterman and Germain 2008) within their denominations. Further, the clergy participants' perception of how they fit within their denominations and how they connect their religious, spiritual, and sexual identities will enable the principal investigator's understanding of the religious, spiritual, and sexual domains of the participants (Miller 2005, 2007; Tajfel and Turner 1979).

INTRODUCTION OF SOCIAL SCIENCE PERSPECTIVES

While denominational literature (as shown above) offers competing theological perspectives that either support the maintenance of purity through the elimination of the sin of homosexuality (i.e., purity) or advance the view that the assumption of a such unforgiving purity view is unbiblical and un-Christian (i.e., justice), contemporary social science adds yet another perspective to the debate: the conceptualization of homosexuality as a social justice issue that is defined by social consciousness, not by church/theological doctrine and belief. The last four decades have brought considerable change to the thinking of the behavioral science community regarding the issue of homosexuality. Toulouse (2000) suggests three stages of homosexual development and (Telford in Via and Gagnon 2003, 4)[9] offers a fourth perspective that has influenced both the secular society and the Protestant mainline denominations.

In general, homosexuals were viewed as degenerates prior to the 1960s in not only the PMC community but the behavioral science community as well. Gudorf (2000) argues that progress in redefining how we view homosexuality is due primarily to the exploration of sexual orientation as a valid attribute of an individual that could be studied for its impact. While there was awareness of homosexual orientation in the ancient, pre-Christian world (Gagnon 2001), the contemporary, postpagan concept of homosexual orientation did not exist in the literature in Europe until the nineteenth century. (For more details on the history of the concept of homosexuality as an orientation, please refer to appendix 1). According to Via, Toulouse, at the time of this writing, continued to pine that probably

---

[9] Dan Via cited (without a book citation) that his friend George Telford suggested that gay people are "differently ordered, rather than disordered."

most mainline Protestants still regard homosexual behavior as sinful but that those "in the muddled middle simply wish that the issue would go away" (Toulouse in Via and Gagnon 2003, 4).

Kinsey's research on homosexuality also significantly promoted the idea of homosexuality as an orientation (Kinsey 1948). According to Kinsey, there are two types of homosexual acts: homosexual perversion and homosexual inversion. According to Kinsey, 37 percent of the males between eighteen years and older had had a homosexual experience to the point of orgasm, but only 4 percent were exclusively homosexual throughout their lives (see Edwards 1984, 17). Based on this, Kinsey concluded that "the vast majority of homosexual acts (33 out of 37 percent) are instances of 'heterosexual perversion'" (Kinsey in Cook 1984, 254). His research focused primarily on Caucasian males and is not generalizable to non-Caucasian men or any females but was considered to be revolutionary at the time of its publication. Kinsey's term "perversion" describes persons engaging in homosexual acts whose basic sexual orientation remains heterosexual. In contrast, homosexual inversion is "not a conscious choice but form determinative factors over which the person has no control. Unlike the pervert, the invert does not decide to become a homosexual" (Kinsey in Cook 1984, 254).

Movement toward LGBTQ Inclusion in the Church

Nearly forty years after Hiltner's presentation on the impact of Kinsey on the church, Olson and Cadge (2008) published a qualitative study on clergy perceptions of homosexuality, in which they interviewed sixty-two Protestant clergy across the United States; of these sixty-two clergy, forty volunteered their views of homosexuality without being prompted. Cadge collaborated with Wildeman (2005), presenting a conference paper summarizing the dialogues that many mainline Protestant denominations were engaged in within the last decade. Their findings indicate that over the last ten years, there has been some shift in overall perception of members in the PMC toward the adoption of LGBTQ inclusion policies/perspectives. Cadge and Wildeman (2005) found that in order for local congregations to engage in meaningful dialogues about homosexuality, their underlying emotions and fears have to be identified and addressed. The result of the self-reflective process reflects a fundamental change in how the issue is now conceptualized; indeed, Cadge and Wildeman (2005) postulate that it represents the rejection of the "cultural war/rules of engagement" theoretical framework that had been fueling the denomination-wide contentious debate. Interestingly, sociology of religion scholars (Ammerman 2005; Olson and Cadge 2000; Luidens 2009) predict that in several decades, only the most conservative denominations will still maintain policies that prohibit homosexual persons from ordination. Indeed, trends suggest that in the North American mainline Protestant denominations, the cohort groups in their twenties and thirties do *not* perceive ordination of homosexual clergy to be a problematic issue or a biblical conundrum (Kaleem 2014). On a similar note, the Public Religion Research Institute, in a 2013 survey, found that up to one-third of millennials had left their faith in the church due to "negative teachings" or "negative talk" as related to LGBTQ persons.

HISTORICAL PSYCHOLOGICAL PERSPECTIVES ON GAYS AND LESBIANS

In 1905, Sigmund Freud is said to have developed the concept of sexuality as independent of an individual's gender in his book *The Three Essays on the Theory of Sexuality*. Thinkers prior to Freud had asserted that homosexual men or male "inverts" inherit some female characteristics that make them sexually attracted to members of their own sex. Freud, instead, promoted the idea that the direction of the sexual drive is independent of inherited sexual characteristics. Freud did, however, continue the psychiatric tradition of labeling nonheterosexual behaviors as "perversions." It appears that Freud's view of homosexual "perversions" contributed to the perspective that homosexuality is a mental illness, which, in the 1950s, continued to be widely held in the United States by the psychoanalytic community (Nelson and Longfellow 1994, 393–393).

Due to the efforts of gay activists in the 1950s, which gained more credibility in the late 1960s at the time of the civil rights movement in the United States, the American Psychiatric Association released the Diagnostic and Statistical Manual-II (DSM-II) in 1973, and "homosexuality" (as stated earlier) was no longer listed as a diagnosis. Instead, "sexual orientation disturbance" was developed to explain individuals who were struggling with their sexual orientation.

Whereas the Bible only speaks to behavior, in contrast, the psychological community speaks about orientation (American Psychiatric Association 1973). According to Stapert (2008), an ordained clergy (male) in the Reformed Church in America and licensed psychologist, this 1973 edition of the DSM-II sparked fierce debate in both the mental health and church communities. According to *Time* (February 20, 1978,), a 1978 poll of the 2,500 American Psychiatric Association members revealed that sixty-nine of their members disagreed with this homosexuality disease an orientation to sexuality.

In 1974, the American Psychiatric Association (APA) dropped homosexuality from its list of mental diseases completely, with homosexuals no longer being defined as having a disorder. However, the APA did recognize a category of "sexual orientation disturbances, which did not include all homosexuals but designated those who were disturbed by, in conflict with, or wished to change their sexual orientation, and those who were subjectively distressed or socially impaired by their homosexuality" (Edwards 1984, 16). After 1974, some Protestant mainline denominational leaders began to regard homosexuals as "differently ordered," rather than disordered (Telford in Via 2003, 4). As noted by Telford, the psychological community's emerging perspective on homosexual orientation began to positively affect the PMC perspective on homosexual behaviors.

With the publication of the DSM-III-R in 1987, the American Psychiatric Association took another step toward full acceptance of homosexuality when it removed the category of "ego-dystonic homosexuality." Lief and Kaplan (1986) viewed ego-dystonic homosexuality as a clinical presentation of an individual who presents for therapy because he or she is uncomfortable with his or her fantasies, behaviors, feelings, and increasing shame about homosexuality. Their treatment involved the choice of "working through the homophobia or the heterophobia." Despite the progress being made, critics of the DSM continue to assert that this concept remains *implicit* within the DSM-IV category of "sexual disorder not otherwise specified" (American Psychiatric Association 1994).

Homosexual Identity Formation

In a contemporary understanding of homosexual orientation, liberal theologian Via (in Via and Gagnon 2003, 4) states, "Sexual orientation means a proclivity or predisposition that is given and not deliberately chosen or subject to the will of the individual" (p. 16). According to the American Psychiatric Association (2008), sexual orientation exists on a continuum that stretches between exclusively heterosexual and exclusively homosexual individuals. However, Gudorf (2000) also asserts sexual orientation is resistant to change even among extremely motivated people and that sexual orientation is fixed early in life. Thus, there continues to be debate in the scientific and religious communities about the ability to change one's sexual orientation (Via 2003).

Sexual orientation is usually discussed in terms of three categories: heterosexual (having emotional, romantic, or sexual attractions to members of the other sex), gay/lesbian (having emotional, romantic, or sexual attractions to members of one's own sex), and bisexual (having emotional, romantic, or sexual attractions to both men and women). This range of behaviors and attractions has been described in various cultures and nations throughout the world. Many cultures use identity labels to describe people who express these attractions (Via in Via and Gagnon 2003, 16).

In the United States, the most frequent nonheterosexual labels are lesbians (women attracted to women), gay men (men attracted to men), and bisexual people (men or women attracted to both sexes). However, some people may use different labels or none at all (American Psychiatric Association 2008). Currently, there appear to be two accepted views of gay/lesbian orientation (Gudorf 2000): an essentialist view and a constructionist view. The essentialist view asserts that gay/lesbian orientation is innate and biologically or genetically caused. The constructionist view maintains that gay/lesbian orientation results from the interaction of psychological and social forces on the individual. Thus, sexual orientation refers to an enduring pattern of emotional, romantic, and (or) sexual attractions to men, women, or both sexes. Sexual orientation also refers to a person's sense of identity based on those attractions, related behaviors, and membership in a community of others who share those attractions. Recent research, however, has demonstrated that sexual orientation exists in ranges. Sexual orientation, especially for women, ranges from exclusive attraction to the other sex to exclusive attraction to the same sex (Diamond 2008). Specific to the debate on lesbian orientation and behavior, Diamond debunks the idea of women as having a set or rigid orientation. Rather, she states there is natural fluidity between being heterosexual or homosexual that defies concrete classification.

RESEARCH APPLICATIONS OF SOCIAL IDENTITY THEORY

Both Canda (2010) and Helminiak (1989) discuss spirituality as involving an evolutionary process that is marked by turning points and developmental milestones. Quackenbush (2008) asserts that individuals have hierarchies among the many labels that they apply to themselves but that some are more central to the core of their identities than others and that the identities they hold influence their choices. Quackenbush (2008) also notes that individuals' spiritual identities are context driven and vary from person to person, and spiritual identities emerge only as individuals understand what needs have shaped their journeys. In other words, for some individuals, their spiritual identity becomes primary, but religious identity remains important, albeit in the backdrop of their spiritual identity, throughout their lives. However, Quackenbush (2008) asserts that it is healthy for individuals to have consistency between religious/spiritual identities and religious/spiritual practices.

Miller (2005, 2007, 2008), who studied the experiences of African American gay men living with AIDS, also presents a logic model for religious, spiritual, and sexual identity formation, which has been used to inform this study on lesbian clergy. Through his research on African American gay men living with AIDS, Miller (2005, 2007) found that spiritual development for homosexual African American men tends to follow their religious development in the black church but that eventually their sexual development becomes dissonant with their religious development. This results in the development of a spirituality that is separate from their religious identity.

Through the lens of social identity theory regarding homosexual clergy, Giesler (2006) presented a paper titled "From Outgroup to Out:

Lesbian Clergy's Self-Perceptions of Leadership" at the annual meeting of the Association for Women in Psychology. Based on this work, Geisler's (2006) social identity theory conceptual framework suggests that dominant groups create outgroups in order to attain identity and thrive.

THEORETICAL CONSTRUCTS OF IDENTITY

Religious Identity Construct

First, the identity theory of religion defines religion as "whatever sacralizes identity or a system of meaning" (Mol 1979). According to this theoretical approach, socialization is similar to the concept of institutionalization, except that it adds "qualities such as untouchability and awe, qualities that reinforce the materials of which the house of identity is constructed" (Mol 1979). Pertinent to social identity theory (SIT) is that the sacralization aspect of religion appears to protect individuals' religious identity as it defines reality "and modifies, obstructs, or (if necessary) legitimates change" (Mol 1979). In other words, the ideologies and practices of many religious groups encourage the development of a self-concept organized around their religious identities (Aremerman 1987). Furthermore, the more indoctrinated or socialized individuals are to their particular religious groups, the less likely they will shift their religious identities over time (Grecas 1981; Greil and Rudy 1984).

Another perspective on religious identity is that the accommodation of discrepant identities, as in the case of Christian homosexuals and specifically Christian lesbians, does not always result in a decision in which they abandon their former identities (religion) while accepting a new identity (homosexual). This type of identity negotiation (Becker 1963; Straus 1976; Gecas 1982) is a process in which multiple identities remain intact. Such religious identity revision is equated with socialization. "Socialization is the process by which the self internalizes social meanings, reinterprets them, and in turn, responds back upon the society" (Gecas 1981 in Thumma 1991, 335). Thus, through this socialization process, individuals interact between themselves and society and create meaning systems that result in individuals' self-concept (Troiden 1984), and the self-concept in relationship to a social situation (Gecas 1981). According to Thumma (1991), in his case study of a conservative, gay, Christian organization called Good News, he wrote that it is possible to reconstruct one's religious identity without abandoning his or her religious identity altogether. Through a process of socialization, he found that gay individuals have been able to renegotiate their religious identities, once their sexual identities are solidified.

SPIRITUAL IDENTITY CONSTRUCT

Both Canda (2010) and Helminiak (1989) discuss spirituality as involving an evolutionary process that is marked by turning points and developmental milestones. Quackenbush (2008) asserts that individuals have hierarchies among the many labels that they apply to themselves but that some are more central to the core of their identities than others and that the identities they hold influence their choices. Quackenbush (2008) also notes that individuals' spiritual identities are context driven and vary from person to person, and spiritual identities emerge only as individuals understand what needs have shaped their journeys. In other words, for some individuals, their spiritual identity becomes primary, but religious identity remains important, albeit in the backdrop of their spiritual identity, throughout their lives. However, Quackenbush (2008) asserts that it is healthy for individuals to have consistency between religious/spiritual identities and religious/spiritual practices.

SEXUAL IDENTITY CONSTRUCT

Both Canda (2010) and Helminiak (1989) discuss spirituality as involving an evolutionary process that is marked by turning points and developmental milestones. Quackenbush (2008) asserts that individuals have hierarchies among the many labels that they apply to themselves, but that some are more central to the core of their identities than others and that the identities they hold influence their choices. Quackenbush (2008) also notes that individuals' spiritual identities are context driven and vary from person to person, and spiritual identities emerge only as individuals understand what needs have shaped their journeys. In other words, for some individuals, their spiritual identity becomes primary, but religious identity remains important, albeit in the backdrop throughout their lives.

THEORETICAL CONSTRUCTS OF BELONGING

Secondly, the life model of social work practice, also known as the ecological model (Bronfenbrenner 1979; Gitterman and Germain 2008), emerges as an appropriate foundation for understanding the issues faced by lesbian clergy. It is anticipated that this model of human ecology will theoretically explain the level of fit that individuals have within their various environments. In other words, through the use of the ecological model, lesbian clergy who are able to remain within their denominations can be explained as having an "adaptive level of fit" within one or more of their various environmental contexts (i.e., their families of origin, their partners, their congregations, their denominations, and their communities). Bronfenbrenner (1979) likened this type of ecological system to Russian nesting dolls with concentric circles that explain human development.

Bronfenbrenner (1979) stressed the interactions of a changing organism in a changing environment. In Bronfenbrenner's view, the environment is composed of one's immediate settings as well as the complex social-cultural context in which we experience relationships across many different settings. The concentric circles include microsystems (spouses/partners, nuclear families, extended families, schools, religious organizations, congregations), mesosystems (interaction of microsystems), exosystems (local governments, work settings, school boards, denominations), and macrosystems (dominant beliefs and ideologies).

In addition, it is anticipated that the ecological model will lend itself to this qualitative research method because it considers "social time" and accounts for the "fit" of lesbian clergy research participants in their environments, including fit between themselves versus their families of origin, their partners, their congregations, and their denominations. This study seeks to examine the person-environment fit within these systemic contexts, exploring the interactions of various systems on the individuals' developments (Bronfenbrenner 1979), their levels of stress (Gitterman and Germain 2008), as well as their perceptions of their social networks (i.e., primarily their congregations and denominations).

THEORETICAL CONSTRUCTS OF OPPRESSION

Thirdly, anti-oppressive (Dominelli 2002) theory will be used to provide a framework for understanding the degree to which each of the lesbian clergy participants are affected by the oppressive nature of the relationships with the individuals and organizations that they interact with on an ongoing basis. Importantly, according to AOT, individuals' identities form as a result of interactions between people. Thus, in applying this theory to this population, the literature suggests that these women will have one of three responses to their denomination(s): (1) acceptance of its theological stance on homosexuality and therefore remain within their home denomination; (2) accommodation to living within the norms and stances of their home denomination *or* within a different Protestant mainline denomination that they proactively sought out because it appears to be more theologically and socially progressive toward LGBTQ persons; or a (3) rejection of their home denominations and departure from religious identity for a time.

ADDRESSING THE VOID OF RESEARCH ON LESBIAN CLERGY

Building on Giesler's findings, this study seeks to further explore the lived experiences of lesbian clergy in four Protestant mainline denominations and to explain how lesbians have sought to fit in to their communities— particularly the faith community. The study seeks to give a voice to their lived experiences and their feelings of isolation, diminishment, or not being accepted or fitting in. The theological, denominational, and behavioral science literatures fail to give an explanation for how the lesbian clergy have experienced institutional oppression by their denominations. Additionally, the literatures fail to provide an understanding of their experiences of oppression in the development of their various identities (e.g., religious, sexual, and spiritual). Finally, the literatures do not provide an explanation for the lesbian clergywomen's tolerances and intolerances of the institutional oppressions that they regularly experience. These gaps give rise to the need for an exploratory research on these questions that involve the lesbian clergywomen's development of their various identities in their denominational contexts, with a mix of positive and negative experiences.

In conclusion, there is minimal knowledge about the experiences of lesbian clergy who professed their sexual identities to their Protestant denominations. This is true from a contextual, theoretical, and empirical perspective. There are many biblical and theological essays and papers on the topic of LGBTQ inclusion and clergy ordination issues but nothing about the experiences of lesbian clergy in ministry. In addition, there are numerous denominational surveys about the attitudes of congregations and denominations toward LGBTQ inclusion and clergy ordination, but again, very little is understood about the lesbian clergy themselves and their unique set of struggles for acceptance and full integration into the lives of their denominations. Thus, the social science research leaves a gap in the knowledge about lesbian clergy's experiences of coming out to their families, their congregations, and their denominations. Lastly, it is unknown what the exact impact on the women's lives is, specifically on their psychological well-being and physical health, due to their experiences of ongoing employment discrimination and institutional oppression.

This exploratory study makes important contributions to the social work literature by addressing these identified gaps in the peer-reviewed social science and theological journals, offering both the positive and negative experiences of the lesbian clergy who attempt to negotiate their passions and ministries within their denominations. In this study, the lived experiences of the lesbian clergy, specifically regarding the confluence of their various identities—their religious, sexual, and spiritual selves—will be detailed.

CHAPTER 3

METHODOLOGY

METHODS

THE NEED FOR RESEARCH

This study seeks to address the lack of qualitative research regarding the experiences of lesbian Protestant mainline clergy, which could inform the debate and potentially assist qualified candidates for the clergy in making positive contributions to the church. Initially, the need for this specific research was indicated due to overall lack of research studies on all aspects of homosexual clergy in general, but it became quickly apparent that our knowledge of the lesbian Protestant mainline clergy population is even more limited. This is particularly true for the Evangelical Lutheran Church in America, the Presbyterian Church, USA, the Reformed Church in America, and the United Church of Christ. This contrasts to Roman Catholicism, which has completed some research on the incidence of homosexuality in the church. Sipe (1995, 73), a Roman Catholic priest and Baltimore therapist, found in his study of one thousand clergy that 23 percent of the Catholic clergy in the United States are gay (Ostling 1989).

The lack of research on lesbian clergy in most Protestant mainline denominations appears to be due primarily to the sensitive nature of the issue (Kaleem 2014). What has been missing, and this study specifically offers, is research that humanizes the experience of what remains currently to be a controversial group, lesbian Protestant mainline clergy. While the human or lived experiences of male heterosexual clergy members have been a subject of controversy, lesbian clergy remain an even greater enigma because they have fundamentally two obstacles in the theological arena: being female and being lesbian.

THE SAMPLE POPULATION

Based on the interviews to be conducted and a review of the documentation supporting this study, it does not appear that the general church population draws a distinction between male and female homosexuals. There are, however, considerable gender differences and life experiences between male and female homosexual persons. For the purposes of this study, therefore, only lesbian clergy will constitute the population being studied across four Protestant mainline denominations.

The heterogeneous sample of lesbian clergy chosen for this study will generate a thick description of the lived experiences of these women. This research offers a new light and understanding of the lived experiences of the lesbian ELCA, PCUSA, RCA, and UCC clergy that will be sampled.

INTRODUCTION TO RESEARCH PROBLEM

Homosexual clergy remain marginalized in many mainline Protestant denominations in North America (Hartford Seminary 1998). This study explores the pathways that lesbian women follow in becoming clergy in the four denominations under consideration. These are the Evangelical Lutheran Church, the Presbyterian Church, Reformed Church in America, and United Church of Christ. Historically, these denominations have not been supportive of LGBT persons becoming ordained. Certainly, the ordination of lesbian, gay, bisexual, or transgender clergy who are open about their sexuality, are sexually active, or are in committed same-sex relationships remains a hotly debated topic within most contemporary Christian Church communities (Reformed Church in America 2012). Along the theological and social continuum of this issue (from which the lesbian clergy were sampled), it appears that the Reformed Church in

America (*MGS*, RCA 2012, 149–150) remains more conservative than its sister denominations, with whom it shares common European Reformation roots (the Evangelical Lutheran Church in America, the Presbyterian Church, USA, and the United Church of Christ). The United Church of Christ remains the most theologically and socially liberal denomination, with the Evangelical Lutheran Church in America and Presbyterian Church, USA sharing a middle position along the theological and social justice continuum. (Table 1, "Views on homosexuality in Protestant mainline denominations," is provided below for the reader's convenience.)

Table 1. Views on homosexuality in Protestant mainline denominations[10]

Denomination	Percent of Those Who See Gay Issues as a Concern	Of Those Who See Gay Issues as Important, the Percent Who ...		
		Support Inclusion	Oppose Inclusion	Have Mixed Opinions
All Mainline Protestants (191)	50%	26%	31%	43%
United Church of Christ	24%	22%	44%	33%
Presbyterian Church, USA	81%	35%	12%	53%
Evangelical Lutheran Church	33%	--	20%	80%
Reformed Church in America	36%	20%	--	80%

As noted in this work's introduction, there is an absence of literature on lesbian clergy that is scientifically rigorous. The literature search performed by the author of this study produced numerous news articles and internet opinion sites that primarily focus on the potential schisms in mainline Protestant denominations regarding the endorsement of homosexuality among its lay members (Ostling 1989; Radin 2005) and the ordination of lesbian and gay clergy. Of the references found on homosexual clergy,

---

[10] The Hartford Institute for Religion Research, 2007.

one was an unpublished conference paper (Cadge and Wildemann 2005), another was a published conference paper (Hiltner 1972), and yet another was a descriptive article (Tucker 1998). In addition, a computer search yielded a limited number of scholarly articles and only seven qualitative research studies (Olson and Cadge 2002; Heskins 2005; Miller 2005, 2007, 2008; Giesler 2006; Hinrichs 2008) about the issue of homosexuality in the church. Only three (Heskins 2005; Hinrichs 2008; Giesler 2006) of the studies cited here sampled lesbian and gays in the church, and only one of those (Giesler 2006) specifically sampled lesbian clergy. The literature search did not yield any quantitative studies on homosexual clergy. Only Miller's studies have been conducted in a social work context.

METHODOLOGICAL CHOICES

From a life model perspective, it is considered imperative that social workers constantly attend with knowledge of and sensitivity to the religious, spirituality, and sexual orientation of their clients (Gitterman and Germain 2008). Ingrained in our code of ethics, social workers should consistently accept and respect each client's (1) race, ethnicity, religious, and spirituality; (2) gender; (3) sexual orientation; (4) age; and (5) particular mental and physical challenges (NASW Code of Ethics 1996, 2008). Such sensitivity requires specialized knowledge about a particular population or person being served by the practitioner and a high level of self-awareness.

To honor these ethical demands, the author is adopting methodologies that maximize the exploratory nature of this study, allowing the participants to find their voice and construct their narrative without being overly constrained by theological or psychological frameworks. Data collection will be accomplished through open-ended questions posed as part of a three-part interview series. The interviews will be administered using a grounded theory (psychology) methodology. Remaining sensitive to the population under study, the data from the interviews will be interpreted using the feminist methodology of the listening guide (Brown et al. 1988; Brown and Gillian 1992; Raider-Roth 2002; Woodcock 2005) and open content coding (Miles and Huberman, 1994).

Theoretically, the study represents a synthesis of ecological (Bronfenbrenner 1979; Gitterman and Germain 2008), anti-oppressive

(Dominelli 2003), and social identity (Tajfel and Turner 1979) theories, which are needed to provide a sophisticated framework for understanding the complexity in which these women find themselves, both from a faith-based perspective and a professional perspective. In turn, this theoretical framework is shaped (and constrained) by the parameters of blended methods of grounded theory and the listening guide research approach that was used by the author to guide the interviewing and analytic processes. It provides the discipline through which to achieve knowledge, while allowing the women being interviewed to find their voice and state their lived experiences as they understand them. For a description of grounded theory techniques, see Creswell (1998) and Glaser (2008). For a description of the listening guide, see Woodcock (2005). And finally, the author synthesizes ecological, anti-oppression, and identity theories discussed in chapter 2 to organize findings into individual constructs and domains being studied.

IDENTITY CONSTRUCTS

The religious, spiritual, and sexual identities of the lesbian clergy are cast as social identity constructs, with ecological theory providing the foundational context within which to explore the identity conflicts that the lesbian clergy have experienced in their ministries, communities, and families. The ecological context that appears to be most important in understanding the lived experiences of the lesbian clergy is believed to be their religious belief systems. Applying identity theory to their stated religious belief systems, the individuals' belief systems will be explored from an outsider's stance, in which the researcher seeks to distinguish the research participants' systems of meaning and symbols by which they defined themselves. In addition, the author uses a phenomenological approach to the exploration of religion with the research participants, first recording their experiences of religion and then classifying their observed experiences into categories such as prayer, ritual, sacrifice, music, rites of passage, and family roles. See Mol (1979) for a description of the methodology. And finally, identity theory allows for the conceptualization of the degree to which individuals are able to successfully negotiate their religious identities.

THE RESEARCH QUESTION

This dissertation seeks to answer the following research question: How do the lived experiences of lesbian clergy in Protestant mainline denominations impact their religious, spiritual, and sexual identities?

Through a synthesis of critical conversation and phenomenological methods, the investigator explores the phenomenon of the religious, spiritual, and sexual identity formation in the lived experiences of the lesbian PMC clergy. For more information, see appendix 1 for a detailed matrix of the research questions and method.

The specific learning objectives that will be addressed in this exploratory study are to:

1. explore the lived experiences of the sampled lesbian ELCA, PCUSA, RCA, and UCC clergy;
2. explore whether and how the sampled lesbian ELCA, PCUSA, RCA, and UCC clergy have experienced "fit" in their families, in their communities, and in their denominations;
3. understand the meanings that the sampled lesbian ELCA, PCUSA, RCA, and UCC clergy attach to their personal histories; and
4. understand how the lesbian ELCA, PCUSA, RCA, and UCC clergy perceive themselves regarding each of the domains of their religious, spiritual, and sexual identities.

By fulfilling these research objectives, the relevance to social work is achieved through the justice themes related to LGBTQ issues in general and lesbian rights in particular.

Lesbian rights are specifically explored in the church as a subculture, and even more particularly as subcultures in the ELCA, PCUSA, RCA, and UCC—four Protestant mainline denominations. This application of social work's life model (Gitterman and Germain 2008) illuminates the little-understood phenomenon of lesbian clergy who are living in the subculture of the PMCs, illuminated through the revealed relationship dynamics that surfaced during the course of this study. The life model and its related ecological model (Bronfennbrenner 1979) enable the author to explore the lesbian clergypersons' experience of "fit" in their denominations. Further, the utilization of both phenomenology research methodology and social identity theory (Tajfel and Turner 1979) can be utilized to explore the meanings that the lesbian clergy attach to their identity formation and the impact, if any, of their identities as it related to their ministerial formation.

In studying this topic of lesbian clergy identity formation, the author utilizes in-depth interviews with lesbian clergy in the PMC (Creswell 2007) who fit the inclusion criteria for the sample and who are willing to complete the informed consent documents. The units of analysis of this study will be the shared meanings that the lesbian Protestant mainline clergy attach to their religious identities, spiritual identities, and sexual identities.

ANALYTIC METHODOLOGY

The design of this study is based on the combined methods of two research methodologies. One is the listening guide (Brown et al. 1988; Gilligan, Brown, and Rogers 1990; Woodcock 2005); the second is a grounded theory (Creswell 1998; Glaser 2008).

THE LISTENING GUIDE

The listening guide is a feminist qualitative methodology, which is being utilized because the study is about power relationships between the lesbian Protestant mainline clergy and their denominational structures. Specifically, the listening guide (Brown et al. 1988; Brown and Gilligan 1992; Raider-Roth 2002; Woodcock 2005) is a qualitative, feminist, relational, and voice-centered method of analysis that seeks to understand the complexities of voice in populations that have not been heard historically. The listening guide evolved out of research with female adolescents at Harvard University in the early nineties and is an interpretive method that centers on voice and relationship with others. It draws on Johnston's work on problem-solving, using *Aesop's Fables* as a means for determining what people know and can articulate as it relates to the logic of justice and solving moral conflicts (Taylor, Gilligan, and Sullivan 1995, 216).

The listening guide is a relational method of interpretative analysis using both literary and clinical processes that identify shifts in voice and perspective (Brown et al. 1988; Brown and Gilligan 1992). In utilizing the listening guide, the transcripts of each interview will be read through as many times as necessary to gain understanding and description of what stories the narratives are providing. By utilizing the listening guide, the author listens to the interviews through multiple, overlapping layers of analysis and discerns the multiple voices in a single text through the use of hand color-coding on the transcript. This method allows the author to delve into the complexity of matters that other methods may not have allowed. Rigor is supported by the investigator's provision of a written trail of evidence that is reflective of the participants' words to support the investigator's interpretations in the final research document.

In sum, the author felt that the listening guide captured the complexities of the lesbian Protestant mainline clergy participants' voices and was instrumental in revealing the nuances of their experiences as practicing clergy in their denominations. The listening guide divulged the ways that the lesbian Protestant mainline clergy made meaning of and reconciled their ascribed understandings of their religious, spiritual, and sexual identities. However, there are two possible methodological limitations of the listening guide. They relied on the participants' ability to articulate thoughts and feelings in patterns of speech, and its trustworthiness rested in the definition of self as "socially constructed" (Brown et al. 1988; Gilligan, Brown, and Rogers 1990).

GROUNDED THEORY

The importance of grounded theory (Glaser and Strauss 1967; Creswell 1998; Glaser 2008) to this study lies in its purpose to generate a theory. The theory being generated will be contextualized in the phenomenon being studied (Creswell 2008). In this study, it is anticipated that the in-depth interviews with the lesbian clergy under consideration will generate a theory that can contribute to the practical theology and social science literatures.

The challenges of using this theory are the following:

1. The investigator needs to set aside her ideas about the phenomenon being studied, so that a theory can emerge.

2. Despite the inductive nature of this approach, this is a systemic approach with steps in the data analysis.
3. The investigator is challenged to determine both when the data are saturated and when the theory is sufficiently detailed.

For this research methodology to be effective, the sample has to become the "theoretical sample" (Creswell 1998, 57) in order to help the investigator form the best theoretical explanation. It is here that the concepts of saturation and constant comparison (Creswell 1998) of the research participants are utilized.

CODING PROCESSES

In open coding (Miles and Huberman 1994; Creswell 1998), the investigator has to form initial categories of information in order to classify the issue (e.g., lesbian clergy in the church) under consideration. Both the typical and extreme cases of the phenomenon being studied are identified. Following the creation of the open coding categories, the investigator has to transpose the data into axial coding (Creswell 2007). With axial coding, the investigator identifies a central issue that explores causal conditions to the issue being studied. Finally, the consequences or the outcome of the strategies and tasks for this phenomenon are delineated.

SAMPLING METHOD

For the purposes of this study, heterogeneity in the sampling will be achieved through criterion and snowball sampling (described below) of research participants from four Protestant mainline denominations, the ELCA, the PCUSA, the RCA, and the UCC. The criterion sampling will be drawn from lesbian clergy of four denominations of many possible Protestant denominations in North America. For a discussion of sampling techniques, see Fortune and Reid (1999), Maxwell (2005), Cresewell (2007), Glasser (2008). These denominations share a relationship through the Formula of Agreement previously discussed above. The rationale for this narrowing of the population to the four Formula of Agreement denominations is fourfold:

- it makes for a "thick description" (Geertz 1973; Lincoln and Guba 1985 in Fortune and Reid 1999, 108) of the lived experiences of the lesbian PMC clergy;
- in the most theologically conservative of the four discussed denominations, the PMC clergy will represent "extreme cases" that may test the utilization of the social identity and ecological theories in understanding the lesbian PMC clergy;
- it will achieve the typicality of the sampled lesbian PMC clergy (Maxwell 2005, 89) more than a random sample of a comparative size; and
- it will allow for comparisons to be made between the four denominations.

The heterogeneous sampling of the lesbian clergy in the Protestant mainline denominations allows for more anonymity of the research participants, as the population for establishing the sample frame would be larger. It also allows for maximum variation to the larger sample size.

Criterion sampling is a type of purposive sampling in which the research participants in the sample will have to meet the parameters of the stated inclusion criteria. The participants will be purposefully selected by the investigator in order to accomplish the study's research objectives. According to Creswell (2007), "criterion sampling works well when all individuals studied represent people who have experienced the phenomenon" (p. 128). In turn, from a philosophical perspective, qualitative methods such as grounded theory are "useful in identifying previously unexamined assumptions" on the part of the primary investigator (Crabtree and Miller 2006, 179). And finally, criterion sampling is justified for this population of lesbian PMC clergy because it serves to ensure the quality of data by controlling for discrepancies that might arise from sampling methodologies in which internal validity is problematic (Miles and Huberman 1994 in Creswell 2007, 127) and because it ensures the attributes under study are part of the comparison process (i.e., comparing differences between the lesbian clergy within their ministry settings) (Maxwell 2005, 90).

Crabtree and Miller (1992) recommend that heterogeneous studies have a sample size of ten to twelve cases. Lincoln and Guba (1985), Marshall and Rossman (1989), McCracken (1988), and Patton (as cited in

Crabtree and Miller 1992) all state that heterogeneous qualitative samples should have twelve to twenty research participants for maximum variation or when testing for disconfirmation. However, for the purposes of this study, the sample size will be driven by a "sufficiency" and "saturation" of data (Seidman 2006, 55).

Sufficiency of data (Seidman 2006) occurs when there are enough research participants to reflect an adequate range of individuals sampled in terms of minorities and experience. According to Douglas (1976), Glasser and Strauss (1967), Lincoln and Guba (1985), Rubin and Rubin (1995), and Weiss (1994), a saturation of data occurs at a point in the study when the principal investigator is no longer hearing any new information being reported.

> The method of in-depth, phenomenological interviewing applied to a sample of participants who all experience similar structural and social conditions gave enormous power to the stories of a relatively few participants ... At some point, however, the interviewer may recognize that he or she is not learning anything decidedly new. (Seidman 2006, 55–56)

STUDY INCLUSION CRITERIA

The lesbian clergy sampled for the purposes of this study were at the time of the study either an ordained ELCA, PCUSA, RCA, or UCC minister (i.e., a congregational minister, a chaplain, a missionary, or a pastoral counselor), a minister serving in one of these four PMC settings, or a student preparing for ministry in one of these four PMC denominations. The inclusion criteria did not specify whether the participants were out to their congregations, colleagues, or families. These inclusion criteria spanned the range of possible years of active service. In sum, it was anticipated that these criteria would specifically highlight the characteristics of the lesbian PMC clergy who would be able to give emic or insider's (i.e., their own perspective) knowledge related to the phenomenon under consideration.

Again, the four PMC denominations from which the research participants would be sampled entered into an agreement in 1997 between the PCUSA, the ELCA, the RCA, and the UCC (RCA, *MGS* 1997). This allowed for an exchange of its ministers' ordinations for the purposes of employment in these four denominations. The denominational stances on the issue of homosexuality and on ordaining gay and lesbian ministers have been discussed in length earlier in this paper. The importance of the denominational agreement is that, despite being able to be employed in any of the denominations, they are not similar in their policies related to homosexuality in the church. Of these four denominations, there is a theological continuum, with the UCC being the most accepting of homosexuality ordination at one end, with the ELCA and PCUSA in the middle range since they recently have allowed homosexual ordination, and with the PMC as the most conservative and likely to deny homosexual ordination. In addition, there remain significant regional differences within each, as ordinations of clergy are determined by the local judicatories in each of these denominations. And finally, it is anticipated that the experiences of the research participants will vary depending on the seminary that she attended, due to theological differences between the seminaries within each of the denominations.

RECRUITMENT OF SAMPLE

Once the University at Albany Institutional Review Board (IRB) approves the start of this study, the principal investigator will begin recruiting the research participants. The recruitment process will occur primarily in the following ways: through advertising in the denominationally sanctioned monthly publication, *RCA Today*, and in the monthly newsletter of the unsanctioned advocacy "Room for All" newsletter and on the Room for All website, through advertising and posting of recruitment letters/brochures at the annual Room for All Conference, and through contact with the director and the board of directors of the advocacy group for full inclusion of LGBTQ persons in the RCA, Room for All, regarding individuals whom they would be able to identify as potential research subjects. Beyond the advertising in the initial RCA publications, it is hoped that the research participants will provide additional names, thereby making this a snowball sample (Patton 1990 in Crabtree and Miller 2006).

The potential research participants will be able to contact the principal investigator by email regarding their interest in participating in the study. According to the University at Albany Institutional Review Board (telephone conversation and email correspondence with Kanako Sumida, administrative coordinator on September 22, 2011), it is within ethical guidelines for the principal investigator to then follow up with her leads by contacting the potential research participants directly by either telephone or email. This will protect any woman who may not be outed yet, allowing her to be the first to initiate contact.

If these individuals express interest in participating in the study, the investigator will send an email to each of the potential research participants, confirming her interest in the study and to set up three interview dates, allowing for two hours each time. Finally, by means of a snowball sampling method, the investigator will request names of other lesbian PMC who fit the inclusion criteria and then in turn contact them through email.

DATA COLLECTION

IN-DEPTH INTERVIEWING

Three theories (i.e., ecological, anti-oppressive, and social identity) will inform the development of the open-ended questions for the three interviews. The three interviews are expected to enhance the validity of the study by putting the participants' responses "in context" (Seidman 2006, 25–26). The prolonged engagement of the participants in the project and the three-interview model fosters what Seidman (2006) refers to as "the external consistency of the passages, the syntax, diction, and even nonverbal aspects of the passage, and the discovery and sense of learning that I get from reading the passage lead me to have confidence in its authenticity" (p. 26). As a final point, the author will use an interview guide that contains nine to twelve questions for each of the three sections with each participant to maintain consistency in the delivery of the questions (Merton, Fiske, and Kendall 1999).

The data collection process is structured by the qualitative method of grounded theory (Creswell 2007; Glaser 2008), which clarifies the meanings that the lesbian clergy participants attached to the phenomenon of their identity formation (i.e., religious, spiritual, and sexual). The participants will be interviewed through three separate interviews for ninety to 120 minutes each, over a one- to three-week period. The principal investigator will utilize open-ended questions. As previously stated, the feminist methodology of the listening guide (Brown et al. 1988; Gilligan, Brown, and Rogers 1990) allows for the principal investigator and the research participants to engage each other during the interview process and to negotiate the meaning of the data.

The three interviews, based on grounded theory methodology, allow for an in-depth analysis that provides an opportunity for the deep meanings to emerge as the participants relay their experiences of being a lesbian PMC minister. These meanings are expected to emerge initially during the reciprocal exchange between two female clergy persons (i.e., the investigator and the research participant) at the time of the interviews.

THREE-INTERVIEW MODEL

Interviewing generally involves three separate interviews about: (1) personal history; (2) lived experience of the phenomenon being studied; and (3) a reflection on the first two interviews (Seidman 2006). (See appendix 1 for interview questions.) Thus, for purposes of this study, the interviews were structured first by the clergy participant's reflection on their own personal story and history (personal storying). Secondly, the clergy participants then reflected on their experiences within their denominations (denominational storying). And thirdly, the clergy participants reflected on their experiences of living as lesbian clergy within the Protestant mainline denominations, while reflecting again on the first two interviews and what the experience of the first two interviews meant to them. Lastly, it also involved either the integration or non-integration of the participants' own stories, including their perception of their fit with their denominations' stories.

The first interview explored the participants' personal biographies that include relational and sexual histories, call to ministry, and identity as a lesbian Protestant mainline minister. The first interview also enabled the research participants to identify where their journeys began toward understanding their religious, sexual, and spiritual identities.

The second interview explored the participants' denominational storying, including the participants' experience of denominational life, roles in ministry, as well as their biblical and theological perspectives of sexuality in general and lesbianism in particular.

The third interview explored the participants' "lived experiences" (Van Manen 1990; Moustakas 1994) and meaning making of being a lesbian PMC minister. It also involved either the integration or non-integration of the participants' own stories, including their perception of how their individual story fit within their denominational stories.

DATA ANALYSIS

Essentially, the analysis that emerged from this study was three-dimensional in structure. It was three-dimensional not only because each research participant spoke in terms of the three identities (i.e., religious, sexual, and spiritual) that emerged but also because there were three interview periods in which the women analyzed their own stories from three different story lines: personal, denomination, and life experiences.

The data analysis of the research objectives consisted of two phases, which are detailed below, both using the listening guide and open content coding. Further, the participant's lived experience and meaning making were given voice and set in an ecological context. The data from the interviews were analyzed using a listening guide method (Brown et al. 1988; Brown and Gilligan 1992; Raider-Roth 2002; Woodcock 2005) to understand the experiences of the lesbian clergy participants.

The first analysis of data involved "sufficient" readings of the transcripts and review of the audiotapes until the investigator had obtained a clear understanding of the data. The second analysis involved open content coding of data about the lesbian Protestant mainline clergy as it related to the three domains of their religious, spiritual, and sexual identity domains (Miles and Huberman 1994).

The Stages of the Analysis

The First Stage

During this listening/reading stage of the analysis, the investigator will synthesize the three interviews for each woman into a life story or plot (Woodcock 2005). In developing the plots, the investigator listens to the narrative of the participants' lives, using the research objectives as a guide. Further, the investigator attends to the literary narrative through recurring words, central metaphors, emotional material, contradictions, revisions and absences in the stories, silences, and shifts in the sound of voice and narrative position (i.e., first, second, and third person stances). The investigator listens to the transcripts until she has a clear sense of the data.

Phase one of the data analysis utilized the first three learning objectives. They are as follows: (1) to explore the lived experiences of the sampled lesbian PMC clergy; (2) to explore whether and how the sampled lesbian PMC clergy have experienced "fit" in their families, in their communities, and in their denominations; and (3) to understand the meanings that the sampled lesbian PMC clergy attach to their personal histories. Using the listening guide method, as described below, the data from the three interviews were transcribed and analyzed across interviews to identify common features of the discourse (Brown and Gilligan 1992). In other words, the transcription of the interviews are completed, and then the words/phrases and other striking features of the conversations between the investigator and the research participants (e.g., silences, tone of voice, and emotion) are hand coded with colored pencils.

The listening guide method of analysis calls for listening to the transcripts rather than reading them (Gilligan et al. 2003, 159). As Gilligan explains, "The need for a series of listenings arises from the assumption that the psyche, like the voice, is contrapuntal (not monotonic), so that simultaneous voices are co-occurring." Once each transcript is listened to and coded, each woman's transcript will be compared to the rest of the women's transcripts. Following the comparison, an overall analysis of the saturated data will be written with the learning objectives in mind.

In utilizing the listening guide, guided by the structure of the interview questions (i.e., the personal storying, the denominational storying, and the meaning making of the earlier interviews), the transcripts of each interview will be read thoroughly and listened to as many times as necessary to construct each woman's story that includes her personal, denominational, meaning-making experiences, as well as data about her three identities (i.e., her religious, sexual, and spiritual). In addition, for each story plot that is written based on the research questions, the investigator attaches a reflexive response (Balan 2005, 8) based on her own "bracketed" experiences (Creswell 2007).

The Second Stage

During this stage, the investigator listens for the first-person voice of the participants to emerge. This is a way of knowing for the investigator, as it creates a window through which to view the participants' knowledge about themselves and the phenomenon of their identities. During this stage, the women's I-poems take shape. I-poems are constructed by reading through the transcript and underlining all the I's and their associated words. It is a subjective process in which the investigator eliminates certain words to maintain confidentiality. Occasionally, other first-person forms of speech are used, such as "my," "me," and "myself." This method provides the investigator with an additional lens through which to interpret the transcripts.

Phase two of the data analysis utilizes learning objective four: to understand how the lesbian Protestant mainline clergy perceive themselves regarding each of the domains of their religious, spiritual, and sexual identities. Throughout this data analysis stage, the investigator's reflective and reflexive responses to each lesbian clergy participant are bracketed (Creswell 2007). In other words, the investigator discusses her own responses to the coded material, based on her framework as a clergyperson, as a woman, as a partner, as a clinical social worker, and as a mother.

During the second phase of data collection, the story plot for each of the research participants will be coded for the identities that emerge in the data. Through open content coding, the nuances of the religious, spiritual, and sexual identities of the research participants are explored (Miles and Huberman 1994). First, the data of the clergy participants are developed into exhaustive descriptions of the lesbian phenomenon for each of the domains (religious, spiritual, and sexual identities) of the female clergy participants. The data are deemed exhaustive when no further explanations can be found through "constant comparison" of each participant's data with the other participants' data (Glaser 2008).

Secondly, an analysis will be done comparing the narratives of each of the sampled women to the descriptions of identity data for the other female participants. The investigator then compares the exhaustive descriptions or narratives of each of the thirteen women to the interpretative analyses for each participant from the above listening guide method analysis stage, as an internal consistency check (Lincoln and Guba 1985). Finally, the investigator includes the bracketed investigator's interpretive reflections on each of the women and on the comparison of the women.

The Third Stage

During the third stage, the investigator listens to additional or alternative voices of the research participants (Balan 2005). The additional voice might be the voice of others (e.g., Bible, denomination, family, congregation) that had been internalized by the woman that emerged during the interviews. By speaking in alternate voices, it is anticipated that the participants will talk about their relationships with others and how they experience themselves in the various contexts of their lives. During the additional listening to the transcripts, the nature of these other voices, which are external to them, should emerge. The possible contrapuntal (Brown and Gilligan 1992) nature or alternate voices will be particularly noted, as it is anticipated that through this listening, the participants might begin to make meaning out of their phenomenon of identity formation as lesbian clergy.

The Fourth Stage

Using the listening guide method, the author composes an overall interpretive analysis, which synthesizes the first three stages of analysis, for each female participant. This analysis utilizes the research questions as a road map for this stage. Excerpts from the transcript will be included in the analysis, which become the "trail of evidence" (Balan 2005, 13).

ISSUES OF TRUSTWORTHINESS

Trustworthiness involves the procedures of credibility, dependability, conformability, and transferability (Lincoln and Guba 1985), which assure the integrity of the findings to the perspectives of the women being studied. The prolonged engagement that will occur through in-depth interviewing (Seidman 2006) allows for the trustworthiness of the data to emerge (Bloomberg and Volpe 2008). The grounded theory (Crewell 1998; Glasser 2008) method will inform the structure of the three interviews and the questions within each interview. It will also check for the internal consistency of the content that will emerge over the course of one to three weeks. By interviewing a number of participants, the experiences of one participant can be compared with those of the other participants (Seidman 2006).

The analysis hybrid between the listening guide (Brown et al. 1988; Brown and Gillian 1992; Raider-Roth 2002; Woodcock 2005) and grounded theory (Creswell 1998; Glaser 2008) will further enhance the trustworthiness of this study. In other words, the use of the two analysis methods enables the investigator to seek consistency and accuracy of the data for each participant and between participants.

CREDIBILITY

Credibility refers to the consistency of the participants' statements recorded in the data (e.g., the trail of evidence in the transcripts) (Bloomberg and Volpe 2008, 77). For this study, the author will look for credibility in each participant's narrative (or story plot), checking for internal consistency and whether there was consistency in the data between the hybrid analysis methods (e.g., between the data of the listening guide and open content coding sections). Evidence in support of credibility in this study takes the form of the following:

- **Prolonged Engagement during the Interview Process:** Prolonged engagement with the research respondents allows for the investigator to gain an understanding of the respondents' social relationships within their own work contexts. Further, prolonged engagement over the course of three interviews allows for the development of amiable relationships between the investigator and the respondents, thereby encouraging further disclosure about their experiences (Lindy 2008 in Given 2008).

- **Negative Case Analysis:** Negative case analysis allows for a constant comparison between the stories of the sampled women during both the interview and analysis process. This technique is necessitated by the spontaneous appearance of data that differs from the investigator's working theories and assumptions (Brodsky 2008 in Given 2008).

DEPENDABILITY

Dependability refers to the ability to track the processes and procedures used to collect and interpret the data (Bloomberg and Volpe 2008). The principal investigator will use an "audit trail" in order to detail how the data is being collected and analyzed. The investigator examines dependability of the data (i.e., sufficiency of the data) in developing answers to the research questions.

CONFIRMABILITY

Confirmability is the extent to which the findings of the study are shaped by the participants and not by researcher bias (Lincoln and Guba 1985). In this study, the author will use the listening guide's trail of evidence (Taylor, Gilligan, and Sullivan 1995, 29). Specifically, the investigator records her first impression and response to the material on a separate worksheet. The worksheet is then used to make a distinction between the research participant's voice and the investigator's voice and interpretations. Bracketing requires the author to record her own experiences and bias as well her responses and reflexivity on the interview transcripts and review them as part of the interpretive data process.

TRANSFERABILITY

Transferability refers to whether the study allows other readers/researchers to utilize data generated from this analytic process in their own settings (Bloomberg and Volpe 2008, 78). For instance, it is unclear how much of this study will be transferable to lesbian clergy in other denominations, as this was really an in-depth study about the experiences and identities of a small sample of women that were unique to these four Protestant mainline denominations.

RESEARCH PARTICIPANTS' CONCERNS, ETHICS, DIVERSITY

Due to the sensitive nature of the research topic, confidentiality will be ensured at the start of the initial phase of the interviews by obtaining a signed consent from each of the research participants. The informed consent describes the risks, discomforts, vulnerabilities, and benefits as well as the rights of the research participants (Seidman 2006, 63–68). The rights of the research participants include voluntary participation, the right to withdraw, the right of reviewing and withholding interview material, and the right to privacy.

In addition, confidentiality of the research participants is protected throughout the study by utilizing coded names and disguised descriptive material that could link them to their denominations or congregations. Although all efforts will be made to assure confidentiality, research participants will be informed of the limits of informed consent in the event of either a judicial subpoena or mandated reporter requirements.

The participants will fully know at the outset of the research what the investigator will be asking of them. They will be informed about the prolonged and in-depth interviews, their possible effects, and how they will be recorded. The investigator will also inform the participants that the results will be used for her dissertation and for possible later publication. Research participants will be informed about the emotional risks involved in participating in the in-depth interviews for them and that there could be some unintended consequences for them that the principal investigator had not anticipated. In the event that a participant becomes overwhelmed during any interview, the participants will be given the opportunity to stop the interview momentarily in order to calm down. Upon noted distress, the research participant will be reminded that the study may provide some healing interventions, and those possibilities will then be discussed.

Following the warnings regarding the possible effects, the research participants will be assured that their identities and therefore their risk to losing their employment will be eliminated. The potential benefits to the research participants are also described, although they will be presented as possibly being intangible. Along with the caveats offered regarding possible risks, it will also be explained to each participant that possibly the experiences of the interviews might be in and of themselves transformative for the research participants (See Morowski in Tolman and Brydon-Miller 2001, 62–63).

Finally, it will made abundantly clear that this research and the potential of the participants' stories being published is for the purpose of reducing prejudice, creating more understanding among the public, and to reach the end goal of an RCA constitutional change to allow gay and lesbian clergy to be ordained within the denomination.

⚜

CHAPTER 4

FINDINGS

OVERVIEW

In this study, the stories of thirteen incredible women are shared as they journey from young women in the church to outing themselves as lesbian clergy in four different mainline Protestant denominations. Here are the stories of Esther, Abigail, Rebecca, Deborah, Mary, Leah, Ruth, Naomi, Eve, Rachel, Sarah, Martha, and Hannah.[11] Although the names of the thirteen women have been changed to protect their confidentiality, the names chosen for the research participants were specifically chosen because they have the attributes of their assigned namesakes in the Hebrew and Christian scriptures (see table 4).

This sample of thirteen lesbian women had all revealed their sexual orientation to their families of origin and to their denominations at a point prior to the interviews. As noted above, each of the women was either an ordained minister of the Evangelical Lutheran Church (ELCA), Presbyterian Church, USA (PCUSA), Reformed Church in America (RCA), or the United Church of Christ (UCC) or a student in one of the affiliated denominational seminaries. Of the women interviewed, twelve

---

[11] The thirteen research participants were renamed to match the biblical women whose stories were reflected in their own personalities and stories.

are Caucasian, and one is black Caribbean descent. At the time of the interviews, the women lived in four regions of the United States—New England, mid-Atlantic states, Midwest, and far west. The thirteen research participants were renamed to match the biblical women whose stories were reflected in their own personalities and stories. (See table 6, "Shared characteristics," for a description of the shared characteristics between biblical women and each of the thirteen participants.)

Table 6. Shared characteristics

Assigned Name of Research Participant	Character Traits	Biblical Reference
Esther	She was a leader of her people and took risks to out herself in a hostile environment, while always honoring her tradition and respecting her parents.	Book of Esther
Abigail	She utilized her wisdom to appear before the approaching enemy (the opposition of her denomination and her various employers) to protect the safety and integrity of her own family and her GBLTQ community.	1 Samuel 25:1–44
Rebecca	She was assertive in a fundamentalist culture that did not support that trait; it enabled her to leave her restrictive childhood culture but disabled her from finding a community in which to fully fit.	Genesis 22:23, 24, 25:20–28, 26:6–35, 27, 28:5, 29:12, 35:8, 49:31
Deborah	She was a leader of various LGBTQ church communities and was continuing to do battle for LGBTQ rights in her denomination at the time of the interview.	Judges 4–5
Mary	She continues to be a disciple of Jesus despite her struggle with mental health issues and ongoing experience of oppression within various church communities for being out as a lesbian clergyperson.	Matthew 27:56, 61; 28:1; Mark 15:40, 47; 16:1–19; Luke 8:2; 24:10; John 19:25; 20:1–18.
Leah	She struggled to feel attractive to men when she was a child and, despite her struggles to feel a part of a community, remained loyal in her faith.	Genesis 29; 30; 49:31

Ruth	She represents the loyalty to her family and her partner, despite feeling much of her life that she was in a "strange country" as a lesbian.	Book of Ruth
Naomi	She continued just prior to the time of the interview to struggle with being deeply depressed and having a crisis/famine of the soul. At the point of the interview, she was at last feeling rewarded by the harvest or her new relationship with a woman, as she had finally come out.	Book of Ruth
Eve	She had a reputation for being sexually provocative in her home denomination, and several subsequent denominations viewed her as not being fit for leadership as a gay woman. She had leadership skills but was viewed in a negative light.	Genesis 2–3
Rachel	She feels that she has lived a divinely guided life and has found God in the ordinary circumstances of life, which has enabled her to become an important lesbian voice in her chaplaincy and parish ministry roles.	Genesis 29; 30; 31; 33:1, 2, 7; 35:16–26; 46:19, 22, 25; 48:7; Ruth 4:11; 1 Samuel 10:2; Jeremiah 31:15; Matthew 2:18
Sarah	She, like Sarah in the Bible, is a noble woman in her denomination and a woman of true leadership in the social justice and LGBTQ communities.	Genesis 11:29–12:1–20; 16, 17; 18; 20, 21, 22, 23
Martha	She had a pattern of being more practical than spiritual for years in her role of obeying her Catholic order and taking on various roles as a caregiver. Her spiritual side emerged when she became comfortable with her identity as a lesbian.	Luke 10:38–41; John 11; 12:1–3
Hannah	She was misunderstood as a woman when her religious tenacity and deep prayer life were judged because she was a lesbian.	1 Samuel 1–2

As noted in chapter 3, the learning objectives of this study were to:

1. explore the lived experiences of the sampled lesbian ELCA, PCUSA, RCA, and UCC clergy;

2. explore whether and how the sampled lesbian ELCA, PCUSA, RCA, and UCC clergy have experienced "fit" in their families, in their communities, and in their denominations;

3. understand the meanings that the sampled lesbian ELCA, PCUSA, RCA, and UCC clergy attach to their personal histories; and

4. understand how the lesbian ELCA, PCUSA, RCA, and UCC clergy perceive themselves regarding each of the domains of their religious, spiritual, and sexual identities.

This chapter presents the findings related to these objectives, summarizing and synthesizing the commonalities found within the thirteen life stories of these women. Chapter 5 then goes on to offer theoretical explanations for those identified commonalities through the lens of anti-oppression, social identity, and ecological theories.

In designing this study, it was anticipated that the meanings of the women's journeys would be explained through the application of phenomenological methodology (see Van Manen 1990; Moustakas 1994) to the three theories used in the study (i.e., ecological, social identity, and anti-oppression). However, rather than a phenomenological perspective, the findings that evolved out of this study ended up offering more of a developmental perspective on lesbian clergy identity. A fitting reminder here is that this study was grounded by the research question about understanding how the lesbian clergy perceived themselves regarding each of their domains in their religious, spiritual, and sexual identities. Therefore, the most significant findings of this study were that all thirteen of the women followed a development path that was informed by social identity theory (Tajfel and Turner 1979, 1985), ecological theory (Bronfenbrenner 1979; Gitterman and Germain 2008), and anti-oppression theory (Dominelli 2002).

In reviewing the narratives, the author found that the women shared a similar journey in terms of the sequence of their spiritual and professional development. Seven unique stages were identified: (1) a conservative formative religious identity within a denominational context; (2) after the early religious identities, many experienced a stage of strong spiritual development in adolescence or early adulthood; (3) following their self-identification as being spiritual, their sexual identity as lesbians or as bisexuals emerged; (4) after the women came out to themselves and to others as lesbians, the women went through a stage in which their religious identities became integrated with their sexual identities; (5) the women were able to recognize their calls to ministry and went through their processes of seminary training, ordination, and employment; (6) for the women who left the ministry, there was an interim temporary or permanent stage in which spiritual identity became primary; and (7) after becoming ordained clergy, some of the women appear to have moved toward an integration of their spiritual, religious, and clergy identities within a context of lesbianism. While their spiritual identity remained constant, it is important to note that their denominational identities changed at various developmental stages: generally before and during the coming out process; at the point of reworking their religious identities; during seminary; during the ordination process; and (or) during the employment process after ordination.

This chapter addresses the developmental pathway that each of the thirteen women underwent, identifying similarities and dissimilarities in their experiences within the church as a result of their sexual identity. Specifically, it addresses objectives one through three above, offering a chronological history of their development of their relationship to church as lesbians, with each stage being examined to assess their spiritual and professional fit at each stage in their maturation process of being lesbian and a minister.

Table 7. Stage theory of lesbian clergy development

Tasks Associated with Stage	Stage	Age Range	Characteristics	Role of Social Identity Theory* (as applied to sexual and religious/sexual identity)	Role of Goodness of Fit** (integration of ecological and anti-oppression theories)
- Feel safe in community of faith - Feel accepted in community of faith - Community of faith is center of social life	**Stage 1: Early Religious Identity***	0–34	- Belief in literal and anthropomorphized God - Allegiance to authority structures - Denominational/ congregational identity important	- Maintain religious/ denominational identity - May be some emergence of awareness of same-sex attraction	- Faith community provides a sense of security and belonging

Stage 2: Spiritual Identity (optional)****	13–48	- Anger, disillusionment with church of childhood/ adolescence - Able to differentiate from the authority structure and beliefs of their early religious identity	*Spiritual practices integrated into daily life (e.g., meditation, prayer, guided imagery, Twelve Steps) *May develop spiritual identity as alternative to religious identity	- Intentionally seeking fit in alternative spiritual communities that are different from the ones they were raised in	- Develop alternative spiritual ideas to replace former religious identity - Able to differentiate from the authority structure and beliefs of their early religious identity - Religious and (or) denominational identity less important than it was formerly

Stage	Age			
Stage 3: Emergence of Sexual Identity	13–48	- Confusion about same-sex attractions - Reflection on childhood literal beliefs in God and become disillusioned with former faith - Begin questioning and differentiating from authority structures	- Further emergence of same-sex attraction - Maintain early religious identity, or seek a new denomination, or leave religious identity altogether - Continues to explore lesbian identity acceptance	- Sense of alienation from faith and peer communities - Exploration of involvement in LGBTQ culture
- Begin to internally accept idea of having a lesbian identity - Engage in first lesbian relationships - Coming out to her family of origin - Desire to maintain sense of self within the religious/denominational community				
Stage 4: Revised Religious Identity	21–52	- Feeling a void that as a lesbian she believes she cannot be a part of a faith community - Seeking to reengage in a faith community (ies) that is GBLTQ affirming - Exploring how she can be a minister and be a lesbian simultaneously	- Reworking her religious identity to include feminist and lesbian perspectives	- Intentionally seeking new denominational identity in a tradition
- Integration of lesbian identity (and spiritual identity) into her religious identity				

Stage 5: Clergy Identity	22-plus			
- Enrolled at a seminary for ministerial training - Goes through ministerial training processes - Coming out to her congregation and her denomination - Becomes ordained		- Sense that her life will not be complete if she does not become a minister - Continuing to explore how she can be a minister and be a lesbian simultaneously - Contemplating call to ordained ministry	- Believing ministry has more integrity when she's out with her lesbian identity	- She finds fit in an affirming congregation - She appears to tolerate a lack of fit in a nonaffirming denomination if she is affiliated with an affirming congregation

Stage 6: Spiritual Identity (optional)****	35-plus	- Contemplates leaving ordained ministry because of feelings of lack of acceptance - Experiences a lack of goodness of fit with denomination	- Maintained religious identity outside of institutionalized church - Developed spiritual identity as an alternative to clergy identity, marked by using spiritual resources in work	- Lack of fit within a denomination due to ongoing experiences - Perceptions of lack of fit and oppression because of lesbian identity
- Find ways to work with LGBTQ advocacy outside of the institutionalized church - Demit from denominational ordination - Leave institutionalized church - Continued a career in counseling or social justice—related work outside of church				

- Incorporation of nontraditional spiritual practices into ministerial practice (e.g., yoga, meditation)	Stage 7: Synthesized Identity*****	35-plus	- More allegiance given to religious identity than denominational identity - Acceptance that there is truth in all the previous religious identity stages but that there is also a sense of mystery and paradox in religion	- Ability to transcend beyond the teachings of her own religious identity to include alternative religious/spiritual identities, while at the same time maintaining her own religious identity	- Focus on social justice work connected to a congregation and communities - Emphasis on LGBTQ advocacy and inclusion in her denomination and society - Emphasis on universal love for community rather than individual concerns

*According to social identity theory, people organize themselves into categories regarding organizational affiliation in regard to religion, gender, and so on (Tajfel and Turner 1979).

** In social work practice, applying an ecological approach can be best understood as looking at persons, families, cultures, communities, and policies to identify and intervene upon strengths and weaknesses in the transactional processes between these systems (Bronfenbrenner 1979; Gitterman and Germain 2008).

***Borrowed from anti-oppression theory, when moving on from this stage to develop sexual identity, the women appear to go one of three ways: 1) to maintain religious/denominational identity; 2) to maintain religious identity / find new denominational identity; or 3) to leave religious identity (this group of women develops a spiritual identity) (Dominelli 2002).

****This stage is *optional* for lesbian clergy development. It appears as a temporary replacement for the women who left their religious identity because they grieve the loss of having a religious identity and community. Further, it seems to function as a placeholder in between both stages of religious identity. This stage is distinguished from the spiritual practices that these women integrate into their clergy identity in later developmental stages.

*****Not all of the women in the sample achieved this stage. It appears that some of the women may not reach it due to exiting the profession of ordained ministry or perceiving ongoing lack of fit in institutionalized ministry. Given the relatively short periods of time since ordination for the women in the sample, it appears that if there were a future longitudinal study, more of the lesbian clergy would achieve this stage.

STAGE 1: EARLY RELIGIOUS IDENTITY FORMATION

This early religious stage is comprised of two findings that appear to be paradoxical. First, the early religious identities were strongly denominational and formative for all thirteen of the women. Second, at the same time, all thirteen women found their early religious experiences within those denominations to be oppressive to some degree. The paradox lies in how this strong denominational identity appeared later on to ameliorate much of the pain of rejection inflicted by those same denominational institutions. This resulted in some of the women choosing to stay within their denominations but others opting to leave.

For all thirteen of the women, their early religious identities, which included either a Protestant, Jewish, or Roman Catholic identity, nurtured their faith and their calls to eventually become ordained ministers (see table 1). During this formative stage, which occurred between the ages of infancy up to thirty-four years of age, the young women did not appear to necessarily distinguish between their religious identity and their denominational identity. Other characteristics of this early stage were belief in literal and anthropomorphized God and allegiance to authority structures (see Fowler 1981; Park 1986 for a description of the impact of belief in an anthropomorphized God). During this stage, it appeared that the young women felt safe in church, that church life was the center of their social lives, and that there was a sense of belonging in the faith community—even if their parents did not participate. Further, these women shared a sense at this stage of development that their denominational identity was very important and in some ways merged with their religious identity.

The women in the sample characterized their earliest religious identities as theologically conservative, ranging from conservative to ultraconservative on the theological continuum. As such, they were all taught in their churches or synagogues that homosexuality was a sin and witnessed the reality that women could not have or seldom had leadership roles as clergy. Nonetheless, despite the shared negative experiences of their formative years, the study supports the finding that the religious identities of these women took root within their individual theologically conservative environments; indeed, all thirteen women perceived their early religious identity as critically formative for their future calls to ministry, noting they did not necessarily equate conservative with oppressive and felt nurtured by a strong understanding of the Bible.

Esther. At the time of the interview, Esther was in her late thirties and the copastor with her wife of a small urban congregation in a large eastern city. From an early religious identity perspective, Esther's childhood and adolescent experience of church and her denomination had been primarily positive and had been a lifelong constant. Throughout most of her life, Esther experienced a fit with her denomination of birth and had a strong denominational identity, as well as a strong religious identity as a Christian. Her father was a seminary professor, and although they moved multiple times during her childhood and adolescence, she talked about church being the common denominator in her life that allowed her to feel a goodness of fit, even during her adolescent years of coming out and during her marriage and ordination processes. What Esther offered in her interview regarding her early stage of development was spoken with great hindsight, noting the incongruities between her early "affirming and positive" experiences as a child and adolescent in her father's faith community, while also being able to provide insight into how theologically conservative her denomination of birth was in terms of its stance on homosexual clergy.

Early Years. From birth until the age of seven, Esther experienced a positive religious identity in an ethnically and denominationally homogeneous Midwestern community and church. With animation, she stated the following about this time in her life:

> I really felt that I belonged there. And I, I, I loved church, and I loved everything about church. We were like twice (sic) on Sunday. I loved junior church.

From the age of seven until fifteen, Esther experienced a positive religious identity in a new church in an eastern state but experienced bullying and oppression for looking like a "dyke" in school. However, Esther shared that she had a wonderful junior high and high school youth group at her church that compensated for her poor fit in her public school setting. It was also in that new church community that she was first exposed to peers who were struggling with their own gay identity and who would influence her coming out process late in her adolescence. Of that church experience, she stated:

> But we were all together and out of that confirmation class there were three or four of us who were gay, as well as the youth group leads as well as another guy who was in the grouping ahead of us. I think in retrospect, at the time, we kind of all knew that it was not a great idea to be gay, but we did not get that from our church, even though we knew, like, I was most worried about coming out what the folks [name of church] were going to think.

Esther's experience of her junior high and early school years was significant in cementing her acceptance of her religious and denominational identities. In retrospect, Esther understood that given the larger homophobic stances of her denomination, which she did not know during the early years, her experience of church was unusual. Despite the anti-oppressive stance of her denomination, she found the early years to be formative in not only the development of her religious identity but her lesbian identity as well. Later, when she and her family moved to a metropolitan area in an eastern state during her later high school years, she again felt that she fit within her church youth group.

As further evidence of her acceptance of her early religious and denominational identities, her college years in a large metropolitan area remained positive. Esther's father intentionally connected her to an open and affirming church in the same city; she made the weekly effort to commute more than an hour to an inclusive gay congregation of the denomination of her birth.

Interestingly, Esther stated that she remembered her father, who was a friend of the pastor and was aware of her sexual identity before she was, encouraged her to become a part of this particular congregation. Within a year of attending this congregation, she started teaching Sunday school and eventually became the director of the youth group as well. Church was a full-day event, and she would return to her dorm at seven or eight at night. Of this period in her life, she stated:

There were a group of folks who were in their late 30s, who looked after me. Right, they were very careful to look after me. We would go out to brunch and go out drinking. The whole time I was in college, I would not go out drinking on a Saturday night. I would purposely not get drunk on Saturday night because drinking was reserved for Sunday after church.

Ministry Years. In recalling her college years, Esther noted that the positive experiences from her college years likely influenced her decision to join the ministry. Within just a few years of completing her undergraduate studies, Esther began her seminary training. It was during this time she met and then married her wife. However, that event caused a cataclysmic reaction within her home denomination toward her father, who had married them. In the end, Esther's father, who was a seminary president, was put on ecclesiastical trial and lost his ordination credentials. During those early years of marriage and completion of her studies at seminary, Esther's home denomination refused to ordain her because of her openness about being a lesbian. Ultimately, she joined another denomination and, after several years of its ordination-preparation processes, was finally ordained.

The artifact of the severe reaction by her congregation was extraordinary, resulting in holding ordination credentials in one denomination but continuing to be the pastor of a small urban congregation in her home denomination. Even then, Esther's status as a minister in her current congregation has continued without the benefit of financial security that would come from being installed as a minister of a congregation.[12]

During the interview, Esther reflected on being a lesbian minister in an oppressive denomination that continues to hold the position that homosexuality is a sin. She now understands that what drives some of the oppression is oddly the same homogeneous ethnic aspects of the denomination that created a sense of belonging for her as a child. Ironically, as a pastor in a large, eastern, urban neighborhood congregation,

---

[12] Installation to a congregation is akin to having the security of employment, as tenured teachers or professors do at the respective academic institutions.

she compared the oppressive nature of her denomination to a Hasidic community that she lives close to:

> I mean, I think there are actually a lot of similarities between growing up in the [name of denomination], I mean the rural kind of [names ethnic group] parts of the [denomination] and growing up in Hasidic [name of community], where it's a lot of community policing.

At the same time, Esther stated that despite experiences of control and oppression, she still loves the close-knit nature of the denomination of her birth and finds it comforting that "we all know each other's business." She stated at another point in the interview that "there's a culture in the [name of the denomination] where people just feel like they need to protect [the groupthink or need to maintain homogenous thinking processes]." For instance, she cited the Goffman book on stigma as a means of explaining her experience of being ostracized in her home denomination.

> The proven Goffman book on stigma. I means there's definitely a ... a ... a stigma in that um, enforced uniformity and conformity is for some reason, which is particularly present in the [name of denomination]. I remember one of the heads of the [name of denomination that ordained her], saying to me, "Wow! What is it in this [name of home denomination] that they can enforce [to hold back] their LGBT folks so incredibly well—like it's very well policed—the silence—the good behavior." Well and it's not just culture; it's not just about LGBT issues, it's about everything. It's about like whether or not you're a good housekeeper. It's about you know life—there's whole set of enforced behaviors that you know when you're not living up to what's expected of you.

Despite her experience of being ostracized by her home denomination, in the months prior to the interview, Esther reported that she was surprised that she felt a resurgence in positive feelings of emotional and theological fit toward her denomination of birth. She attributed this to healing from her experiences of oppression. As a result, she had begun to attend events in the denomination of her birth, which happened also to be the denomination of her current congregation.

The literary device of the voice poem comes out of the listening guide methodology and attempts to highlight the research participant's struggles (Brown et al. 1988; Brown and Gillian 1992; Raider-Roth 2002; Woodcock 2005). The following voice poem articulated a composite of Esther's struggle to be accepted in her home denomination. Consistent with her sense of fit in church, Esther from the beginning of her time in her current congregation, more than ten years before she participated in this study, felt a sense of fit and acceptance. She attributed that to her openness from the beginning about being gay. This, however, is not without the cost of loneliness and being cut off from the rest of the local denominational judicatory that does not fully accept her ministry because she is gay. Yet Esther described her congregation that she serves as a great fit:

> They were
> They were
> They're really supportive

She compared her congregational fit as being in sharp contrast to her experience of denominational oppression:

> They don't want to associate with me
> Ostracize you
> Abandon you
> They feel afraid
> They don't
> They don't have the capacity to handle it
> You know
> I mean
> So when I say it's pretty lonely
> Yeah it is really lonely
> But the lonely (inaudible), lonely

In summary, Esther revealed that she has experienced a good fit with her spouse and children. She and her wife copastor the same congregation, able to negotiate the incongruities of the denominational homophobic oppression while living as a lesbian within a traditional family structure of marriage, with two biological children. In addition, she has continued to experience a good fit within her open and affirming congregation, despite it being embedded in a denomination that has continued to uphold institutional oppression toward individuals in same-sex marriages. Esther had been the pastor of her congregation for almost ten years at the time of the interview and continued to be deeply involved in social justice ministries both within the congregation and in the community, as well as LGBTQ inclusion.

Sarah. At the time of this study, Sarah was in her midthirties and serving as the solo pastor of a downtown city church in a large Midwestern city. Like Esther, Sarah consistently had a Christian religious identity and the same denominational identity throughout her life. Sarah was raised in the Midwest in an ethnic denomination in what she called a very theologically conservative region of her denomination. She participated in all the traditional church events for young girls during her developmental years. Later, she attended a denominational college and spent her summers working at a denominational church camp.

> Ok. Um, let's see. I grew up in a small town in [names Midwestern state] a um outside of the [names region] in a big [names denomination] Church. And really knew that church to be a family. I mean, it's a big congregation of probably 1,500 people.

Early Years. Also like Esther, church and denomination provided very positive forces in Sarah's early life and were predictive of her chosen profession in becoming a minister, despite later experiences of oppression. She was in eighth grade when a close family friend observed her at an ecumenical Thanksgiving dinner for the homeless and mentioned to her that she should be become a minister.

And really I think I, in my call story, the one thing that you write about and tell about and all the rest, I think mine goes back to eighth grade um serving a meal on Thanksgiving Day in our small town to—like an Ecumenical gathering. I would assume to people who didn't have anywhere else to go on Thanksgiving Day but to the Catholic Church basement. I was wiping tables which waiters are often assigned to do, um just the thing you did and wiping tables and later someone came up and told me, who had been a Sunday school teacher and a close person to the family, said, "You know. You should really think about becoming a pastor." And that very statement, "You should be a pastor" was sort of the beginning of the turning inside me to a gift I probably already had, but I just never thought about it before.

The quote above conveys Sarah's early call that emerged at a young age because of Sarah's positive experience of fit and acceptance of her early religious identity, which she has never left. Sarah was ordained in 2010 in her home denomination.

Ministry Years. Like Esther, when Sarah went through the ordination processes of her home denomination, her experience of homophobic oppression spiked. However, her high allegiance to her home denomination enabled her to accept her denomination's regulations about LGBTQ ordination. In other words, in order to be ordained in her home denomination, she needed to go through a parallel ordination process that had been established for LGBTQ persons. Sarah waited for ten years and was ordained by a denominational alternative process, which her denomination had established as a mandatory policy for LGBTQs to get ordained. Sarah appeared to be able to tolerate the long wait for ordination, despite what many would consider a process based on homophobia, in order to push forward the ordination of LGBTQ persons in her denomination. In order to ameliorate the sense of oppression, Sarah stated she became involved in a movement to enact policy changes regarding the ordination of LGBTQs. As Sarah reported, this process has been both exhilarating and exhausting because of the mix of oppression and the ability to be a change agent within her denomination.

> But it's very fine for me to be ordained now that my ordination was transferred to the [names denomination] and I was welcomed by the [names denomination] so I'm now a [names denomination] clergy person on my [denomination's list of clergy] It was, they called it a Rite of Reception. So they received me onto the denominational (sic) roster with the bishop's thing and a big ritual and they did it in September of 2010. So it was a full year a little more than a full year after the [name of denomination] changed its policies at the church wide assembly. And then I was part of, there were a couple of us, 3 of us in particular who did the negotiating with the Bishops and the [name of denomination] church wide staff. So once policy change occurs, it's wonderful. But then how are you going to make it look? How are you going to write the rules so that all of us who are in that gray area don't get left behind or thrown under a bus? So we were really active in writing that policy stuff with them and to be the faces during that process. Which is really exhausting, but very empowering to be a part of it. I was grateful for that chance.

Sarah had been the pastor of a small inner-city congregation for eleven years at the time of the interview. At the time of this study, Sarah remained impassioned for ministry. She also has continued to be involved in social justice work with the homeless in her community, as well as being involved in LGBTQ advocacy work in her denomination and performing World Council of Churches work. Sarah articulated her perception that her denominational leadership may have used her public profile to push forward the LGBTQ ordination issue. In other words, because Sarah was so public in being out in her denomination, the proponents of LGBTQ inclusion in her denomination eventually used her as their poster child to push the issue to the fore for the entire denomination.

We are pushing international issues such as sexuality that was becoming more and more of a conversation. I could just be that person at the table. I think the [names denomination] was using that space for that to happen. Of course they never said that. They would never say that they were using that space, but that's part of the package. You get me, you get that too. Um and that was positive.

Sarah indicated that perhaps the biggest manifestations of homophobic oppression she encountered in her denomination were the boundaries that denominational policies placed on LGBTQ clergy. Sarah declared feelings of *great relief* and *great joy* to finally having been ordained within her denomination, while simultaneously expressing feelings of weariness with the political "stuff." She noted it remained a conundrum for her on how to be a part of a community that provided her with such joy but at the same time proselytized policies that she did not want to be a part of or support.

While there was a sense that Sarah has minimized some of her oppression, she certainly presented without bitterness. She added that, compared to most LGBTQ clergy, she felt fortunate in that her oppression has been minimal. When Sarah shared that her oppression was minimal, it appeared that it was difficult for her to fully acknowledge that her home denomination, to which she remains very loyal, could still hold onto its hurtful policies. It seemed that what Sarah called "minimal oppression" had to be understood in light of the consistent support she had from her family of origin, her partner, her church, and her ecumenical connections. In sum, at the time of this study, Sarah perceived that her experiences of oppression as a lesbian clergy were much less than most, and as a result, her outlook was positive.

However, regarding oppression, in contrast to her overall relief on being ordained and having a congregation, she recognized that her marketability outside of her congregation would be limited. Sarah said that it would be very difficult to find another call in the Midwest, because of her lesbianism.

> And yet at the same time, I don't think I experienced a lot of the really yuck stuff. I've never been thrown out of a church. I've never been defrocked. I've never had to live in the closet. I've never been personally physically hurt.

I've never felt what a lot of my colleagues have felt which they tell some horrible stories about.

Abigail. At the time of the interview, Abigail was in her midforties and serving on the ministerial staff in a midsized town on the East Coast as the part-time social justice minister. For Abigail, the themes of fit and oppression are opposite sides of the same coin. From an anti-oppressive perspective, Abigail had not been able to find a church position in three of the four formula of agreement denominations—taking more than twenty years for Abigail to find her place (niche) in ministry. At the time of this study, Abigail had been in her position as a social justice minister at a church that is outside her denomination for two years. Abigail stated multiple times during the interview that this position was a powerful fit for her, but, as an example of the limited opportunities arising from the oppression of lesbian ministers, it was part-time. She supplemented her income with three other jobs: as a hospital chaplain, as a dog trainer, and as a pastoral therapist.

Early Years. Abigail's religious identity as a Christian was lifelong. In referring to her religious identity, Abigail stated that "her key concepts of faith have been a constant throughout her life." She stated that for as long as she could remember, her parents were "committed conservatives" who frequently changed independent nondenominational congregations to find the one that was the most conservative.

> Christian conservatives. I would consider them Fundamentalists. I don't know if they would claim that themselves. I grew up in a non-denominational Church going Sundays, Wednesdays, Saturdays—often—often.

One of her early memories of religious gender oppression was when, while still in high school, as a late teen, she was told that women cannot go to seminary and instead that she could only become a Christian educator or missionary.

> I was talking about [going to seminary] back when I was at the [high school church]. I was talking about wanting

to be clergy, but was told gently and kindly that you can't do that, but you could go and be a missionary and preach in, in, another country.

Ministry Years. Interestingly, despite encountering early prejudiced and discouraging advice, Abigail was the only woman in the sample to go to seminary immediately following her undergraduate education. Abigail credited several religion professors in college as supportive and countering her experience of male domination in her home denomination. Although her college was religiously conservative, its biblical department was not. And it was in college that she found female mentors who encouraged her to fulfill her call to go to seminary. Although Abigail experienced antifeminist oppression while attending the fundamentalist Christian college, she credited two female mentors, both religion professors, who introduced her to feminist theology and encouraged her to enroll at a seminary.

As such, Abigail's undergraduate educational experiences were formative in terms of leading her to her calling by introducing her to more progressive forms of Christian thinking. Further, although Abigail later would experience some aspects of her denominational seminary to be homophobic, the fact that she was exposed to feminist and lesbian theology scholarship in college was critical in bringing her to "accomodationist" solutions (see Dominelli 2002).

For Abigail, her call to ministry and coming out processes were intermingled as she attended seminary school.

> So, I came to an understanding of sexual orientation and identity during Seminary, which wasn't a real place either at that time [to come out].

During her first year at seminary, her sexual identity as a lesbian emerged as she became increasingly involved in reading feminist theology and social justice ministries. Because she was raised in several conservative Christian denominations, Abigail believed, looking back on it, that her sexual identity as a lesbian had previously been repressed. Specifically, she stated that she had had some thoughts in high school that she might be a lesbian but repressed them because of her conservative religious identity. After she came out, she felt that the oppression she experienced in seminary was more due to the conservative era than the policies of the denomination in which she was ordained.

It was also during that same period that Abigail met her spouse, who also became an ordained minister. Abigail's spouse had served the church as a minister at the time of this study for twenty-two years. Abigail shared her experience of falling in love with her spouse at seminary and acknowledging the fear of being a lesbian in a church-affiliated environment that was not open or affirming to LGBTQs. Here are Abigail's poignant words about her fear of coming out and being open in her lesbian relationship while attending seminary in an era when the issue of LGBTQ clergy was not yet on the radar of most mainline denominations.

> Terrified. Terrified. In a relationship so when we finally realized there was something between us we both kind of freaked out and I called the one person I thought who could help us on campus who was the one professor who we kind of knew was a lesbian but it wasn't like, "Ah I'm a lesbian!" and I called her and she knew right away without my having to say anything. I called her and I was very nervous. It was one of those put down the phone real fast and call again saying, "a friend and I are having an issue and we really need to talk to somebody (laughs) and you know, you don't know me or, but we really need," and she welcomed us to her home.

Here, Abigail reflected on the pain of coming out in an era when denominations and seminaries had barely discussed the issue of LGBTQ clergy. She remembered how scary it was to come out, knowing she might not be able to get ordained if she was fully out. Abigail's instincts about not being able to get employment in a church proved to be true, as she was not able to get a full-time position. Another example of oppression, she stated, was the fact that she was ordained into one of the formula of agreement denominations right out of seminary, only because she was closeted. Eventually, she was ordained as a chaplain at a battered women's shelter.

Her oppression experiences prevented her from getting a church job, so she worked at multiple jobs as chaplain and went on to get her MSW. Upon seminary graduation, she had anticipated a call to a congregation, but that was not possible until almost two decades after graduation. She experienced discrimination multiple times by congregations within her own denomination. She stated that she also experienced discrimination from congregations that professed to be open and affirming to the LGBTQ issue. She stated during one interview that one of the churches that was a leader in the LGBTQ movement within her denomination sent her a rejection letter that stated simply, "Because you are a lesbian, we cannot hire you."

Abigail then tried to go to a more liberal denomination but was rejected by them because she had not grown up in their denomination. Because of her more than twenty years of experiencing oppression and rejection from multiple churches, she stated that she was less drawn to a particular denominational identity than she was to her religious identity. Because she was not tied to a denomination, Abigail joked that she considered herself to be a "denominational mutt," because she has been involved in so many denominations.

Ruth. At the time of this study, Ruth was the solo pastor of a midsized congregation in a rural eastern community. Like Abigail, Ruth had maintained her religious identity as a Christian throughout her life and switched denominations several times as an adult as she attempted to find a goodness of fit for her ministry. Unlike Abigail, Ruth had a twenty-year gap between her undergraduate training and her seminary education. In her early fifties, Ruth was ordained as a minister in the decade prior to this study.

Early Years. Ruth, who was adopted as an infant, was raised as a Roman Catholic. She believed that her mother promised her birth mother to raise her as Catholic. She attended Catholic schools from kindergarten through her first master's degree in pastoral ministry, and she emphasized the importance of her Jesuit education while in college and graduate school. Regarding her formative childhood faith, Ruth stated the following:

> Ultimately, I grew up with a very strong interest in faith
> and in Christian religion. I read these little books about
> the lives of the saints when I was young.

Thus, Ruth's journey toward eventually becoming a Protestant minister was rooted in her strong religious identity as a child. As a young child, she played priest with her brother and remembers wanting to be a Benedictine nun. During one interview, Ruth chuckled about the irony of wanting to live in a community of women, noting she did not fully come out as a lesbian until she was nearly forty years old—after her ordination.

After completing her master's in pastoral ministry and relocating to a new geographic region with her husband and two young children, she was unable to find a Roman Catholic parish in which she felt a goodness of fit. She soon discovered that Roman Catholicism was very different outside of a Jesuit university. Of the time of her leaving her denominational ties to the Roman Catholic Church and seeking or accommodating a new Christian identity in a Protestant church, Ruth reflected in her poetry:

> It was a swan dive onto the pavement when I was trying to
> find a church here, uh, that had some sense of a connection
> that being a woman you are a valued member of being in
> the church.

Ruth's conversation with a local priest who was dismissive of women's issues was the final tipping point for her as a feminist and her leaving the Roman Catholic Church. She stated that the views of the local priest, however, should not have surprised her. Regarding the role of women in the church and social justice issues, Ruth recalled the words that a Jesuit priest said to her when she was in graduate school.

> Well, honestly, women's issues such as birth control,
> ordination. Well, you know, in the grand scheme of
> things, those issues really aren't important.

Ministry Years. After she left the Roman Catholic Church, Ruth went on to experience a fit in two denominations. After a year of searching for a church, she found employment as a director of Christian education at an

Episcopal church, and then after another year, she began her employment at another church. It was during her work as a director of Christian education at the second church that she also joined that denomination, eventually becoming ordained. Within two years, she began commuting three hours several times weekly to seminary.

During this era of church shopping, Ruth increasingly felt that she was bisexual. She still was deeply in love with her husband of ten years, but she had experienced three crushes on women. After one of the women moved away, she became clinically depressed. At this point, she disclosed her attraction to women to her husband but remained in her marriage for three more years. Just as she was completing seminary, her husband told her he was leaving her for another woman, and they began divorce proceedings. Within three months of her marital separation, she started dating a woman she had known in town for several years. At the time of this study, Ruth and her partner had been in a committed relationship, without marriage, for more than eight years. In one of her interviews, Ruth spoke about feeling a strong connection with the woman who became her partner after she and her husband separated. In reflecting upon the importance of coming out, Ruth drew on not only the religious implications but also the physical impact that being closeted had had on her.

> But I haven't had bronchitis since [name of husband] and I spilt up. I just feel like I was just living the wrong life you know. I mean, I'm still grateful for my children. I wouldn't change any of it. But he left and I knew that I could think about, *Is there a guy around here I could date?* You know, I did think about that. But I knew in my heart, if I had another relationship, it would be with a woman. And by … he left in February. And by June I went for drinks with this woman [name of partner] who I had kind of known very casually for many years. She was my framer (chuckles). She owns a little shop in [town where she lives] called the [name of shop]. And so I called my friend, who is an all-out lesbian who is a friend from seminary and …

Approximately two years after her divorce from her husband, Ruth had told her children and certain friends in her community about her lesbianism. However, she felt reluctant to come out to her congregation, and due to fear of oppression, she waited until her contract with her congregation was secure. Also, in fear of losing her contract, she did not live in the parsonage but instead received a housing allowance. At the same time, Ruth stated, she and her partner frequently were seen together in town having dinner and so on.

> Meanwhile, [name of partner] and I were not exactly skulking around. We went out to dinner together, we went out to movies together and we held hands in the movies. Uh and in a very certain group we were very well known together. But uh, I was never there. You know, I got a housing allowance instead of using their Manse. Um, so finally, once [her son] knew, by a few months later, um my daughter (sic), uh, I got a call from a friend that seemed to indicate that word was out. Someone else said, "Did you know [names her] was gay?" And my friend called me and said, "I didn't know what to say. I didn't know how many people knew." And once I kind of got the feeling of Uh, Oh, it's out, I told my daughter as well. So both my kids found out in just a few months of each other. And it was actually really good because they had each other to talk to and they had my ex to talk to. I told him actually much earlier than that.

Soon after this, Ruth knew that she needed to risk coming out to her congregation. She had signed another two-year contract, so she felt like it was time, as they had fully endorsed her ongoing ministry with them. Although in contrast, as an example of oppression, her denominational judicatory would not install her because of the theologically conservative nature of the judicatory in which her more liberal congregation is located.

The issue for Ruth was that a contract was not as secure as a call. The call includes installation of an open-ended pastoral relationship, and an installed call position of a minister to a congregation is analogous to a teacher or professor getting a contract in which he or she is protected once tenured by the institution. Here, Ruth described her angst about coming out, although she knew she had a solid relationship with her congregation. After she came out to her congregation, Ruth was supported by the majority but did experience some micro-oppression by several people leaving the congregation.

The excerpt below is Ruth's teary recalling of being affirmed by her congregation when she came out to them.

> The relationship was there. They knew me. And all but four people in the congregation—it's a reasonably small congregation. It was about a 169 at that point. All but four people in the congregation, the relationship was there. It was solid enough. Um—the four people—now that's not to say that others weren't concerned or were worried or didn't feel that this went against their understanding of scripture. There were about ten who expressed that to me directly. But the ones who expressed it to me directly, expressed it to me directly. They were, they stayed in relationship with me. They let me come to their homes. They asked me questions. I didn't—I didn't offer my interpretation of scripture to anyone unless they asked. Um—and then I explained to them how I understand the Gospel. Um—and they stayed in relationship with me, they prayed with me, they prayed for me. The people who left are the people I called and would not pick up the phone or people who would not let me visit them. They simply withdrew and four people left. Two actually had us remove their names from the rolls. The other two didn't. They just stopped coming. And they came to a funeral a couple months ago and they said to me, "We would like to come back." So they actually came back. So um, so actually …

As evidence of the simultaneous nature of oppression and fit, Ruth expressed her contentment about the manner in which the majority of her congregation supported her coming out process. However, Ruth reported that she experienced prejudiced comments by colleagues in her denominational judicatory. The significance of this was that she was at risk at that point of losing her ordination because this is the level of ecclesial government that manages the ordination and installation process of ministers.

She stressed at several points in one interview that in her identity now as a lesbian minister, she is "happier right now probably than what [she] has been in [her] entire life." However, in the conclusion to her final interview, Ruth talked about much more work in her denomination needing to be done around LGBTQ inclusion.

> We still have some miles to go on this [LGBTQ inclusion issue in the Protestant community].

Naomi. Naomi was in her early fifties and in the process of leaving a two-year pastorate in a rural northeastern community at the time of this study. Like Abigail and Ruth, Naomi maintained her lifelong religious identity as a Christian. However, as an adult, she found a new denomination when she and her first husband moved to New England. In this new denomination, she found a goodness of fit, and it eventually was the denomination in which she was ordained.

> We went to a congregational church and I didn't know they were [name of denomination]. We went to this congregational church and then we got very involved within the life of the church and started thinking very early on about the possibility of going to seminary.

However, unlike Abigail and like Ruth, Naomi went to seminary several decades after completing her undergraduate education and while she was still married to her first husband. Naomi, like Ruth, was adopted as an infant. But in contrast to Abigail and Ruth, Naomi's early conservative religious identity appeared to have caused her to be more delayed in both her ministerial call and coming out processes. Naomi stated that growing up in an affluent southern church family with prescribed views on women precluded her from knowing that she did not want to get married young, at twenty-two, or that she wanted to go to seminary. She put it this way:

> Um, because I think I am late to my own party in terms of being clear about. Yea. About who I am, I look back (sic) no one ever suggested to me that I should have any agency about what I wanted.

Early Years. Naomi continued to explain more about how her background prevented her from knowing what her religious or sexual identities were to her thirties and forties respectively.

> I grew up in a very churched family. My mom's family was Baptist and they were part of the founding members of the Baptist Church in [name southern city]. My dad's family was Methodist and my dad's family were founding members of the Methodist Church and before that. But none of them (sic) even though some of those denominations were ordaining women, because the Presbyterians and the Methodists had starting ordaining women when I was a little girl. I didn't ever meet any of them. But I had no idea when I was a little girl that being a pastor was something that a woman could do.

Naomi spoke about the experience of knowing what she called "apartheid" in her southern town and being nurtured by a black maid. She equated her growing-up experience to that of the Caucasian author Kathryn Sockett, who wrote *The Help*. In contrast to the love of her maid, she experienced her mother as being emotionally unavailable and her father as being physically unavailable because he traveled a lot and was in national politics. However, her life as a child and adolescent was focused on her father's public career as an attorney and politician.

Ministry Years. As further evidence of a formative Christian religious identity, Naomi stated that, as a child, she spoke about wanting to marry a minister. She recognized now that this was an early repressed call to ministry that she believed she could not act on. She did not realize then that she had been repressed by the expectations of her culture and social class to both not become a minister and not come out as a lesbian.

> I started to want to marry a minister. I had a boyfriend when I was in high school and college who I was convinced, oh my gosh, convinced that he was called to ministry. In other words, I was called to ministry and he (voice trailed off) …

In this way, Naomi suggested that she was repressed by her traditional southern culture both in church and community. Despite her feelings of not having found her place/niche in any of her congregations, it appeared that her early religious identity had been predictive of her call to ministry. In her story, it became apparent that Naomi's experience of trying to comply with the southern cultural expectations of being a traditional woman—with a husband, children, and no career—eventually became a conflict for her. So much so, she noted, that she eventually developed an autoimmune disease as a result of the internal conflict and serially married two abusive men. Naomi said the following about the expectations for women she was exposed to early on:

> And [the expected roles as a southern woman] had an impact on me in my call to ministry or the lack thereof and my understanding of my sexual orientation or my lack thereof.

Despite her struggle to accept her call, during the early religious identity stage, Naomi went to seminary for fifteen years with three children, while commuting to another state, but after graduating and becoming ordained, she still did not find a full sense of fit in her ministerial positions. For instance, Naomi served a series of eight congregations in a period of a decade, in the capacity of an interim pastor. During the interview, Naomi had insight that she had not connected well to any of her congregations, which she attributed to the intentional short-term work of her ministries. Further, it was certain that Naomi could not fully connect to her congregants because she had not fully come out and therefore was not fully able to be fully honest with them. Indeed, it was as if Naomi continued to suppress her lesbian identity both from her congregations and herself in her early ministry years.

Naomi's final realization of her sexual identity occurred at the end of her marriage to her second husband, when she developed an autoimmune disease of rheumatoid arthritis four years prior to her participation in this study. Only a year prior to this study, Naomi had come out to her congregation and become engaged to a female minister of another church. Her wedding was planned for six weeks after the interview, and she was moving to the mid-Atlantic region to live with her future wife. As Naomi put it so succinctly, she said things now are better for her than ever. Although as evidence of more oppression, she believes that she will not find a position within her denomination in that region because it is much more theologically conservative than the New England region. Of her goodness of fit with her soon-to-be-wife, Naomi said the following:

> Exactly. Exactly. So now, I'm a fifty-one year old woman with three pretty-much-grown-up children with a chronic disease, but I've never felt better in my life.

In summary, Naomi came to both her ministerial call and her lesbian identity in middle age. Until her forties, Naomi had repressed her true identities due to her early religious identity. Only when her physical health had deteriorated so severely was Naomi able to discern that there might be a connection between her physical deterioration and her suppression of her true identity, such that she then decided she could no longer repress her clergy and lesbian identities. Her physical and mental health issues appeared to be the catalyst for self-realization, allowing her to move beyond the expectations of her conservative culture.

Rachel. Like Esther, Sarah, Abigail, Ruth, and Naomi, Rachel perceived that her early conservative religious identity foreshadowed her call to ministry. Her call came in her thirties as a second career, following her first career in music theater. Rachel's foundational upbringing as an observant conservative Jew was formative to her call as a multifaith chaplain. Although Rachel left her Jewish identity for a Christian identity because of being drawn to the power of its redemptive message, she too accommodated to a new form of religious identity rather than leaving her traditional religious identity altogether.

As the only study participant who was born as a Jew, Rachel was a long-tenured hospital chaplain at a large medical center in a metropolitan eastern city. In addition, she was a part-time interim pastor at a local congregation within her denomination. Demographically, Rachel was raised in the mid-Atlantic region. However, she moved to a large eastern city for work, once she had completed her undergraduate education.

Early Years. Rachel converted to Christianity, without the initial knowledge of her parents, at the age of seventeen. Thus, Rachel is also unique to the sample in that she has two early religious identities, which served her well in her ministry when she identified herself as having multiple faith identities. She has written extensively as a hospital chaplain and has been published multiple times. Below is her explanation of what it means to her to identify as a multifaith chaplain.

> And, and I should send you the chapter of this book I wrote about my theology. It's, it's a book for pastoral care, ummm, of about when I am with someone, I am really of a dual mind. And dual heart because while that person may be Jewish I'm still, while I may be helping them to verbalize their own religion and their own belief system. It has not (sic) my belief system has gotten broad enough that I can welcome that. (Sic) And that I can honor who they are and honor their own religious beliefs without them impinging on my own. (Sic) While at the same time being faithful to their own religion with them.

Rachel spoke fondly about her earliest faith community in Judaism that nurtured her earliest religious identity and how it influenced her in positive ways but also addressed how it became oppressive by her early teen years. For instance, she joked about the family nature of her synagogue, which was so strong that if she was disciplined at Hebrew school, her parents knew about it before she walked in the door at home. Rachel described the family-like nature of her childhood faith community and affiliation very powerfully. Another characteristic that was similar for Rachel with

Esther, Sarah, Abigail, Ruth, and Naomi was that Rachel's early religious faith community promoted a homogeneity in thought patterns and an authoritarian clergy pattern.

> The rabbi was like, was like the Messiah. In some ways, he controlled a lot of things. Umm, And I can remember coming home from Hebrew school and my parents knowing if I had done something wrong or said something wrong before I walked in the door. Umm, no privacy. And I didn't even realize until around fourth grade that there was a religion other than Judaism. Umm, because I had been—I was so—closed. Yeah, in a lot of ways.

Rachel was aware of her own mixed feelings gleaned from a fundamentalist faith community: on the positive side, she was drawn to the family affiliation, while, on the negative side, she was hurt by the strong judgments that often evolved from the homogenous groupthink patterns. Rachel's eventual election to leave Judaism and go into Christianity was done without the knowledge of her rabbi or her parents. Her exposure to Christianity came during her last three years of high school when she was hired to sing in a local Christian church by her high school music teacher.

She remembered being drawn to Christian ideas, although she was still very much involved in her local synagogue at that point in her life. As she drove herself to her Sunday singing job, her parents had little awareness of her involvement with the charismatic youth group at the church when she was sixteen years old. Rachel reflected on the early impact of Christian ideas, noting that her early Christian identity was that the Creator was a personal God, rather than a distant or academic God, as was presented by her Judaic training. It was this part of her training that she had found oppressive by her adolescent years.

> And I started hearing about this God who was not the God of the Jewish people and it was not a God who was out there somewhere. Because when I was young, I never prayed to God, for me. If I had a problem, it never would had occurred to me to. Nope. Nope. It was all

about—you know the prayers are in the prayer book and I could daven—you know pray—with the best of them. I knew it backwards and forwards. Didn't know what I was saying, but I knew it. It was all in Hebrew. And umm, it would never have even occurred to me to turn to God when I had a problem. Never even. So, umm, I started hearing about this God, who was inside of people and not just outside. Umm, And, and, I started questioning. And I had been raised never to question. Umm, you are to never question the adults. You just accepted things as they were and umm, you were expected, I was expecting to tow the line with my family and with Judaism. You know, with everything. And then, umm, so I started questioning. You know, "What's going on? Why do we have to pray in Hebrew? Doesn't God understand English?" You know, those kinds of things. So …

At the age of seventeen, she intentionally went across the country to the West Coast for college. She enrolled in a BFA program in music theater. While in college, Rachel began to consider conversion from Judaism to Christianity. For Rachel, her exposure to liberal Christianity was refreshing in that it offered the idea of universalism, in that all persons could be a part of God's kingdom, which was in sharp contrast to her childhood understanding that only the chosen people or Jews could be a part of the kingdom. Her knowledge of the stories of the Hebrews felt limiting, while learning of Christian scriptures for her told the rest of the stories she had learned as a child. Though she was still drawn to the warmth of her family-oriented synagogue, she recalled how she had found it to be restrictive and judgmental to non-Jews by the time she was in high school. This was part of her trajectory toward becoming a Protestant minister, which foreshadowed some of her later experiences as a multifaith chaplain.

Through her college years, Rachel attended several liberal churches on the West Coast and eventually converted from Judaism to Christianity officially, still without the knowledge of her family. As Rachel put it, her collegiate academics did not so much influence her conversion, given she had made the decision to eventually convert while still in high school, but she had needed the physical space from her family to finally actually do it.

Ministry Years. After college, Rachel moved to a large metropolitan Northeast city, where she started working as a stage manager. Then, by 1980, she found her way to a large church. She was shocked when she was told, "We welcome anyone here." She was shocked but drawn into that community because she was already involved with her long-term same-sex partner at that point. Although the introduction of Rachel's same-sex partner appears abrupt here, it is because Rachel has a limited coming out story of falling in love with her longtime partner, whom she referred to as her soul partner, moving quickly from being exclusively in heterosexual relationships to wanting to share her life with this newly found partner.[13]

Rachel's call to ministry came at the height of the AIDS epidemic in the 1980s, when she attended to her friends who were dying. It led to her friends and pastors of her church beginning to ask her when she was going to go to seminary. In much the same way, her colleagues encouraged her to become a hospital chaplain. She resisted becoming a chaplain for a long time, stating that she hated hospitals, and in much the same way resisted becoming ordained. But in both regards, colleagues and mentors convinced Rachel that this was what God was calling her to do.

Deborah. At the time of this study, Deborah was in her late forties and had just taken on a church planting position in a suburban New York metropolitan community. By way of explaining church planting, Deborah's denomination had hired Deborah to create a new congregation that was both multicultural and LGBT inclusive. Importantly, Deborah is the only black woman, who happens also to be of Caribbean descent, in the sample. She was raised in a large family of eleven children.

Early Years. Deborah had identified religiously as a Christian, with a period of two decades of spiritual identity (stage 2), when she tried multiple non-Christian churches in between her experiences of not feeling a goodness of fit at Christian churches. She was raised as a Roman Catholic while a child in the Bahamas. Deborah believed that her clergy identity originated in this early religious tradition that did not ordain women. Like

---

[13] In her research, Diamond (2008, 175) found that half of her sample had experienced "person-based attractions."

Ruth, who also left the Roman Catholic Church, Deborah had been drawn to the powerful stories of the female saints, the humanity of Jesus, and the idealistic teachings on charity and justice for all persons.

Deborah came out around the age of sixteen or seventeen during her early college years in the United States, having started college early because she was so precocious. Deborah gave her coming out very little time during the interview. In analyzing the reasons for this, it was as if she was comfortable with being out when very young during her early college years. This supported her assertion that she did not have a difficult coming out process, either with her friends or family of origin. In contrast, she experienced extreme difficulty in finding fit as a lesbian in various Christian and spiritual communities.

Deborah perceived that the Roman Catholic Church laid the foundation for her clergy identity. She stated that Catholicism had taught her to love Jesus, and the teachings on charity and giving to the poor were particularly important to her. She had even wanted to be a priest, but Deborah had to face during her college years that the position of ordaining women in the Roman Catholic Church was intractable. During the interview, Deborah's anger and disappointment at her childhood church still seemed evident. In the end, it appeared that Deborah found an inability to affiliate as a minority black lesbian in the Roman tradition. Thus, she needed to leave the Roman Catholic tradition in which she had been raised because she was unable to find a niche where she could be fully herself as an openly out lesbian who happens to be black.

> Well, at that point, there was the whole issue of women in leadership, then the position of the, um, the Roman Catholic Church with regard to gays and lesbians, then there was the Anita Bryan protest, I think this was like, a lot was going on.

After college, Deborah was in search of a faith-based niche. She had left the Roman Catholic Church because the teachings did not support female leadership or inclusion of LGBTQs. After that, Deborah searched sincerely and earnestly, through a process of accommodation (Dominelli 2002), wanting to maintain her Christian identity but leaving many congregations and denominations. She notes that this was due primarily to micro-oppressions (e.g., not being able to wear pants to church) or for being black, lesbian, or a woman. For the next two decades after her search for a fit first began, Deborah seemed unable to find a home in a denomination.

This sense of struggle to find a denominational affiliation became a long struggle, resulting in her participation in more than fifty denominations, some for a day and some for as long as eleven years. She reported that her religious journey became an ongoing denominational affiliation search, attempting to find her fit. In each denomination, Deborah has been *seeking Jesus in the sanctuary* in terms of worship style, social justice issues, inclusiveness of women and LGBTQs, diversity of various cultures, and warmth.

Retrospectively, Deborah recognized that God had a plan for her life to eventually go into ministry, even though her religious journey had begun in a Roman Catholic Church and ended up in a denomination. Deborah finally intentionally chose the denomination in which she is affiliated because of her positive experiences of inclusion and affirmation as a black lesbian in one particular congregation, not because she had researched the theological statements of the denomination.

> Yes, it's just amazing. I would say God is very creative just so creative because, the trajectory I had my life on was just like very straight and ...

Ministry Years. Deborah's ministry call came late, as her third career, in her forties. After a near-fatal automobile accident in 1988, which included multiple surgeries and extensive rehabilitation, Deborah began to discern her call to ministry. She believed that her accident helped her to reengage and pursue her call to ministry that she had first felt as a college student when she thought she wanted to be a priest. During her physical and emotional recuperation, Deborah perceived that her experiences of being ministered to by caring medical personnel, both educated and uneducated, reminded her of the importance of being a caregiver and kind. She felt ready to leave her top financial position in higher education to enter into a world that promotes healing and justice.

My healing process, that whole accident was like an epiphany for me and transformative.

During her recuperation time, Deborah became involved as a leader in a nationally known LGBTQ denomination. After several years more of recuperation, Deborah eventually attended a prestigious northeastern seminary that was affiliated with her denomination. Paradoxically, and as referenced above, in seeking a field education placement during seminary, Deborah found herself in a congregation of a denomination that did not endorse or support LGBTQ ordination. Within a year of this interview, Deborah had become the first declared lesbian woman to be ordained in a mainline Protestant denomination that does not nationally endorse LGBTQ ordination.[14]

In speaking about her specific call within her progressive denominational judicatory, Deborah was clear that her role as the first lesbian ordained within a judicatory of this denomination was to promote justice and inclusion for other LGBTQ persons seeking ordination. Her call was in a theologically conservative denomination, to plant or start an open and affirming congregation to LGBTQ persons.

While Deborah spoke of her local call to help with movement toward an open and affirming church, she did not address the larger LGBTQ discussion that was occurring in denomination about its homophobic policies or the fact that her ordination had been appealed to the national level of the church. It was as if Deborah's way of coping with the discrimination all around her for being an open lesbian minister was not to speak or focus on it but rather to focus with tunnel vision on her local tasks. In terms of identity, it was as if her religious identity, which had created her call, triumphed over all her other identities as a lesbian, a black woman, and a denominational minister.

---

[14] As a point of clarification, Deborah was ordained by the regional judicatory of this denomination; the judicatories of the denomination are able to make independent decisions about ordination even if the national governing body of the denomination has statements about homosexuality being a sin. Within this and the other three denominations, historically this is the way that controversial issues get pushed forward (e.g., women's ordination, LGBTQ ordination). Other judicatories have the right to appeal the decisions, however.

> Someone has to fight that struggle to make sure that people can realize the gifts of the spirit, and if I'm called to be that person at some point, I'll be that person, but for right now, the Holy Spirit has called me to get [name of church plant] to a point where individuals can see the good news of the Gospel in [names town], to provide, uh, different opportunities to fellowship and bond as a congregation to move towards structure and leadership and outreach, to establish a mechanism to become, um, financially independent, self-sustaining, you know, we got a lot of work to do here.

Within five months of interviewing Deborah, she was called to be part of a new church just starting up. Ironically, the new congregation that Deborah is serving is not totally clear that it will make an open and affirming statement to the LBGTQ community. But through her spiritual resources and outside support system of clergy who do support her, Deborah sustains her ministry in this setting. In expressing her ability to minister in a denomination that does not affirm her sexuality, Deborah spoke about being open to divine guidance because of her gratitude for having survived a near-fatal automobile accident earlier in her life. Thus, in terms of her sense of fit in this particular congregation, she stated the following:

> It may be me, I don't, I don't know, I just, you know, just, God is creative, you know, um, after I almost lost my life I, um, I said two things—I said, you know, whatever God wants me to do, that's what I'm going to do, because at that point I felt like I was [not existing]. (Voice barely audible.)

The heteronormative and male normative policies toward female clergy in the Roman Catholic Church caused Deborah to leave that branch of the church, but from an anti-oppressive perspective, for two decades she attempted to accommodate and find another Christian denomination with which to affiliate. Despite significant differences in the stories of

Esther, Sarah, Ruth, and Naomi, Deborah attributed her early conservative religious identity to laying the foundation for her call to ministry.

Mary. At the time of this study, Mary was a graduate student seeking a faith-based master's degree in a pastoral counseling program. She was living in the mid-Atlantic region of the United States. From a demographic point of view, Mary reported that she was raised in a rural part of an eastern state. Her family of origin was blue collar and did not place expectations on her to get an education but instead expected her to get married and have children at a young age. Despite becoming aware around the age of ten that she was not attracted to boys, at the age of sixteen she found herself in a culturally expected heterosexual relationship, which led to marriage. After eight years, she left her alcoholic husband because she did not want to repeat her family of origin patterns of dysfunction.

Early Years. Mary reported that her Christian identity came at a young age, in both Anabaptist and nondenominational churches. Her mother sent her to several local denominations, although her family did not attend church with her. Mary's mother was an alcoholic, and her home life was inconsistent. Mary stated that although these childhood church experiences were formative as a child when she needed support, they also became homophobic and oppressive to her when she came out to her female church friends in her twenties. Like Deborah, Mary reported ongoing experiences of rejection in the church. Thus, it was as if these experiences of congregational rejection trumped all the other stories of her narrative, including her formative religious years.

> Uh, initially I was going to Sunday school at the Mennonite Church, (Sic) which they were very nice to me as younger child you know, before I had a sense of my sexual identity or anything like that. And then from there, my mother started sending me to the [names mainline denomination] Church and it came time for me to be confirmed, she connected with the [names denomination] Church and sent me there. And I went through confirmation class there. I sang in the choir and that stuff. So I really felt that that was really a formative experience for me. At times I really didn't have a close family or anything um …

In this sample, Mary was perhaps the woman who most struggled with maintaining her religious identity because at the end of the interview, she revealed that she had left the denomination in which she was ordained. She cited ongoing experiences of oppression and lack of fit, which appeared part of the same issue as her reasons for leaving. More will be said about this in stage 6, when Mary entered into a second optional stage of spiritual identity.

Mary reported continuing to struggle with oppression in religious communities throughout her adult life. Throughout her life, she rarely experienced a sense of fit with a Christian denomination or in an intimate relationship with either a man or a woman. As a significant factor in Mary's lived experience, this study found that Mary's chaotic family of origin also contributed to her minimal experiences of fit in a faith community or in intimate relationships.

At the time of her marital separation, a bridge for belonging and fit was her connection to a small Bible church. Through her two best female friends, who remained her close friends at the time of this study, she began to attend an independent fundamentalist church with her daughters. This connectedness through the church provided her with a "family of choice," a term that Mary borrowed from Al-Anon. In addition to her church, Mary found significant support from her community in Al-Anon, which she attended after her separation from her alcoholic husband.

Within this church community and with the aid of her female friends, Mary raised her children. However, also at the time of her marital separation, Mary felt that she wanted to explore her burgeoning sexual identity as a lesbian. After her marriage broke up, Mary had serial relationships with women that each had lasted for five years. During this same time, in this postseparation church, she first experienced heteronormative oppression when some friends from her church told her that they had a house they would only rent to her, with the stipulation that she could not live there with another woman. She experienced significant hurt when some of her friends at church interpreted her burgeoning lesbian identity as one in which Mary was looking for a nurturing mother figure that she never had as a child.

At this point, she had a church crisis, which caused her to leave the church altogether for a time. Mary continued to maintain her Christian identity, but after experiencing this homophobic oppression at her church, she remembered praying, "When the time is right, God will call me back." When Mary's third relationship with another woman broke up after five years, Mary entered college. At that point, she reopened her religious seeking of either a religious or spiritual community that would embrace her as a lesbian woman.

Ministry Years. Evidence of how her early Christian identity influenced her return to church was Mary's determination to find a goodness of fit in a church as a lesbian. This journey back to church began at Barnes and Noble one day on her lunch hour. She remembered being drawn to a book in the religion section, a Spong book titled *Why Christianity Must Change or Die: A Bishop Speaks to Believers in Exile*. She wistfully remembered that she had hoped the church had become more LGBTQ affirming and inclusive; she wanted to reenter the church as a lesbian. Mary longed for the principles and connectedness of the family-like churches she had attended as a child and as a young adult.

> And I really did have a powerful understanding of God's presence and God's love. You know, and um … when this happened in the other church, it was hard for me. It was difficult to make the decision to leave. It felt that was the right decision, but that was hard. You know, it was painful.

Mary longed to return to a Christian community or religious identity where she would be accepted as a gay woman and that was more in line with her faith tradition. However, she had continued her metaphysical church connection throughout this time. Thus, after a short period, she sought a gay Christian denomination, because she wanted to return to a Christian tradition for worship. Based on the ideas from Spong's book, Mary felt called to ministry. She felt called to revolutionize the church in a way that would be inclusive of LGBTQ persons.

> Well, he [Bishop Spong] was talking about Christians that were living in exile. And you know, how the church really needs to change to become more accepting of people with different theological views, of people with different sexual

orientations, an you know, there are people who do believe in God but are not coming into the church because the church is not really meeting their needs and the church is being really exclusivist.

Prior to going to seminary, and after seminary, Mary developed a pattern of maintaining multiple allegiances to both non-Christian and Christian congregations. At this point, Mary began to discern a call to ministry, believing that her call to a clergy identity would be part of this movement to change the church. It is interesting to note, however, that she had not experienced a call to a particular denomination.

Interestingly, Mary applied to a prestigious denominational seminary in the Northeast with triple congregational identities that included the church in the gay denomination, the nondenominational church, and the church sponsoring the seminary. She started her training in 2005, was open about her sexual identity as a lesbian, and chose to align herself with a theologically progressive denomination for endorsement purposes. Despite struggles within her denominational judicatory about being endorsed as an openly lesbian seminarian, her ordination committee did approve her for ordination with her call to hospital chaplaincy in 2007. During her chaplaincy training, she again experienced oppression as a lesbian clergywoman from her male clergy supervisor.

Despite the oppressive experience with her supervisor, toward the end of the interview, Mary stated that she had at last found a strong fit and achieved a master's in a pastoral counseling program. In that program, Mary began to integrate her spiritual, religious, and sexual identities, at the time of this study. Mary had again left her religious identity as Christian but was identifying as a spiritual counselor because of her inability to find a goodness of fit as a lesbian minister in her denomination. As such, Mary was an exemplar of a research participant who left the church at multiple periods in her life—including having decided to leave professional ministry just prior to being interviewed—because of what she perceived to be significant experiences of homophobic oppression.

Rebecca. At the time of the interview, Rebecca was in her second year at a prestigious denominational seminary in the Northeast. Her decision to go to seminary was years in the making; in looking back, she recognized that she had felt called to ministry since she was an adolescent.

Early Years. As a child, Rebecca's parents brought her to church. Although her parents did not attend church when she was young, her experience of religious identity as an adolescent drew her into church. Since she grew up in the Midwest though, in a theologically conservative denomination, women in ordained ministry were not on her radar. Through her musical talent though, Rebecca participated in church throughout her elementary, high school, and college years, playing piano and doing youth work.

She remembered being drawn to leadership and was employed in youth ministry during her postcollege years. As was found in the lived experiences of other women in the sample, for Rebecca, it was the same theologically conservative context that was nurturing for her as a child and adolescent (in her case, by providing structure and rules that her parents had not) that later became oppressive to her as a young college woman.

Using the literary device from the listening guide (Brown et al. 1988; Brown and Gillian 1992; Raider-Roth 2002; Woodcock 2005) methodology, Rebecca's own words make several voice poems below that reflect the ministerial formation that occurred in her early religious identity stage.

> I started going
> I'd do Sunday school
> I think it was just an hour thing
> I got older
> I got more and more involved
> I started to go more and more
> I got involved
> I had some freedom
> I could go to church
> I was baptized
> I was in the sixth grade

She spoke about having developed a "more stringent moral and ethical system" than she had gotten at home. She joked that she was amazed that she still had friends when she found empowerment in telling them what they were doing wrong.

I think
I began developing a really more stringent
Then I would have gotten
I think
We do the things
We do
We say, "this is how it's supposed to be"

During high school, she continued in music and youth leadership. It was at this stage of her life that she "began considering ministry as a vocation." However, she also knew that pastoral ministry was not an option, and youth ministry was an option by default because that is all she knew at the time. In addition, for women of her denomination, youth ministry for women was just beginning to be possible.

I was really involved in the Youth Group
Once I hit Youth Group
I was there every time
I was just a total
I always had really close relationships with Sunday school teachers
I was just that kid
I loved
Even as I got older
When I was in high school
I was really involved
I felt like it
It was just everything I knew
I felt a sense of
I was entrusted with leadership
I really started
I think
I really got into that
When I was in high school
I began considering ministry as a vocation

In fact, Rebecca had never participated in worship as a woman—other than through music—prior to becoming a part of a mainline congregation in the Northeast. In her home denomination, ordination was not necessarily a step toward ministry; therefore, Rebecca remained on a theological journey of determining if she was called to ordained ministry at the time of this study. Rebecca was also still on a journey to discern if she was called to be a part of a particular denomination.

Within the context of her home denomination, Rebecca experienced a lack of acceptance as a woman in youth leadership in the churches in which she worked postcollege. She had recognized that men on the staff had better pay and more clearly defined roles than she and the other female staff members. Thus, the reasons Rebecca left church for a period of time were around issues of antifeminist oppression rather than homophobia.

> But yeah, but, I yeah, so I was working full time at this church and doing youth ministry and it began to get um, once I became full-time, I sort of began realizing how different my experience as at this church then the two other male associates, there was a head youth pastor and a huge staff and all men except for the children's minister and her associates. Yeah, I started to see things happening. I started to see how I wasn't as entrusted to do things as the guys were and it went to being this thing on paper that I know that my church does or says to this, whatever believes it, to this abstract thing, to this thing that was happening to me and really pissing me off and I don't think I was emotionally in a place to handle it well (chuckles) because I think I felt so inferior.

Rebecca, reflecting on that time of her experience as a female staff member, noted her sense of being significantly different from a male staff member at the churches where she was working. Beyond the fact that she did not have a title, she realized that the female staff were, quite plainly, not considered equal to the male staff. Rebecca's questioning of her lack of recognition in her role in the church as a female staff member resulted in her leaving the church altogether for a time. Rebecca poignantly stated the following:

> I was angry at him [the senior pastor] and then I was angry at every other pastor out there—I was angry at the church. And ugh, on top of that, I was just angry (chuckles). I just started getting angry. Right and um, just decided I am just gonna take a break and figure out what I'm goon do so, I took a job.

Rebecca transitioned smoothly from a religious identity to a spiritual identity during the next ten years of her life. During this same decade, Rebecca was employed at a secular, gay-friendly, national corporation. During her employment at this corporation, Rebecca found more community than she had in her church. In addition, she was increasingly aware during this period of her life that she was exclusively attracted to women. It was in the context of working at the gay-friendly, national corporation that she met her future spouse. Eventually, she and her future spouse took a corporate transfer together to the Northeast.

Ministry Years. After she and her partner moved, they found an open and affirming congregation by word of mouth in the gay community. She and her partner began attending church there, and through the efforts of the gay pastors, Rebecca again experienced a sense of fit in church. She then quickly became involved in church leadership at this same congregation. Soon after arriving at this congregation, Rebecca and her partner were married, and she experienced a reignited call to ministry. The personal meaning for Rebecca of finding a church that was both gay and female friendly is reflected in her words:

> Oh gay minister, that's great. So they just sort of took us in and I don't think it took long before she was like, "Hey you need to learn some [name of denomination] liturgy. Why don't you help me with the liturgy this week?" It was just, you know, she very quickly folded me into what was going on and so, um I preached for the first time at [name of congregation] before I came [to Seminary],

which was weird to me. I'm like; I can't believe this was
my first time at the pulpit except that when else would I
have been invited to a pulpit?

Within several months of being married, Rebecca and her wife again
relocated to another part of the metropolitan New York area, so that she
could attend a denominational seminary. At the time of this study, she had
a religious identity with significant spiritual practices. Although Rebecca
left the church for a decade and entered into a spiritual identity stage, her
early religious identity stage was formative for her in terms of its sense of
community and its biblical teachings. Having longed to reconnect to a
nurturing community, Rebecca found her way back to the church. This
was despite her lived experience as a young adult of finding her church's
rules oppressive in terms of the pressure to comply with heteronormative
and male normative ways of thinking about church leadership.

Eve. Eve was in her late forties and living on the West Coast at the
time of this study. She had a bachelor's in broadcasting journalism and
had just completed her master in divinity degree. She was in the process
of completing the ordination requirements for her denomination. Like
Rebecca, Eve was a seminarian who had come to a ministerial call in
adulthood as a second career. Like Rebecca, Eve left her early religious
identity, although it was formative for her later ministry, when she
experienced it had oppressive views toward women and LGBTQs.

Early Years. Like Rebecca, Eve had attempted to maintain her
formative early religious identity, but her experiences of oppression in the
churches she was involved with early in her life drove her out of church
for a while. Also, like Rebecca, for a decade Eve had a spiritual identity
that eventually replaced her early religious identity. Here Eve reported that
her strong ethnic roots were tied to her church life, much in the same way
that Esther and Sarah reported. Unlike Esther and Sarah, however, her
home life was not intact and did not assuage her significant experiences
of oppression in church. Further, Eve's stories of oppression may also have
been more severe because her denomination is more authoritarian than
those of Esther and Sarah.

> So church life and spiritual life, religious affiliation was very much intertwined into the fabric of who we were. I went to a Christian school which was [names denomination] so basically everyone I knew was [names ethnic group] and [names denomination].

Like her Christian identity, her lesbian identity took multiple twists and turns. Eve acknowledged that she "was very late in [her] development." She said that she was not necessarily attracted to men or women in her teens and early twenties. Through her religious beliefs, she had wanted to be "really quite sexually pure." She had been raised with the sexual teaching of remaining a virgin until marriage.

Thus, she did not explore her sexual identity until almost her mid-twenties. Eve said she first had a sense that she was a lesbian when she was twenty-four years old. After her first lesbian relationship ended, she dated men for a while, whom she was certain were gay in hindsight—and she, therefore, felt "pretty safe." She then fell in love with one woman but broke up with her because she was conflicted religiously. She returned to dating men for about seven years and then got back together with that woman and was with her for twelve years, and they became domestic partners. Eve came out to her family at the age of thirty-one to thirty-two, and it seriously shook them, per her report. However, noting her late age, she said they took her seriously and eventually began to accept that she was a lesbian.

Eve identified as a Christian throughout her entire life but had not always been involved in church. Her coming out process occurred during a period as a young adult when she was involved in church, but she left the institutionalized church, believing that she could not have both a lesbian identity and a denominational identity. Before coming into her current denomination, Eve tried multiple Protestant denominations and then was outside of any church connection for a period of ten years.

Eve had many losses that impacted her Christian journey. Her first major loss occurred when she was eighteen and her parents separated. Given her conservative religious context at the time, her parents were the first people she knew who were divorced, and she and her mother felt judged by their congregation. In addition to the loss of her relationship with her father,

Eve also experienced the loss of her first marriage to a woman. Further, before the period that Eve lived outside of any church connection, she experienced multiple changes in denominational affiliations as she sought to find a denomination in which she did not experience oppression. Thus, Eve's many denominational relationships have resulted in both resiliency and an accumulation of pain in response to her multiple experiences of congregational and denominational oppression. Although she does not remember a specific sermon being preached against homosexuals, she did have a sense during that time in the eighties of LGBTQs being very marginalized in the congregation. At that time in that congregation, she said, "we were so marginalized, we didn't even talk about it."

Through the use of the listening guide (Brown et al. 1988; Brown and Gillian 1992; Raider-Roth 2002; Woodcock 2005) methodology, Eve's following voice poem poignantly expresses only a portion of the oppression she experienced as a lesbian in various Protestant churches. These experiences of loss were primary in driving Eve from the church as a young woman in her mid-twenties.

> I would never come out to them
> I didn't want to do this
> I was the biggest leader of the church
> The biggest donor of the church
> I decided to come out to the pastor
> We believe it's against biblical principles
> I want you to stay
> You can't be in any kind of leadership
> I want you to stay
> But you can't do anything
> I can't do this
> I can't

Ministry Years. During that ten-year period in which she did not attend church, Eve had a strong spiritual identity. Contrary to what might be expected though, it was during this period that Eve experienced a calling back to the church and to professional ministry, albeit while being outside of a church affiliation.

Eve's call experience is interesting in that it came to her when she was a television producer of a popular sitcom. When one of the crew died suddenly at the age of twenty-two, the director called her and asked her to do a funeral sermon of sorts for the crew. The production assistant had been a person of faith, and Eve realized that the crew knew that she was too, as she had shared enough of her faith experiences over the years. After the quasifuneral, the crew began to ask her when she was going to seminary.

> And the cast asked me to act as the minister for the funeral. And I said, "No. I can't do that." I think they had known a bit about my spiritual life even though at that time I wasn't going to a church. I had been—I returned to the Baptist Church after about a seven-year absence. I had gone to a different Baptist Church and had gotten kicked out when I came out. Yeah. In television show. A secular position television show where I think I must have shared enough of my faith with people that they then asked me to be the pastor for the funeral. And I knew they were right. Its seven years tonight that I was called to be the pastor for tomorrow.

As a context to understanding Eve's struggle to find fit in a denomination, it is important to understand that she was raised in a homogeneous ethnic community, like Esther and Sarah, where she only knew people from her denomination and ethnic group. As the first generation of an immigrant family that attended a primarily immigrant congregation, Eve joked that it was scandalous to date Americans when she was in junior and senior high school. In addition, she was raised in a denomination that took the Bible literally and where you had to have a personal conversion. Eve named her conversion experience when she was around twelve but had been raised in the faith and had sort of "accepted Jesus Christ as [her] Lord and Savior kind of thing-language." In describing the homophobic and antifeminist views of the denomination of her childhood and adolescence, she stated the following:

> They [her home denomination] still don't ordain women
> and they have been doing homosexuality studies for thirty
> years. They keep saying that they need to keep studying
> it. Um, they are quite anti-gay. And quite nervous about
> women's leadership. Um, it continues to be a real struggle
> for them.

In her frustration and hurt regarding the homophobic regulations of her childhood denomination, Eve was recalling how her home denomination was still struggling with LGBTQ inclusion at the time of being interviewed. She contrasted this with her new denomination, which she stated was open to LGBTQ inclusion. That being said, Eve, like Sarah, still has to go through an alternative ordination route that is designed for LGBTQ persons. For Eve, this is progress and makes her ordination a possibility, whereas it was not a possibility in her home denomination or in many of the other denominations that she tried along her journey.

At the time she started seminary, Eve's denomination was not yet ordaining gay people. Thus, for a time she dropped out of the ordination process, but she "refused to go back into the closet," and like Sarah, Eve was willing to tolerate the process because she felt strongly about her current denominational identity, which is just starting to allow LGBTQ persons to be ordained through an alternate route. In her geographic region, her denomination was incredibly open to gays being involved in the life of the church, and that gives her hope for her ability to do ministry in the future.

Hannah. At the time of this study, Hannah was a co-pastor with her wife at a small urban church in another denomination from her own. She was living in a large eastern metropolitan city, had just completed her master's in marriage and family therapy, and had plans to supplement her small income as a pastor with a counseling practice.

Early Years. Hannah's early religious identity was formed in her Southern Baptist roots in part of the Midwest and then the West Coast. Hannah, like Naomi, believed that her call to ministry first appeared when she experienced a yearning to be a minister's wife. Like Rebecca, Eve, Naomi, Abigail, Ruth, and Martha, ordained ministry was not on her radar at that stage of life because her childhood denomination did not recognize women's ordination.

Hannah later experienced this formative time of religious identity development as antifeminist and homophobic, as she entered into her later teens, when she came to see that her Christian context endorsed an antifeminist and anti-homosexual theology.

> Like, and I remember, like, in our church there would be sermons against it, against homosexuality.

Her family of origin supported this theologically conservative way of thinking as well. Thus, Hannah's parents, like the other parents in this third group, did not support her coming out processes when that occurred, or her critical thinking about their church experiences as she got into her adolescent years. In the end, it was precisely Hannah's experience of homophobia as an adolescent, when she had a burgeoning development of her sexual identity, that drove her away from her church. She recalled experiencing oppression much the same way as she had a sense of being oppressed by her mother. As Hannah stated, her mother was steeped in the teachings of the Southern Baptist tradition.

Below is a story about eleven-year-old Hannah telling her mom that she did not see anything wrong with a gay singer that her friends were making fun of. Hannah relayed how her mom reacted to thinking she (Hannah) was gay.

> No, I couldn't connect. Like I was thinking ok so he likes men, and they're calling him gay, and I'm just thinking, you know, here I am, this little blonde girl, and like I just couldn't, um, it just seemed like such an outlandish thing that they were describing, you know? And I was like but I don't remember feeling like necessarily bad about it, but then I mentioned it to my mother, that some of … that there was some discussion of some boy in class and I mentioned something to my mother about how I might feel like that. Not like a definitive "oh I'm gay" but like a … something like that and she completely freaked out at me. Big time. Um … This was when … I think this was when it was either ten or eleven, 'cause it was when we

lived in Mississippi. And, um, she completely freaked out. Um, which I will hop ahead in the story and say that she has had her own very lengthy journey in dealing with this and is in a totally different place now. But she had been raised Southern Baptist she lived in the Midwest and the South and her reaction was, "there's something wrong." She started reading books about, like, um, like Focus on the Family kinds of books.

During her spiritual identity development, Hannah spoke poignantly during the interview about how during her adolescent years and her twenties she drank and used drugs to repress her emerging sexual identity as a lesbian. Hannah shared that her substance abuse also numbed her excruciating emotional pain of having rejected her family of origin and her home church, as well as her experiences of being internally conflicted about her sexual orientation and the conservatism at home and at church. All in all, Hannah was away from the church for a decade.

Eventually though, Hannah was able to get sober and worked toward maintaining her sobriety. For Hannah, early sobriety was a time when her religious, spiritual, and sexual identities coalesced. Sobriety was also the time of her coming out as a lesbian and beginning her journey to understanding her internalized homophobia. Hannah's journey to becoming a lesbian minister meant that she had to explore her underlying repressed lesbian, religious, and clergy identities before she could eliminate the addictive substances from her life.

In this part of Hannah's transcript, she articulated how Alcoholics Anonymous (AA) was a spiritual place for her, which eventually provided a bridge back to church, and how in recovery she no longer felt the need to hide her lesbian identity.

> Yeah, so I stopped dating men. Um, that wasn't like some big conscious thing it just felt like, well this is pointless and I'm … I also just at a certain point felt like I wasn't being very kind to the men I was dating because it was kind of fake. You know? I mean some guys went out with me for 2–3 years and I knew the whole time there was no

real relationship, you know, no real emotional connection happening—but you know what I'm saying? Like I felt at a certain point like I was being really inauthentic. Um— When I was in recovery it stopped. I'm saying this is kind of like; once I was in recovery I really couldn't do that kind of ... of ... It felt like. There was a lot of relief in that like ... there was a lot of relief in begin more of a real person, so I started attending, um, an AA meeting that was a meeting for gay folks ... And it was held at [name of] Church. I started teaching Sunday school there. I actually, but then I think also, for me, a big part of my spiritual development happened, um, in working the 12 steps in AA actually—what really is my spiritual connection.

Thus, after a decade of being outside of the church and in a spiritual identity stage (stage 2), Hannah ultimately returned to the institutional church, where she even rediscovered her latent call to ministry and then acted to pursue that call.

Ministry Years. Within a few years of substance abuse recovery, Hannah went to seminary in order to fulfill her call to ministry. Hannah attended a theologically conservative denominational seminary for two years and met her wife there. After her two years at the seminary though, she transferred to a nondenominational theologically liberal seminary for her third year, after she again experienced homophobic oppression by her new denomination.

Hannah's institutional oppression as a gay clergywoman had continued to the time of this study. After graduation, Hannah joined her wife as co-pastor at a small, urban, open, and affirming church, which is affiliated with a theologically conservative denomination. This same denomination, though, denied her ordination, and she sought ordination with an open and affirming denomination. Although she experiences a good fit at her congregation, she continues there without the benefit of installation by the local denominational judicatory. The implications of this are that Hannah receives minimal remuneration and has not been installed at the church she pastors.

However, Hannah remained at her current ministry site, believing that she would find few congregations that would accept her as their minister because she is a lesbian. Thus, despite such gifts as her huge capacity for empathy and her sincere longing to help and be of service to others as a minister, Hannah perceived that within both of her affiliated denominations, her options for ministry were limited.

Part of Hannah's experience of institutional oppression was what sealed her decision to move toward bivocational ministry. At the time of being interviewed, Hannah had just completed her master's in marriage and family therapy. Finally, Hannah indicated that she felt she had a good fit with her spouse and her children, as well as with her in-laws. She reported that she now has a better fit with her family of origin since her children were born, but up until that point, she felt rejected by them due to her sexual identity. She and her wife seek to live within a traditional family structure of marriage with the two children whom Hannah birthed.

Martha. At the time of this study, Martha, in her sixties, was a retired minister. However, despite being in retirement, Martha reported that she was still working part-time for her denomination. Martha was the oldest research respondent in the sample.

Early Years. From a demographic perspective, Martha was raised by a single mother, whom she described as being progressive for the time, in the Midwest. Martha described her mother as Roman Catholic but progressive in her ideas for the era. Martha identified her father, who had a minimal presence in her life, as a Primitive Baptist [name of a denomination] from Appalachia. Like Deborah and Mary, Martha focused very little on her early years as a Roman Catholic schoolgirl. Because of her early decision at the age of seventeen to become a Franciscan nun, Martha did not have a sexual narrative until her thirties, when she came out and subsequently left the order.

Martha went to Catholic elementary and Catholic high school and then entered the Franciscan Order to become a cloistered nun at the age of eighteen. She would go on to become an elementary school teacher and eventually an elementary school principal as nun. She remained a nun for seventeen years. Her Roman Catholic education was formative in her early religious identity. In interviewing her, it was revealed that, from her religious identity development, what was most significant to her was the structure it provided for her life, because her personal life at home, by contrast, had been chaotic. Her parents had separated and divorced when she was young, and her mother moved the family frequently. Martha spoke of her background with a touch of humor.

> Oh absolutely. Roman Catholic. Umm, So the bingo piece may have been a clue about that (she laughed) Absolutely. But she [her mother] had us moving all the time. We were always moving for some reason. Umm. (As if contemplating what to say next). Went to Catholic grade school, high school, entered the Franciscan Sisters at age eighteen.

Martha had a complex religious identity history, which included having been a cloistered nun during her late adolescence and early adulthood. Martha's religious identities were part of a religious journey, which she called a pilgrimage. They included an early part of her life as a Roman Catholic Franciscan nun, then a transition to Protestantism and the ministry—and then still, an integration of Franciscan principles into her Protestant ministry. Nonetheless, for purposes of this first developmental stage, Martha recalled that her early religious identity was formative but that it later became oppressive not as much from a lesbian perspective as from a feminist point of view.

In addition to her childhood religious identity, Martha maintained the principles of St. Francis in her life after the order, throughout her early adult years (which for Martha was still during the first stage). For instance, at this point in her identity as a minister, she stated that St. Francis taught that in doing the simplest things, sometimes even the ugliest things, you find joy like you have never found anywhere else. For her, these Franciscan principles of her early religious formation were not incompatible with becoming part of a Protestant denomination. Thus, Martha never fully abandoned Francis's Rules of Life. In other words, Martha resonated with the spirituality and structure that St. Francis laid out in his Rules for Life. According to Martha, these Franciscan principles include the spiritual practices of service, prayer, simplicity, and humility—which St. Francis called spiritual practices. Thus, Franciscan principles from Martha's early religious identity influenced her later return to church and her call to Protestant ministry.

> I was a Franciscan. I loved Francis. Loved everything about him. He was as nutty as a fruitcake, but he had, he had a way about him. He was a pilgrim too! [I embraced the] fact that he just accepted where he was. He, his simplicity was not ignorance or anything else. His faith was not blind faith. He was just a very simple person who saw life as it was, saw nature as it was, and was very clear about things.

In the early 1970s, when she was in her mid-thirties, with the permission of her mother superior, Martha began PhD work in theater in an eastern city. During this time, Martha went through significant developmental transitions in her life in which she became increasingly aware of her attraction to other women and her growing lesbian identity, as well as her recognition of how oppressive Catholicism was for her.

After seventeen years as a nun, she abandoned her Catholic identity and developed a spiritual identity (stage 2) as a theist. Concurrent with Martha's emerging spiritual identity was her emerging lesbian identity. During her time of living in the east, she lived in a halfway house with mentally ill women who were transitioning between a psychiatric hospitalization and independent living. During this time, she came to understand that many of these women were lesbians. As a historical backdrop, Martha stated that during this period in the early 1970s, the psychiatric community still considered homosexuality to be a mental illness. At the halfway house, Martha observed that many residents demonstrated same-sex behaviors. At this point, she also began to recognize her own repressed sexuality identity. She stated, "I think I began to understand myself as a lesbian being with them."

Martha related that her coming out process was progressive over time and was parallel to her leaving her identity as a Franciscan nun. Martha left the Franciscan Order in 1973. Martha left the order because she had experienced that life was oppressive on many levels, including theologically, socially, emotionally, and particularly in terms of gender and sexual orientation prejudice.

> Yeah. And Catholicism took a different—the repressiveness of Catholicism, just in some ways—the smallness of how things of, of necessity of how we lived was not, was not agreeable with my new understanding of myself. Part of that had to do with when I left, when I finally left the convent, I was 35 and I really had a breakdown. I wasn't hospitalized. I had to continue to work, but I felt like I should have been hospitalized. I went to therapy. [What came to a head was] Life transitions, but also when you were in the convent at that time you were—you were given a number. The 1st book you read was "Pride: Thief of the Holocaust." You were not an "I." You were a "We." Every sense of ego was to be gotten out of you (sic). Because you had to act as a member of a community. Now we know to be a member of a community, you have to have a good sense of yourself in order to be productive. So I left the convent. I was up here (gestures over her head). I decided to stay in [names city]. Struggling mightily to work and (sic). This is 1973.

Thus, for a thirteen-year period, Martha experienced a faith crisis when she left the order. At this time, Martha believed she lived with a spiritual rather than a religious identity, identifying herself as a theist. However, she perceived that in leaving the order, for a time she was without any religious identity and was in a faith crisis, having experienced a breakdown. During this thirteen-year period, Martha worked at multiple jobs in the corporate world.

Another historical backdrop was that Martha's spiritual identity journey coincided in the 1980s with the height of the AIDS crisis. Thus, she extensively volunteered at a Catholic-run AIDS program. During this time, Martha began dating a woman who was an art therapist, and who, at the time of being interviewed, she had been in a relationship with for sixteen years. Toward the end of her thirteen-year spiritual identity journey, Martha did not have a full awareness of it at the time, but in looking back, she realized that she was beginning to be drawn back to the church. During the revised religious identity phase, it appeared that Martha wanted to return to the foundational principles that offered a sense belonging and structure, which she had experienced in her earlier religious life.

Ministry Years. Having progressed through her religious identity phase, Martha felt called to do ministry again but this time within a Protestant context—a context where she had experienced minimal homophobic and antifeminist oppression. Martha reiterated that the Franciscan Rules for Life were foundational for her and drew her back to the church, but she knew she could not do ministry in a Roman Catholic Church context because of its history of being oppressive toward women and lesbians. The answer for her was to intentionally seek out a theologically progressive Protestant denomination. Throughout that time, Martha utilized the Franciscan Rule of Life to help reconcile her lesbian and religious identities.

> Yeah, yeah. And I think prayer is so important for self-acceptance and that's—you go through it with yourself. And that's where a Rule of Life is helpful. I don't talk about self-acceptance because I'm not a therapist per se, but I can talk about prayer and how supportive and how enriching it is for your life no matter whom you love.

When she was ordained in the year 2000, Martha had already embraced her lesbian identity. She felt as though she was easily able to integrate her sexual identity into her clergy identity. From an anti-oppression theory perspective, Martha stated that her ministry experiences had been, for the most part, positive.

Leah. At the time of this study, Leah was in her late forties. She was raised in a very large Roman Catholic family in New England. She was the youngest of five children and one of thirty-eight first cousins on her father's side alone. Although there was a great deal of substance abuse among her brothers and her father, she described her family as loving and supportive and as religious. From her father, Leah said, she received the gift of religiosity. From her mother, Leah said, she received the gift of spirituality.

Early Years. Regarding her early religious identity, Leah quipped that she was "happily Catholic for a while," until she got swept up in the "born-again Christian movement" for a year when she was in the eighth grade. Leah spoke of her born-again experiences during her early adolescence as providing her with structure and rules. But upon further reflection on that time, Leah said that she believed it was a means of escaping her burgeoning sexual identity that seemed so polar opposite to her Catholic upbringing.

> Very common for these [fundamentalist] churches to come into a little Podunk town and just sweep through and you know—Yeah, [it was another Great Awakening] (laughs) and convert a bunch of people out of fear you know. And or, into fear. Into fear I should say. It was— you know, it was horrible. And I think that I had some inkling. I had some inkling that I was different anyway. Maybe—Yeah. Yeah. I was obsessed with my best friends. I felt like something was different or maybe even wrong at that point. So the born-again Christian thing felt like a good way to save myself, my soul, if I thought it needed saving. So—Yeah, I did [need saving]. Plus there was a lot of alcoholism in my family. I think I was reaching out for help and that hand just came along and I just grabbed it.

During her college years, Leah abandoned her religious identities (both her Catholicism and her fundamentalism) for a period when they became too internally conflictual. In her confusion, during high school and college, Leah abused drugs. Like Hannah, in response to feeling different sexually, Leah had begun to fall into her family's substance abuse patterns by the time she was in eighth grade. First, she began to drink like her father and brothers, and then she also began to smoke marijuana on a daily basis (one of her brothers grew it openly on the family property). Her substance abuse patterns continued until the summer before her senior year of college.

Put simply, Leah's confusion had its source, like Esther, Abigail, and

Hannah, in her struggle to reconcile her lesbian and Christian identities. It was when Leah perceived that her burgeoning lesbian identity conflicted with her Catholic belief system that she left the church. After that, she focused on what she perceived to be her calling to become a journalist. During and immediately after college, Leah continued to try to make sense out of her sexual identity. She dated a man for a couple of years and loved him but knew "something was wrong."

Leah spoke almost with loose associations as she shared how, like Hannah, her substance abuse patterns in high school and college dulled the pain of managing her internal confusion about being a lesbian and how to integrate her Christian and lesbian identities. Hannah was aware that her substance abuse patterns and her growing lesbian identity coexisted.

> It didn't feel like a fit. Exactly. I don't know what my deal is. You know, so I umm. Yeah. Yeah. And you know, I was still very pulled by the whole Catholic thing. So I just started drinking like a lot. And then, I wasn't going to mass at that point and I wasn't part of any faith community. I wasn't going to mass. No. I wasn't. I was not—I was not part of any faith community. Yeah. I left. The born-again thing too. After I left the born-again thing, I kind of went back to the Catholic Church through high school. Yeah, in college, I just chucked religion out of the window.

Although Leah had told one of her best friends she thought she was a lesbian when Leah was a senior in high school, her friend told her she was "just going through a phase." Later, being a natural athlete, when she went to college in New England, Leah met a lot of lesbians on the volleyball team, but she did not feel a fit there either. She said they were "too butch" for her, and they "scared" her.

Further evidence of being aware of her coexisting substance abuse patterns and budding lesbian identity occurred in 1986 when a drunk driver killed a close friend of Leah's. She immediately got sober and went to a therapist, telling her therapist during the first session that she had been drinking heavily because she was a lesbian. After starting therapy, she immediately started going to AA, which contributed to her full integration of her former Catholic beliefs with her lesbian identity. From that time on, Leah continued to attend AA. She perceived that she started having a spiritual identity again through AA, and in particular LGBTQ AA meetings. She met her first girlfriend at an AA meeting, whom she had a relationship with for four years, and which she felt a good fit. Although she stated they were young and mutually ended the relationship, she glowed when she shared that she has been with her current partner for sixteen years.

Ministry Years. Leah's call to ministry came during the post-college period, when Leah was working as a journalist. During this same period, Leah recalled relating to her spiritual identity (stage 2). Leah was drawn back to her early religious identity because it had given her permission to view life through a spiritual lens. Her return to her religious identity also enabled her to value acts of mercy and social justice functions. Leah spoke about her call to ministry growing out of her calling as a journalist to write on spiritual and religious subjects. Interestingly, as a journalist, she wrote almost exclusively about religion and social services. Eventually, she researched and then wrote an article on clinical pastoral education and hospital chaplaincy.

> And it was like a calling [ministry] that came out of a calling [journalism]. You know, that's the way I look at it. You know, um, I had considered journalism to be a calling but it started to lose meaning for me. Yeah.

In 1996, it was not surprising that Leah entered a dual four-year program in which she got her seminary degree and MSW. By that point, she had found herself involved in a large church in a New England city, which was open and affirming. She felt a strong fit with this particular congregation's denomination and decided to pursue an ordination track. Leah graduated from her dual program in 2001 and was ordained in 2003.

Like Rachel, who incorporated her Jewish prayers into her chaplaincy work, and Martha, who incorporated her Franciscan ideas into her congregational work, Leah brought her emphasis on the early mystics into her work as a hospital chaplain.

Yeah. Majorly integrated [her Catholicism and Protestantism]. I would say that most of my spiritual life is still very much Catholic. And a lot of what I learned about my own mystical experiences I have gathered from my own Catholic studies, you know. Once receiving her ordination, Leah worked both in HIV and psychiatric chaplaincy programs. She proudly shared that she is one of eight Clinical Pastoral Education (hospital chaplain) supervisors whose specialty is psychiatry. Leah, like Abigail, Hannah, and Mary, found that a second master's degree in a mental health discipline enhanced their ministry.

STAGE 2: SPIRITUAL IDENTITY

Of the thirteen participants, only Deborah, Mary, Rebecca, Eve, Hannah, Martha, and Leah entered into this optional stage 2 spiritual identity, which occurred during a span of thirteen to forty-eight years. They had differentiated from their early religious identities, due to their experiences of heteronormative and antifemale oppression in their early faith communities. In contrast, Esther, Sarah, Naomi, Abigail, Ruth, and Rachel did not enter this second stage and were able to come out in the sexual identity stage with their religious identities intact.

For the seven women who did enter into this stage, their spiritual identities appeared prior to their coming out and helped reconcile the internal conflict they experienced as a result of incongruities between early religious beliefs and their growing recognition of their lesbianism. In large part, this stage paralleled their coming out process, with their spiritual identities providing this group of women with a safe context to come out in ways that their religious identities could not. The spiritual identity stage functioned as a protective period—allowing them a non-church-based space in which to suspend the critical judgments of their early religious affiliations and reconcile their spiritual beliefs and sexual orientation. In a sense, the women who entered into this stage of spiritual development created a community through work, friendship networks, or twelve-step groups that replaced church for that time.

The junctures and insights associated with this stage are the following: 1) the women developed alternative spiritual ideas to replace their former religious identities; 2) they developed spiritually based practices (e.g., meditation, yoga, prayer, guided imagery, twelve-step traditions); 3) they were able to differentiate their beliefs from their early views of authority structures and values; 4) their religious and (or) denominational identities began to hold little meaning for them; and 5) they intentionally sought alternative spiritual communities to replace their early religious identities (e.g., twelve-step groups, metaphysical churches, Buddhism). The characteristics shared by the women in this spiritual identity stage were anger and disillusionment with their churches of childhood and adolescence and an ability to differentiate their internal belief structure from the authoritarian belief structures of their early religious identities.

Offered below is the contrast found between the women who experienced a discrete stage of spiritual identity and those who did not. The narratives demonstrate how the spiritual identity stage was important in the lesbian clergy development of seven of the thirteen participants and how this stage appeared to have ameliorated the loss of their religious identity for which they grieved. The functions of this spiritual identity stage were that it seemed: 1) to serve as a bridge for these women between the early religious identity (stage 1) and a later revised religious identity (stage 4) that emerged prior to the call to ministry process; 2) to enable these seven women to come out in a safe context outside of the institutionalized church, as it preceded and then paralleled the emerging sexual identity; and 3) for two participants, the women had several periods of experiencing sexual relationships with both men and women before becoming clergy.

Spiritual Meaning within a Corporate Setting

Rebecca, Martha, and Eve all shared the experience of having found spiritual meaning in the corporate world. These experiences of meaning and community functioned for them in two ways: 1) as a space to make more sense out of their sexual identifies; and 2) as time to begin contemplating professional calls to ministry. Primarily, during this time outside of the church, these three women had the freedom to come out, and they had the freedom to explore their feelings about their spirituality as well as their early religious identities. They each continued to grieve the communities they had when they were in their religious identities. However, they did not think at the time that they would be able to enter back into a religious community they had experienced as oppressive because they were lesbians. Martha and Eve exemplified those who felt called to ministry prior to returning to church (more will be said about this in the revised religious identity in stage 4). Similarly, Rebecca found significant community in the corporate world, where she felt safe to come out, and which appeared to serve as a bridge back to church.

Rebecca. After experiences of antifeminist oppression in church, Rebecca's religious identity as a Fundamentalist Christian had become ego-dystonic for her. Instead, she found spiritual identity at a secular corporation where she worked for a decade as she transitioned through the spiritual identity stage. This phase of spiritual identity allowed her space and permission to acknowledge her sexual identity as a lesbian. Rebecca shared that she did not want to acknowledge that she was a lesbian at the beginning of this stage, when she first left her church employment and her early religious identity. As long as Rebecca was employed at a church, she felt as though she did not have the emotional or spiritual freedom to explore her sexual identity.

> Um that's when my involvement in the church pretty much dropped off. I just because I think I accept, yeah, you know, what you're right, but I don't know what to do no like I've already eaten the forbidden fruit and I don't know.

She stated that when the church was no longer a safe place for her and it no longer felt like a family, her new employer, the coffee company, "stepped in" for her. Rebecca was a seminarian at the time she was interviewed, and she stated that she had a goal of bringing several important principles into the church that she had learned in the corporate culture. Here, Rebecca cited her learnings from the coffee company, which was gay friendly.

> Right and a place to feel welcomed and to feel because it's a very ugh it embraces diversity and they love gay people

Pamela Pater-Ennis, PhD

> and they are big supporters of that and same sex marriage
> and [name of wife] and I have had insurance on that
> policy for years before we were married and it's just a good
> safe place for us to be and I think it taught me a lot about
> community and the value of hard work maybe even more
> than the church ever did and the value of working out,
> you know, your own journey [sigh]. Working out what
> you believe and working out what you [voice trailed off].

During her ten years with this coffee company, Rebecca learned about the gifts of hospitality, embracing diversity, creating safe emotional environments, and the value of a strong work ethic. Rebecca did not know fully at that point, but she came to realize later that these were the gifts that God was calling her to use when she was called to ministry.

Martha. After leaving her cloistered Franciscan Order, where she had been a nun for seventeen years, Martha entered into a thirteen-year spiritual identity stage. During this period, Martha became increasingly aware of her lesbian identity, her lived experience of oppressed Catholicism, and her abandonment of her Catholic identity. In leaving the order, she believed that she was having a psychotic break due to the stress of the repressiveness of the order, more than homophobic oppression specifically.

> Yeah. And Catholicism took a different—the repressiveness
> of Catholicism, just in some ways—the smallness of how
> things of … of necessity of how we lived was not—was
> not agreeable with my new understanding of myself. Part
> of that had to do with when I left—when I finally left the
> convent, I was thirty-five and I really had a breakdown. I
> wasn't hospitalized. I had to continue to work, but I felt
> like I should have been hospitalized. I went to therapy.

At this time of her recovery from a life of repressive Catholicism, Martha believed she lived within a spiritual rather than a religious identity. Also during this time, Martha began dating a woman with whom she would go on to have a relationship with for sixteen years. Martha did not

140

have full awareness at the time, but she was drawn back to the church toward the end of this spiritual identity stage.

Almost unexplainably, one morning she called a local seminary to begin an admissions process. She entered seminary later that year. Martha, like Rebecca, did not have full awareness of the ministerial journey she was on at that point. However, her time in the spiritual identity stage enabled her to heal from her oppression and reenter social justice work in a religious context that was open and affirming to LGBTQs.

Eve. Eve experienced a discrete period of spiritual identity in the decade that she was not in church. Eve was not at church because she had been sanctioned due to being a lesbian. Here, Eve recounted yet another instance of being asked to leave a church because of being an out lesbian.

> I had been—I returned to the Baptist Church after about
> a seven-year absence. I had gone to a different Baptist
> Church and had gotten kicked out when I came out.

Yet, during that same period, Eve still considered herself to be a Christian and, in contrast to Rebecca and Martha, longed to be in church. For instance, when she came out in her early thirties, she experienced significant oppression from multiple churches and left the institutionalized church when she could no longer tolerate the level of homophobic oppression she had to endure. However, during this decade in her thirties to forties, when she was "denomination-less," she would periodically attend big churches and stated that she would "disappear," just so she could be anonymous during worship.

Eve remembered that during this painful spiritual identity era, she longed to be back in church but did not know how to reconcile her lesbian and religious identities. She spoke about how she had hoped that she could maintain her religious identity without the benefit of the institutionalized church. However, during her spiritual identity stage, Eve found that she could not have a deep religious identity without the benefit of church.

> Yeah I think so. I—you pointed it out—I never thought
> I could not be a Christian. I thought for sure that I
> could have a relationship with God. I thought for sure

that relationship could be maintained without being in a formalized structure and so yeah. I think spiritual identity was always there. I'm a little freaked out. I'm a little alarmed. Like I have a really deep religious identity now that I identify as [names denomination].

During the decade when Eve did not formally belong to any church, she implied that she was sensitive to her coworkers' spiritual needs. She frequently spoke to those around her at work in television about faith, and she increasingly realized that people were drawn to that spiritual part in her. She also increasingly realized that she was comfortable talking to her coworkers about existential issues. When she performed the funeral on her television set, mentioned earlier, for the cast member who unexpectedly died, Eve felt called back to the church and called to ministry (clergy identity: stage 5).

In summary, Rebecca, Martha, and Eve found a sense of community outside of the institutionalized church, which they had previously left because of being deeply wounded by homophobic and male-normative oppressions in their home congregations or denominations. For these three women, their spirituality was expressed in terms of the genuine connectedness with other women and in their capacity to both receive and give to others. For Rebecca, her community was her coffee shop; for Martha, it was her social service work; for Eve, it was her television broadcasting staff. These spiritual communities functioned as bridges for Rebecca, Martha, and Eve back to the institutionalized church. None of these women were aware of it at the time, but they longed for the deeper religious beliefs they had been taught. These spiritual communities gave them the freedom to come out and the freedom to understand that some Christian traditions are LGBTQ affirming.

FINDING SPIRITUALITY THROUGH AA

For Hannah and Leah, it was this initial spiritual identity stage that became the placeholders for them when they left the institutionalized church because of their inability to reconcile their Christian and lesbian identities. They left their childhood and adolescent churches because they had experienced both external and internal forms of homophobic oppression, making staying in their early religious identities intolerable for them. Yet they both found spirituality in their gay Alcoholics Anonymous meetings, which essentially became the bridge for them back to an organized Christian church.

Hannah. Like Eve, Hannah, occasionally sat in the back of churches during this spiritual identity stage, in anonymity, because she longed to be a part of a faith community. At that time in her life, she did not think it was possible to be both a lesbian and a Christian. Hannah's spiritual identity seemed most significant in the period when she was not attending church, between the ages of sixteen and twenty-five. From a social identity theory perspective, her spiritual identity served as a bridge between two periods of religious identity and the context for her budding sexual identity. As such, her spiritual identity marked a transition between two periods of religious identity and a context for her burgeoning lesbian identity.

Specifically, the twelve-step program provided a transition from a spiritual identity back to church for her. Prior to this point, Hannah's spiritual identity dominated her religious identity, as she thought that her religious and sexual identities could not coexist. Here, Hannah reflected on the pain of homophobic experiences in church, which were the push factor for her in leaving church life. Yet Hannah also experienced significant loss in leaving her early religious identity (stage 1), because she perceived that her early church background formed her faith.

> I had some really negative feelings about the [names fundamentalist denomination] church, but obviously there was some—I mean I learned a lot about my faith there and that, you know, I think—and that's where some of that faith did help me get through that situation. But anyway, in 1999 I'm 25 years old. I get sober, and at that point I …

In her own voice poems from the listening guide (Brown et al. 1988; Brown and Gillian 1992; Raider-Roth 2002; Woodcock 2005) methodology, her spiritual identity replaced her religious identity for a time. Her spiritual identity enabled her to sustain a belief in a higher power throughout this substance abuse recovery period. Here, through a voice poem, Hannah reflected the pain that she experienced in leaving behind her religious identity in her late adolescence and college years:

> So I, essentially
> I knew that
> I was really very connected to the church
> I stopped
> I mean, uh, when I went to college
> I didn't go to church anymore at all
> I totally, and, um, was sad about it
> I felt like there wasn't a place for me, really

For Hannah, this spiritual identity morphed into her religious identity when she started attending a church where her AA meetings were held, in a large metropolitan area. Her voice poem (Brown et al. 1988; Brown and Gillian 1992; Raider-Roth 2002; Woodcock 2005), set out below, described her internal processing during her spiritual identity stage. She remembered, while being interviewed, the time when she had recently become sober and was beginning to see that her lesbian and religious identities did not have to be mutually exclusive.

> I had some more financial success
> I wasn't doing anything I was excited about
> I was able to live
> > Having a good time, I guess theoretically
> I, um got sober
> I was 25 ...
> Like I was like, 40 years old
> I just thought that something felt really wrong
> I just felt really like, suicidal
> I couldn't figure out how to make my life work at all
> I was spending all my money on drugs
> I just was feeling so hopeless
> I look back it's very much a God moment
> I went to a therapist

I did go I, to, uh, a 12 Step program
I had had a reliance on God in the past
I had this kind of moment
I was like
I
I do believe in you, God
I don't think you created me just for this
I got sober
I'm very grateful
I felt about a hundred years old
Like I felt like my life was over
I might as well try anything because it was so bad
I got sober
I really felt like
I wanted to go back to church
I felt like it
I needed
I was missing something
I really wanted to go back

Despite her pattern of abuse in her home denomination, Hannah longed for reconnecting to a deeper understanding of what God could mean for her as a lesbian Christian.

Leah. Spiritual identity for Leah had four different phases: (1) it ran parallel to her religious identity until late high school when she came out; (2) it was a discrete entity from her religious identity during the decade when she left the church; (3) it was strengthened by her participation in Alcoholics Anonymous; and (4) in ministry, it was integrated into her religious and sexual identities (revised religious identity: stage 4).

According to Leah, in contrast to her father's fostering of a religious identity in her, her mother, who was an artist, fostered in her an appreciation for nature and the divine.

And you know [my mother] taught me so much about my spiritual life, you know. She really imbued a lot in me. So I feel now that I have a lot of liturgical, sacramental, and spiritual, natural, super-natural, you know, all-encompassing spirituality. You know, when I hear people say, "I'm spiritual, but not religious," I understand that.

Further, growing up on a farm, Leah said that she had an enhanced appreciation of nature, which she stated heightened her spiritual awareness at a young age.

[I had a] very strong sense of the divine from the time I was a little kid—like a sense of nature and the divine.

In fact, while being interviewed, Leah remembered fondly that her family teased her by referring to her as "a weird little kid" because she was always "hypersensitive to [the] spiritual." In line with both anti-oppressive (Dominelli 2002) and ecological (Gitterman and Germain 2008) theoretical perspectives, Leah denied that this experience of teasing was oppressive, yet there was a sense that due to her spiritually having such a strong intuitiveness and insight into nature, she felt that she did not fit in with her family or peers at times.

Leah's twenties marked her time of early recovery from alcohol dependency, and it was a time when her spirituality was enhanced. Like Hannah, AA became a bridge between discrete periods of religious identity. Leah's AA spirituality enabled her to again begin exploring Christianity but in a new context of seeking affirming and inclusive congregations in a Protestant context. During her studying of spiritual books and practices, Leah began to reexperience "serious mystical experiences." Thus, Leah, during this spirituality identity stage in her life, dabbled in yoga and Buddhism and did a "little bit of everything" but still identified as a spiritual Christian. Leah emphasized at several points in the interview that most of her spiritual life was very much Catholic. What she referred to was her connectedness to the early church fathers and mothers, because of her lifelong mystical experiences. To offer context, Leah had a traumatic brain injury as a child, and one of her neurologists believed that her injured brain made her more receptive to mystical experiences.

MULTIPLE PERIODS OF SPIRITUAL IDENTITY PRIOR TO RETURN TO CHURCH

Deborah and Mary were exceptions to the other six women (Rebecca, Eve, Hannah, Martha, and Leah) who had developed one discrete spiritual identity (stage 2), in that Deborah and Mary had multiple periods of spiritual identity at crisis points in their lives when they were not involved in a Christian faith community.

Deborah. Deborah's periods of spiritual identity could be characterized as her means of coping with difficult events. This was particular to her experiences of oppression as an African American woman and as a lesbian, as well as having had a near-fatal automobile accident in her early twenties. From an ecological theory perspective, Deborah perceived that she did not fit into fifty different congregations/denominations due to being an African American lesbian. Thus, her spiritual identity appeared to have sustained her during these times of crises or these times of transition between her three careers and the many denominations that she had affiliated with for a time. Of her coping style, she said, "I just hang in there, whatever it is. You know the race isn't always to the swift."

Deborah reported multiple stages of spiritual identity for a two-decade period between her late teens and her early forties and in between her periods of religious identity as a Christian. These periods are: (1) the time she left the Roman Catholic Church in college and did not have a denominational identity; (2) the time immediately following her accident and prior to assuming a religious identity; and (3) the times in between denominations when she was seeking fit in a faith community or had experienced oppression in a faith community.

A significant part of Deborah's spiritual and religious identities appeared to be blurred as she struggled to find fit where she did not experience oppression as a black lesbian. Part of the blurring was her sense that she needed to find a community where social justice occurred. Immediately after her accident, being in a Christian congregation was not as important as fit and justice, but eventually she returned to a Christian identity when she recognized that she missed her connection to Jesus-based theology. For several years, she was involved in a non-Christian church that practiced HIV and AIDS intervention and prevention. She cited that she had a pattern of leaving congregations and denominations because she could not find explicit expression of a Christian identity in those places. Her way of expressing this was the following simple statement: "Jesus was not in the sanctuary."

During the few years after her accident, Deborah utilized her spiritual identity as a means of coping with her consequent losses in both her fast-paced business career and physical functioning. After the accident, Deborah continued to utilize her spiritual identity, including her time in a non-Christian denomination. In sum, Deborah's spiritual identity sustained her through significant periods of ongoing suffering. Deborah stated that the accident was a transformative event that allowed her the time and space to evaluate her values. During this time, she returned to her education and received a doctorate in education in two and a half years.

In the end, Deborah's spiritual identity stage brought her back to her Christian identity. The accident functioned as an index event, which transitioned her from having a spiritual identity toward a religious identity. Deborah's core beliefs—that God does not give you more than you can handle, and what happens to you happens for a reason—were her primary coping mechanisms. Specifically, regarding her coping with a difficult situation during her accident rehabilitation, she stated the following:

> The Holy Spirit just redirected me to, and I went into before going into education, the people who helped me to walk again, to feed myself again, and care for myself, were people who, maybe a month or two later, or, prior, I would not have even know they existed.

Mary. Mary's Christian identity came at a young age. However, it was her spiritual identity and practices that allowed her burgeoning lesbian identity to come to full fruition as an adult, beginning at age twenty-four. Like Deborah, Mary had continued to the time of the interviewing to struggle with oppression in religious communities. Throughout her life, she had rarely experienced a sense of fit with either a Christian denomination or in an intimate relationship with either a man or a woman.

> My friend was going to this church, you know this sort of
> Metaphysical church. So we went to this [metaphysical]
> church and you know, I really liked it. Um, I still think
> I was struggling very much with my sexual orientation.

In her experiences in the metaphysical or spiritualist church and her experiences in LGBTQ-affirming Christian church, Mary ultimately did not find a goodness of fit. Mary expressed her emotional pain on not experiencing fit in either a spiritualist or Christian church context like someone who was stranded:

> And I thought, maybe the church has really changed.
> And I felt that I had nowhere to really talk about [my
> sexual orientation]. So I wound up going to the [names the
> denomination] Church and um, I found that the pastor
> was not very friendly toward me. I got the feeling that they
> only wanted people in their church that really could bring
> up the church and that could really bring in the church
> financial and really could bring in church ministries and
> this and that. And I didn't feel like I could particularly
> come there in my brokenness and, um, mostly by the
> pastor.

Interestingly, despite her incredible pain and experience of rejection from multiple churches, Mary spoke in a limited way about any sort of spiritual identity. She did not have a lot of language for this spiritual identity stage. Instead, Mary utilized Christian language to describe this time in her life. Her language about her spiritual identity seemed to be reflective of her longing to fit into a church community as a lesbian minister. She also reflected the grieving that Mary experienced in not feeling that she could fit into a Christian context as a lesbian with the following words:

> And I really did have a powerful understanding of God's
> presence and God's love. You know, and um, when this
> happened in the other church, it was hard for me. It was

149

difficult to make the decision to leave. It felt that was the right decision, but that was hard. You know, it was painful.

In summary, Deborah and Mary had extensive histories of homophobic oppression in multiple Christian church settings. Although their multiple spiritual identities seemed to enable them to heal from either health, faith, or church crises, in the end, they remained unsettled.

NOT HAVING A DISCRETE STAGE OF SPIRITUALITY

Unlike the women discussed above, it does not appear that the remaining six participants required the interim, discrete stage of developing a spiritual identity in order to come out during their sexual identity stage and to achieve ordination. Esther, Sarah, Abigail, Ruth, Rachel, and Naomi each reported that they remained constant in their denominational identities throughout their lives. These women appear to have skipped the spiritual identity (stage 2) and entered into the sexual identity stage (stage 3) following their early religious identity stage (stage 1).

Rather than having a discrete period of spiritual identity development, Esther, Sarah, and Abigail reported periods of utilizing spiritual practices further along in their developmental process toward becoming lesbian clergy. Specifically, they appeared to have utilized spiritual practices to cope during periods of homophobic oppression from their denominations that occurred later in the context[15] of the clergy identity stage (stage 5).

Esther. To understand the relative absence of Esther's spirituality is to account for her extremely strong religious and denominational identities. Esther reported minimal spiritual identity, except as a means of explaining her daily practice of prayer and scripture reading that historically sustained her in her coming out period as a lesbian. She reported that her spiritual practices also sustained her when being oppressed as a lesbian clergy by her denomination of birth. Lastly, for Esther, her social justice practices are her spiritual practices.

---

[15] This is consistent with Quackenbush's (2008) assertion that spirituality is context driven and can vary from person to person.

Esther referred to spiritual identity only one time in the interview, which points again to a later stage of clergy identity (stage 5), when she spoke about some of her ministerial colleagues who were not out. Her conversation about her spiritual identity was distant and seemed to be outside of herself. In regard to spiritual identity, she stated that remaining closeted "doesn't allow you to be fully yourself and that remaining closeted as a minister gets in the way of your spiritual life." Esther asserted, in regard to spiritual identity, that her practice of being fully out to the denomination, congregation, and community constituted her identity. This is connected to Esther's strong calling to do social justice ministries, which will be discussed further during the synthesized identity stage (stage 7).

When speaking about spiritual identity, Esther became almost inaudible. For Esther, there is no disconnect between her religious identity and her spiritual identity, but for her, it is more of a spiritual practice. However, she noted that the full expression of her spiritual practice connected her to the pain of homophobic oppression in the church.

> Well [they] remain closeted for fear of being ostracized, or kicked out makes you really less than capable. It doesn't allow you to be fully yourself. I don't think they "have, have the love of Jesus down in their hearts, down in their hearts" (singing a child's song).

Heteronormative oppression in the church made Esther angry at the church for oppressing out LGBTQ colleagues and angry with her closeted LGBTQ colleagues who were afraid to come out to their congregations or denominations. For Esther, remaining closeted limited one's authenticity as a minister and, therefore, limited one's spiritual practices of prayer, preaching, and leading worship.

Sarah. Like Esther, Sarah spoke minimally about having a spiritual identity. Regarding spiritual identity, she said, "I don't know." She further said that her spiritual identity was not huge. Thus, Sarah was fairly adamant that she did not have a separate spiritual identity stage as distinct from her religious identity stages. In speaking about her spiritual identity, Sarah spoke enigmatically. "It's not even super important to me, but it is important to me."

Sarah stated that she purposefully studied in Europe during her seminary years and was exposed to the world church there, which included a variety of expressions of faith. Further, her ecumenical training overseas also enabled her to borrow principles from feminist theology and from Buddhism. However, for Sarah, it was the Christian rituals, which were particular to her denominational identity, that were important to her. Sarah stated that her spiritual identity was more about the traditional faith practices that emerge out of the denominational tradition that she was raised with and that she continued to practice.

> I've always been sort of happily Christian. Not sort of, I am Christian. I don't always like the Christian church. I struggle with all that stuff politically and all those trappings of it. And I sort of borrow of all traditions as I find it helpful. But I think something from Buddhism is helpful.

In addition to her Christian practices, Sarah, almost as an afterthought, stated that she thought some Buddhist practices might enhance her Christian practices.

Abigail. Like Sarah, Abigail's spiritual identity is in the form of faith practices that she has continued to develop in her journey toward becoming a lesbian minister. In fact, Abigail's spiritual identity evolved out of her growing comfort with her sexual identity. Like Esther and Sarah, for Abigail, her spiritual identity never emerged as a separate phase but rather was a parallel process to her constant and evolving religious identity. Her spiritual identity has enhanced her religious identity. For Abigail, a developmental theorist and clinician, her spiritual identity has increasingly been integrated into her religious identity. In other words, for Abigail, the terms spiritual formation and spiritual practice feel more accurate than spiritual identity.

Ruth. Like Esther, Sarah, and Abigail, Ruth stated that her spiritual identity was not a discrete entity from her religious identity but rather a way of making meaning out of particular events in her life.

> The spiritual stream is there, but I think in the context of
> the narrative [pauses as if thinking], and events.

Specifically, Ruth's spirituality has enabled her to primarily focus on feminist biblical criticism and theology. For Ruth, her study of feminine images of the divine has strengthened her friendships and connections to female clergy colleagues.

> One of the most powerful experiences that I had in terms
> of spirituality was when I discovered feminist theology.
> When I discovered feminist biblical criticism, and started
> looking at these biblical characters with fresh eyes.

In order to further explore her spirituality, Ruth also stated she regularly explored art and prolifically studied spiritual formation and spiritual direction books. To further illustrate this point of spirituality being in her narrative, Ruth cited the following life examples: as a child, she wanted to be a cloistered Franciscan nun or a "Poor Claire," and in one of her churches, she became concerned that its weakest asset was its "passionate spirituality." Additionally, concerning her spirituality, Ruth stated that she feels increasingly drawn to the spirituality of the early Christian mystics.

Rachel. Rachel does not believe that she experienced a spiritual identity as a discrete period in her life. Like Esther, Sarah, Abigail, and Ruth, her spiritual identity takes the form of faith practices that she utilized in her work as a chaplain (see stage 5). What is unique to Rachel is that her spiritual identity is marked as the outward manifestations of her religious identities in practices of prayer from both Jewish and Christian traditions.

Rachel's spiritual identity appears to be more of her outward expression of her dual religious identities as both a Jew and as a Christian. When she was in training as a hospital chaplain, and prior to being ordained, a rabbi chaplain gave her permission to develop her own unique brand of spirituality in relationship to her experience of God. He stayed until six thirty in the morning, conversing with Rachel as they sat vigil, waiting for a patient to die. In leaving the hospital, the rabbi gave her a blessing, which enabled her to begin embracing her dual religious identities. During the interview, Naomi did not make a huge distinction between her religious and spiritual identities.

> You can develop your own spirituality in relationship to God. Umm, so we, we failed a whole generation of you. It's been an interesting blessing talking the whole night. Christianity's gain is Judaism's loss because you are clearly going to be a wonderful chaplain. And we are the lesser for it.

Naomi. Like the other women in this group, Naomi maintained that she did not experience a discrete spiritual identity stage prior to becoming ordained because she never left the church prior to ordination. Naomi spoke with a lack of clarity about whether or not she had a discrete spiritual identity stage. Technically, she did not leave the church or her ministry at that point. However, during the interview process, Naomi had the insight that her spiritual identity had functioned as an alternative voice to her religious identity voice, keeping her sexual identity repressed.

Naomi referred to, in what appeared to be confused voice, her inability to make a distinction between her religious and spiritual identities. In this section, Naomi quickly noted that her spiritual identity had functioned to keep her sexual identity repressed, but at the same time, she also noted that her spiritual identity had resulted in a positive discovery about her relationship with God and those truths about herself that she had formerly been afraid to look at.

> I probably would have separated those out. Yeah. I think that's true. Um, spiritually—what's interesting is even though I was churched my whole life, with how much I identify with a secret identity and that there was something more to find. I didn't realize it was just as much about finding myself as it was about finding God. I mean God was there all along and ...

However, Naomi brought a unique position to this study in that, as Naomi contemplated for a moment the possibility of having a spiritual identity, she said she thought she may have had a spiritual identity that had both enabled her to maintain a secret identity for years as a lesbian, as well as eventually functioning more as a spiritual bolstering for both her clergy and lesbian identities during her period of coming out. When Naomi's voice trailed off while being interviewed, the listener had the sense that Naomi still could barely say out loud that she is a lesbian, for fear that it may reify it more for her. During the interview, Naomi noted for the first time, it appears, how she has used spiritual language, rather than religious language, to talk about being a lesbian.

> Yeah. I think that's true. Um, spiritually [pause]—what's interesting is even though I was churched my whole life, with how much I identify with a secret identity and that there was something more to find. I didn't realize it was just as much about finding myself as it was about finding God. I mean God was there all along and [voice trailed off as if in deep thought]—my perspective would be that God always knew and um [voice trailed off] …

One last note here is that Naomi almost seemed to be entering a discrete period of spiritual identity (stage 6) at the time of the interview. She used the interview to give voice to her depression and her transition to a region of the United States where she believed she would experience homophobic oppression for the first time in ministry. Therefore, Naomi was contemplating leaving professional ministry and perhaps the institutionalized church for a time (see stage 6 for more discussion on this).

STAGE 3: SEXUAL IDENTITY EMERGES

The emergence of the women's sexual identity stage in this study was found to overlap with the prior early religious identity stage (stage 1), which occurred between the ages of zero and thirty-four for a portion of the sample. For these women, who remained in their early religious identities (stage 1) without entering a spiritual identity phase (stage 2), their lesbian identities emerged while they remained in their religious identities. For those women who were unsuccessful in adjusting their early religious identities in order to accommodate their newly emerging sexual identities, they eventually abandoned their religious identities altogether and entered into a spiritual identity phase (stage 2). In these latter instances, the stages of spiritual identity (ages thirteen to forty-eight) and sexual identity (ages thirteen to forty-eight) were found to be parallel processes, occurring simultaneously for the women who had left their early religious identities (stage 1).

Characteristics and Tasks

The women during the sexual identity stage were characterized by the questioning of their literal belief structures (Fowler 1981; Park 1986) and by their struggles to adjust their religious beliefs to accommodate their emerging same-sex attractions. In addition, the women in this third stage of developing their sexual identity began to: 1) internally accept their lesbian identities; 2) engage in their first lesbian relationships; and 3) negotiate with their own desire to maintain themselves within their religious or denominational communities. For six of the women, staying within their early religious identities was difficult during their coming out processes. Thus, there was a questioning of and differentiating from their religious authority structures, while they simultaneously became aware of their same-sex attraction during this emerging sexual identity stage.

With the exception of Naomi, the other twelve women in the sample came out prior to forming their clergy identities. Naomi did not come out until the age of forty-eight, which is the high end of the age range when the participants came out. However, Naomi began seminary in her midthirties, while her children were young and she was married to her first husband. Thus, Naomi was part of the group (together with Hannah, Eve, Martha, Rebecca, Leah, and Ruth) in this study that perceived that their coming out ages, as well as their calls to ministry, were delayed by their allegiance to their conservative religious identity.

Naomi. Although Naomi's immersion in traditional church cultures in both the South and New England appeared to prohibit her call to the ministry, nonetheless, her call to ministry seemed more feasible to her in her thirties after she had become involved in a much more liberal denomination that had already been ordaining women and homosexuals.

Naomi attributed her pattern of hiding her lesbian and clergy identities from herself as an attempt to fit into her proscribed culture. Generally, from ecological and anti-oppression theory perspectives, Naomi tried to fit into her family of origin and her marriages because of what she thought was expected of her. However, her attempts failed, as she experienced oppression from her mother and father (in the form of not being accepted fully as an adopted child), her husband, and then from her denomination when she moved to a theologically conservative region.

Naomi's first memory of seeing a male homosexual couple came from a movie that she watched with her mother when she was in elementary school. Naomi's mother told her that homosexuality did happen, but Naomi got the understanding that it could not happen for women. In hindsight, she remembered that her mother did not express homophobia at that point, but she believes she may have started to repress her homoerotic attractions from that time on. In her thirties, Naomi re-watched this movie that left her unsettled. Naomi indicated that seeing that movie about the gay couple could be identified as the index event in her eventually knowing she needed to come out.

> So there was this movie with Martin Sheen and Hal Holbrook about a gay couple. The son of one of them is figuring out that his dad is gay. And believe it or not this was the subject one summer of a teen movie in 1973. I watched it with my mom and I remember at the end of it saying to her, "Can that really happen?" And my mom said, "Oh yes." Like it was no big deal. But what I didn't expect from all that was it could also be true for women so I went off to college thinking only men could be gay, not women. Only girls couldn't. And you had already thought that you were gay at that point? Or if I did [think I was gay], I did a really good job of covering that up.

This movie continued to leave Naomi troubled, and she later knew she could no longer deny her lesbian identity. However, initially she denied both her calls to ministry and her lesbian identity. Naomi stated that she did what was culturally expected of her; she married a man at the age of twenty-two after she had completed college. She then became a housewife and had three children. Using Troiden's (1989) concept of denial, Naomi married young, without conscious knowledge of being a lesbian, and then married a man a second time as a way of avoiding dealing with her burgeoning sexual feelings. From ecological and anti-oppression theory perspectives, Naomi tried to fit into her family of origin and into her marriages because of what she thought was expected of her.

> So I think that probably has a pretty significant impact on understanding my journey to ministry and understanding my journey to understanding myself. Um, so I grew up in settings where there was (Sic) a lot of expectations, so in some ways I felt like I was ten years behind in understanding what women's roles were. I had a very old fashioned sense of what a girls roles were supposed to be as a Southern girl. And that had an impact on me in my roll to ministry or the lack thereof and my understanding of my sexual orientation or my lack thereof.

However, generally Naomi felt like she experienced a lack of fit, which again slowed her explorations of her clergy and lesbian identities. She stated she did not find fit with her adoptive mother, which may have also made her more susceptible to the feelings of depression in her adult life. Naomi's relationship with her mother seemed to foreshadow her sense of not having a goodness of fit as an adult with her spouses and her church life until she came out. Regarding her formative relationship with her mother, Naomi stated the following:

> I just never really felt like I fit. I couldn't get it right whatever it was. You know, I couldn't get it right. I was my mother's daughter. I couldn't get it right even though I was good I was a very good girl.

In talking about her repression of her lesbian identity, Naomi referenced the time in between her two marriages to men when she briefly was aware of being attracted to a woman.

Um, and I presumed if I ever did, it would be a man because that's all I had known up to that point. After that, I had met a friend, and in the contact in the relationship with that friend, we began to have feelings that were really unexpected for me (voice trails off).

As another example of her lesbian identity repression, Naomi shared that she had written in journals for many years about feeling attracted to and falling in love with various women. She was reminded of how long she had buried her lesbian identity when she found them carefully tucked away—in a bottom drawer in her big closet—when she was cleaning out her house to put it on the market. In the journals, she found that she had torn out pages, which she recalled she had burned because she had written negative things about her first husband and about women she found attractive. As if to bury her burgeoning lesbian identity even further, she wrote her feelings about being attracted to women on floppy discs. In preparing for her move, she and her fiancée found her floppy discs with proof of her buried same-sex attractions. The discs dated back to 1982.

It [a reference to same sex erotic crush in her early twenties] was a relationship that never developed into anything beyond a friendship, but that I reflected on a lot and never talked to anyone about it. Um, in fact I still have files on my computer that I saved from a floppy disk. I converted those files to have them on my laptop now. And I even wrote in the computer file, "I'm not writing this in my paper journal because it doesn't feel safe." Right, I'm a journal keeper. Yes. Yes. In fact, this past Thanksgiving weekend, Catharine, who's my fiancée, and I were starting to pack up things in my house. And I went through a bottom drawer in my big closet and I found carefully tucked—I knew they were somewhere, but they were carefully tucked away journals that went back to 1982. Not that they were consistent, but they were journals from about 1982 to about 2001. And I (sic) tore all the pages out of them and burned them 'cause the stuff I had

written about my children's father you would not want
your children to ever find. It was, but my point being,
there's nothing in those paper journals about how I felt
about [names a woman] and about other women I found
attractive. If I didn't have this computer file, I would
not have any proof of it for myself. So then, I turned
around and did the same thing, the same thing, that's not
right [referring to her second marriage]. Basically, I talked
myself out of it and I reread the document and saw that
it was all there because I knew we would be talking so
it's fresh in my mind. [I] read through it [in preparation
for the interview]. Yeah. Things that I haven't read since
1999. Um ...

Despite her repressed sexual identity as detailed here in her old
writings, prior to being ordained, Naomi still avoided her lesbian identity.
She convinced herself that it would be difficult to come out to a student
care committee that knew her as "straight." At the point of returning to
seminary a second time to complete her degree in her forties, Naomi still
felt unable to disclose that she was a lesbian. The irony of that was that she
was affiliated with a denomination that was already ordaining LGBTQs.
Still, Naomi shared that she continued to deny her lesbian identity.

Sure, sure it does because if I had been brave enough to
talk to anybody about this, I don't think I would have
been able to have been (sic) in denial about all this. I mean,
I probably could have still tried, but, ah, I remember
going back to uh, when I was thinking about going back
to seminary at the end of '99, when I was going to go
back in early 2000, I remember having a very rational
conversation with myself and I said, "Well, its ok to be gay
in the [names denomination], but wow wouldn't that be
confusing for the committee I'm going in front of because
they think of me as straight."

The final part of coming out for her was when she became clinically depressed and developed an autoimmune disease. The gravity of her disease process enabled her to finally face who she was and come out to herself and then to a group of female clergy colleagues. In that group, the most supportive person would become her fiancée.

For Naomi, the years of repressing her lesbian identity eventually caused her to develop both mental and physical symptoms. For instance, Naomi had a major depression (which included suicidal intent and a hospitalization), as well as rheumatoid arthritis. Through her support group, Naomi came to recognize that not being out contradicted the integrity of her ministry because she was not being authentic about her own sexual identity. The reflections here grew out of her ecumenical female clergy support group, which at last gave her permission to come out.

> Anyway, so the thing that changed in my life that opened up the door for me to know who I am was that doing my work in ministry, I kept saying to people, because this is a deep theological fight for me. I mean, your salvation is in your authenticity in becoming the person that God wants you to be. And I can't keep preaching that over again and tell people that they have value in the way that God made them, without having that rub off on you eventually. Although I was pretty stubborn in accepting that for myself. Um, and I got involved in and Ecumenical Clergy Women's group. I was part of the founding it and running of it and made friends in other parts of the country in other denominations and they actually thought I was pretty awesome and loveable and that didn't stack up to what I was getting at home or any home that I was ever in except for my kids. And it caused me to kind of evaluate the kind of relationship I had and why in the world I was in this committed relationship since he just didn't seem to value me in any sort of way. Um, and I got sick. And, um, I was diagnosed with arthritis about four years ago.

At the time of this study, Naomi stated that she continued to struggle with daily arthritic pain. However, she maintained that her coming out had made her happier, healthier, and more authentic than ever. A year prior to being interviewed, Naomi had come out to her congregation and become engaged to a female minister of another church. Her wedding was planned for six weeks after being interviewed, and she was moving to the mid-Atlantic region to live with her future wife. As Naomi put it so succinctly, she said things now are better for her than ever. In closing the interview, Naomi reflected as follows:

> Exactly, Exactly. So now, I'm a fifty-one year old woman with three pretty-much-grown-up children with a chronic disease, but I've never felt better in my life.

It is interesting that Naomi's strong fit with her adult denomination did not ameliorate the experiences of her early conservative religious identity. Apparently, Naomi had so strongly internalized her denominational and familial expectations of being a housewife and stay-at-home mom that it very significantly slowed her coming out. Her marriage to a man, who had these same traditional values as those of her family of origin, further slowed down her coming out and call to ministry processes. Additionally, Naomi's experience of poor fit with her mother and, subsequently, two husbands functioned more to delay her coming out process than her open and affirming denomination of adulthood. Finally, both Naomi's coming out and call to ministry processes were delayed because she was unable to look at alternate ways of thinking about sexuality and religion until she was in her thirties and forties. In other words, Naomi was not able to differentiate from the early religious identity (stage 1) beliefs that she was taught as a child, even at the end of her adolescent years.

Delayed Coming Out Due to Early Religious Identity

Naomi, Ruth, Martha, Eve, Rebecca, Hannah, and Leah are all examples of women whose coming out processes were delayed because of their early religious identities. The women in this group came out in the age ranges of thirty-one to forty-eight, as compared to the remaining women in the sample who came out in the age ranges of sixteen to twenty-six.

Like Naomi, Ruth came out in her forties, with the experience of moderate oppression in her early faith community as a Roman Catholic. Also, similar to Naomi, Ruth had remained in the church her entire life and therefore came out while actively involved in church work. Unlike Naomi, Ruth came out prior to her ordination as a minister. Ruth did not fully come out to her first congregation until she had been there for two years.

Also like Naomi, Martha came out in her late forties, after she left her early religious identity as a Roman Catholic, following the experience of high oppression. Like Ruth, Martha came out prior to her ordination, but Martha did not come out to the first congregation she served, for fear of being rejected by them, even though she had come out to others during the period in her life when she was outside of a religious identity and in a spiritual identity.

In contrast, Esther, Sarah, and Abigail were among the youngest to come out. They all came out in the context of a supportive faith community. As discussed in stage 1, Esther and Sarah remained within their home denominations and found the support of ministerial mentors during their coming out years. They both had experienced the support of the congregations they attended when they came out.

Abigail came out through the encouragement of an academic mentor at her seminary, but unlike Esther and Sarah, she was not involved in a supportive congregation when she came out. Esther and Sarah had come out also with the support of their families of origin, but Abigail experienced significant emotional cutoff from her family of origin when she came out. However, Abigail's oppression by her family and by her seminary appeared to be tempered by her partnership during seminary with her now wife.

Ruth. When Ruth reflected on her childhood, she remembered two things that may have pointed to her latent lesbian identity. One was her first sexual experience with a girl at the age of twelve.

> In terms of sexuality, my first sexual experience was at age twelve with another girl, which I was always told it was normal. That's like a normal adolescent experimentation thing, so I kind of put it in that category. Ummm, but anyway, (Sic) married very young. My college sweetheart

and I got married at twenty-one and he was twenty-two. Right after we graduated.

Her second experience, both a religious and perhaps a sexual one, was her desire to be in a cloistered order with a community of women.

Um, when I was a child I was to be a Cloistered Franciscan Nun. I wanted to be a Poor Claire.

She wondered out loud during an interview if really she was bisexual. Ruth stated that she had truly been in love with her husband when she was married but that the longer she has lived with the lesbian identity, the more she lives into the experience of that identity. Ruth's coming out process took more than two decades, from her mid-twenties until midforties. Part of her delay in coming out was that for those twenty years, Ruth's religious and sexual identities developed in separate streams that did not intersect and existed as mutual entities. In stage 4, when Ruth's religious and sexual identities intersected in a revised religious identity, it paved the way for Ruth's clergy identity to emerge in stage 5.

The following markers led Ruth to acknowledge that she was lesbian:

1. At twenty-four, she became so infatuated with a woman while she acted in community theater that she quit the play because her feelings were so uncomfortable.

And uh, in the midst of all this [faith development and vague sense of call to ministry], my first kind of crisis in my marriage was when I was twenty-four. I have also been very active in theatre my whole life. I'm a singer and an actress. And I was in a production of "Sweeny Todd" in uh, [name town in New England]. You know, a community theatre type of a thing. And I fell kind of head-over-heels—I wouldn't say in love, but (sic) was very attracted to a woman in the chorus with me. And it was so upsetting and disturbing to me that I quit the play. Um, rather than be with her. I did not know what to do with it. I had dinner with her a couple of times. I invited her to my house. I've been in her apartment, which was this incredibly—God, I can feel like these physical echoes of how thrilled I was and how horrified at the same time with this physical reaction thinking about it now.

2. At the age of thirty, soon after finding her way to an Episcopal church, she fell in love with a woman and became clinically depressed when the woman moved away.

And in '90, so after a year or so of trying to find a Catholic church, I started going to an Episcopal church. Um … and then within the next couple of years, I had the second kind of shock to my system in terms of my sexual identity, which was I fell in love with a woman. I mean, I truly fell in love with a woman. Not just an attraction or a crush. Um, she was a good friend of my husband's. She had become a good friend of mine through his graduate program. And I was just bowled over. And I walked around, kind of in a haze trying to be with her as much as I could, apparently never speaking about my feelings to her or to anybody. She decided at some point to move to California. The day, literally the day before she left I went to her apartment and told her. And (Sic) didn't do anything with that information. She was very sympathetic and yet at the same time very principled that you know "I wouldn't do anything to hurt your family. I love you all and you know, thanks for telling me, but this is not going to go anywhere." And then she left and I really went into a depression.

3. At the age of thirty-seven, after finding her way to a church, she fell in love with the closeted lesbian pastor

Um, at this point I am working as the Director for Christian Education for an Episcopal Church and then for a [names denomination] Church, where I eventually had a massive crush on the lesbian Pastor, who was closeted herself. Um and ...

4. At the age of forty, she enrolled in seminary and commuted three hours one way. During her commute, she would cry and pray to God for God to take away her lesbian identity. Ruth, by this point in her religious development when she was in seminary, denied that she struggled with same-sex love, but she struggled because she was in a committed relationship to her husband. In the end, it was her seminary training that enabled her to come to terms with and find compatibility between her religious and sexual identities.

    So my son is thirteen. My daughter is eight. Um, and I commute back and forth to New York City and I meet more lesbians than I've ever known my entire life. And this begins to feel a little like Paul's thorn in the flesh for me. This begins to feel like something I can't shake. And I mean I can tell you, humph, whoa, (Begins to cry) I'm surprised that this is so emotional for me, but I can tell you that I had times driving down to the city when I was literally crying in my car saying to God, "Take this away. Take this away please."

5. She told her husband toward the end of seminary that she believed she was a lesbian. After her internal struggle with God about being lesbian and not wanting to violate her commitment to her husband, Ruth had an external struggle with her husband and fought to save her marriage. Although within weeks of her husband moving out, Ruth stated that her confirmation about being lesbian was that she did not have her annual psychosomatic reaction of getting bronchitis, which she believed was due to the stress of being married. She never again got her terrible bronchitis that would result in her being knocked on her back for a week or two or three. She then could admit to herself that living as a lesbian was living the right life for her.

But I haven't had bronchitis since [name of husband] and I split up. I just feel like I was just living the wrong life you know. I mean, I'm still grateful for my children. I wouldn't change any of it. But he left and I knew that I could think about, *Is there a guy around here I could date?* You know, I did think about that. But I knew in my heart, if I had another relationship, it would be with a woman. And by—he left in February. And by June I went for drinks with this woman whom I had kind of known very casually for many years.

Thus, Ruth's life, at the time of being interviewed, had fallen into place, and she had been with her current partner of eight years. Within several more years, she came out to her two adolescent children and then to her congregation. Although out to herself and dating her partner of eight years at the time of this study, Ruth was not initially certain that she would retain her employment if she were to come out to her congregation. When she believed her contract with her congregation was secure, she came out to them. Ruth reported that she was continuing at the same congregation, noting that although her denominational judicatory would not install her, her congregation fully endorsed her ministry.

I knew I was coming out to them. I knew it was going to happen. And I continued to blog the readings all through lent. And they were all … it was all about coming out. That that was it. (Sic) It was all from my spiritual discipline from that point on. I had set the date in May because I had, I mean, I did have a bit of a paranoid scenario of you know getting up in the pulpit the next Sunday and being covered with rotten tomatoes and you know, slinking away and … But I hoped it wouldn't be that. Um, and I guess was the date I called a special [church board] meeting. I wrote a letter, which I put in the mail that afternoon for the whole congregation, but brought it before the [church board] that night so the session had the letter the night before the congregation was going to receive it. Um, it is, it was the most scary thing I have ever done in my entire life. Scarier than anything. It is scarier than giving birth, scarier than getting on a plane. Scarier than anything. Um, one by one. We went around the table basically and everyone said some sort of version of that. The [church board] was unanimous.

Martha. Like Ruth, Martha's latent coming out may have been related to the mixed streams of conservative Roman Catholic and burgeoning lesbian identities that ran at odds with each other. Still, Martha began to explore her repressed lesbian identity while she was still a nun. During her graduate work in the late seventies, while she was still in the order, as already explained earlier, she lived in a halfway house with mentally ill women. Martha discovered that many of them were lesbian and how terribly oppressed the women were by society and their families of origin. Through the community she developed with these women, Martha discovered her latent lesbian identity.

But everybody came together at night and we kind of formed a community with those women. So the freedom that the lesbians had when I was living with them, just kind of set up a frame work and then when I got to [names city], I fell in love with another woman. I'm like, "Well, it was just a progression."

Although she had also explored her heterosexual identity while still in the convent, by the time she left the convent at the age of thirty-five, she was comfortable with her lesbian identity.

I had boyfriends and even when I was in the convent, the priest and I were very close and we talked about getting married one time, but we decided to stay in our religious vocations. So I kind of got a sense there. When I came to [names university] to study for my theatre degree, I got an M.A. and then just knew I could not go back to [names

Midwestern state] so I stayed in [names eastern state].
Umm, [I] engaged in my first lesbian experience.

Simultaneous with leaving the convent, Martha left her religious identity for a period and entered into a period of spiritual identity. In other words, from a social identity theory perspective, it appears that perhaps one of the push factors for Martha to leave the order was that she did not think that it was compatible with her new sexual identity.

And my [Catholic] theology and my sense of who I am
and who God is in my life conflicted with my being a
lesbian.

However, when Martha returned to church in approximately 1996—for her second epoch of Christianity (and for purposes of this study, a revised religious identity in stage 4)—this time it was to a theologically liberal protestant denomination. At that point, Martha reported that her theology no longer conflicted with being a lesbian.

Martha denied that coming out was ever an issue for her. Perhaps this was because she had come out during her time when she was outside of the church, and when she reentered church life, it was to a theologically progressive denomination. She equated her time of coming out with a sense of liberation and without reports of oppression but also acknowledged that leaving her first thirty-five years as a Roman Catholic enabled her to begin a new life as a lesbian that she could not have while living in a convent as a nun.

Ultimately, Martha's comments about coming out offered hints of both a struggle to come out and threads of coming out with little experience of oppression. It seemed that because Martha's sexual identity had been so latent, with her coming out in in her midthirties, and because she was not ordained until the age of fifty, she had not yet had the opportunity to understand the intersection of her religious and sexual identities. Martha seemed, due to her allegiance to Franciscan ideals of suffering, to tend to minimize her coming out struggle. Martha said, at different points while being interviewed, that she both struggled and that she did not struggle to come out. Her statements about having a struggle appear in the following:

> Yeah, I just feel like my being a lesbian is, um, as being integrated, naturally integrated as, the natural integration of my being a lesbian has really been a fight to me. And I'm grateful I didn't have to suffer like a lot of people.

On the other hand, her statements about not having a struggle appear in the following:

> It [being a lesbian] just seemed to make—it was never an issue. I never thought it was an issue with God (laughs). You know, it's not even life, "Well, God made me this way." I didn't even go there. It's not even like God. I don't' want to say God can't be bothered, God doesn't care. It's not that at all. God would say "Of course. Of course you are."

Martha did state, however, like Ruth, that she struggled to come out to her first congregation. She said she had been with her first congregation for seven years but had never come out to them due to advice from a mentor. It appeared that this was a form of denominational oppression that Martha experienced early in ministry.

> Oh. Very! Yeah. She was my mentor. Umm, she said, "This is your first congregation and they are older and it might be better if you just didn't make an issue of your sexuality." And I said, "Well, I wouldn't, because it's me and it doesn't affect how I minister and whatever." And she said, "Test the waters. And don't say anything."

After that position, Martha came out to her second congregation, believing that she could have more integrity in ministry being out. Martha met her partner at the seminary she had attended after she returned to Christianity—this time to a theologically liberal denomination, and it was in this context that Martha began to integrate her lesbian and revised Christian identity (stage 4). Martha shared that at the time of this study, she had been with her partner for sixteen years, but sadly, her partner had been diagnosed with stage 4 metastatic brain cancer one year earlier.

Eve. Eve acknowledged that she was a lesbian very late in her development. An important theme that emerged from Eve was her complicated sexual history of wavering between homosexual and heterosexual identities throughout her twenties and thirties, until she fully accepted her lesbian identity in her early thirties. She came out at the age of thirty-one. She acknowledged that it was late for coming out, but she said the good thing about it was that her family took her seriously at that point.

> And I was more mature. I was ready to come out. And so it was the time that I got back together with her that I came out. Yup. Early 30s, which again is pretty late for coming out for a Christian or not, but, Yeah. But the good news about me coming out around 31–32 was that my family took me seriously. They knew that it wasn't because of faith. Because coming out at 31–32 meant that I was serious.

Eve's early religious teaching that adolescents had to remain virgins until they were married delayed her acceptance of her identity. In addition, Eve recalled that her home denomination placed a great deal of emphasis on being *quite sexually pure.* She said that she was not necessarily attracted to men or women in her teens and early twenties. Eve, therefore, remembered that she was not consciously aware of being attracted to men or women. Because of this, she did not explore her sexual identity until she was in her midtwenties, which she cited as being due to her religious teaching as a child and adolescent to be chaste until marriage.

> So I was just very late in my development. So it's not like I was having all this attraction to men and then or women. That was just not really happening either. Um, I think religiosity [kept me from exploring my sexuality to men or women]. Um, a deep commitment to virginity until marriage. And um really not wanting to go there. I think really believing that I was really quite sexually pure.

Eve said she first acknowledged to herself that she was a lesbian when she was twenty-four years old. However, upon reflection, she remembered being attracted to women in high school. She also remembered after coming out to herself that she had two prior significant attractions to women—one at sixteen and one at eighteen—but said that nothing had happened. She said that they were fleeting attractions.

Finally, at the age of twenty-four, Eve stated that she had a girlfriend for thirteen months in which they were totally closeted. At that stage, she and her girlfriend struggled, Eve stated, because she was so religiously conflicted. As a result of her religious confusion at that point in her development, she proceeded in her mid-twenties to date mostly men. Eve did not articulate this, but it appears that her dating of men may have been a way to further repress her emerging lesbian identity. Here, Eve described her complicated and repressed dating history in her teens and twenties with both women and men:

> Yeah. I was probably twenty-four and got into a relationship with a woman and went, "OH!" there were two other women that I had intense attractions to. We had friendships, but looking back they were attractions that I had at sixteen and the other first when I was eighteen, uh, that nothing ever happened with. The one is actually a lesbian now. The other one is not. Uh, but not even close to anything ever happening. They were just fleeting attractions. That realization didn't even occur to me. I wasn't just very developed in my straight life either. I intentionally didn't date a man or woman until I was twenty-four. My first experience was with a woman and then I left her and then went with men for a little while.

After college, Eve left her home church/denomination due to experiences of oppression and then experienced more heteronormative oppression at yet another Protestant church in her twenties. She added that her career in broadcasting enabled her to leave the church and enter into a stage of spiritual identity. She stated the following:

[In broadcasting] where not a lot of faith was discussed, made it easy to slip away from church and [either] be a lesbian or not a lesbian any more.

After seven years of dating men, Eve returned to a relationship with the same woman who she had previously dated for thirteen months. For twelve years, they were domestic partners. When she was thirty-one, she said, "It was that time that I got back together with her that I came out."

She and her first partner broke up after extensive couple's counseling because of financial struggles and a difference in faith values. After a very painful breakup with her first wife, Eve started dating her second and current wife. They had been together for four and a half years at the time of this study. They had been recently married but had a four-year-old foster son. Eve met her wife at a Christian retreat for LGBTQ persons.

> I met [name of wife] at a retreat for Gay and Lesbians that her church was sponsoring. And I went just to sort of meet new people and to try just a little bit of a spiritual retreat because I was absolutely heartbroken [due to the ending of a prior relationship with a woman]. And so [name of wife] and I met and we were drawn to each other and we both went "Ohhh. I'm so not ready for this."

Rebecca. Being gay was not anything Rebecca had ever thought about in high school. She stated that it was never discussed in her community or in church. However, like Eve, Rebecca's internalized religious ideal was to remain a virgin until she married. Yet, in referring to her experience with her college/post-college girlfriend, Rebecca stated that, in hindsight, her lesbian identity had been burgeoning since junior high school.

> I feel like once like it happened that I, my eyes were open to the idea of having a relationship with a woman it made me look back at all of these, I had had, I would never have called them crushes or infatuations at the time but I look back particularly women like that were older than me in my life throughout from Junior high to—from puberty on

and there was always a woman in my life, outside of my family like through church or whatever, there was always someone that I was particularly fixated on.

During college, she had her first gay experience with her roommate, which she stated was somewhat physical and not particularly sexual in nature. She stated that she had never before "been with women in [her] life." Yet, she began at this time to recognize that all of her mentors, whether in church, in college, or at the coffee shop, had been women whom she was attracted to at the time.

Rebecca said that this woman and the next woman she was intimate with were both church connected, but neither of them were willing to discuss the connections between their religious and sexual identities. Instead, these two relationships were hidden from the public. In her early twenties, Rebecca reported that she had an intense relationship with another woman that did not become sexual, but it heightened her awareness that she was most likely a lesbian. Here Rebecca cites the confusion and pain of her first lesbian relationship while she was still in her early religious identity stage. This relationship ended shortly before she left the institutional church for a decade and entered into a spiritual identity stage.

> Right but, and I think that but, I think that if she had I had been in a healthy sort of partnership and explored it in a healthy way—I mean I think it could have easily turned into something like a functioning relationship but it quickly became an, uh emotionally abusive relationship because I wanted to sort through this stuff. I wanted to talk about it and I wanted to like deal with it because I felt completely buried under it and her uh reaction was, "oh we're not talking about it and you need to like get your shit together ..." (Chuckles) "like you need to stop worrying about it," and, "do you have any idea how much this would ruin our lives if anyone knew about this?" and it was constantly adding just fuel to this fire of guilt.

Still, during this time, she continued to work in a theologically conservative church, and she did not know how to reconcile her religious and sexual identities. Thus, during this emotional turbulence with this female relationship, Rebecca began to have a faith crisis. She stated that "it was just a really dark time" in her life.

This final experience intensified Rebecca's religious guilt and movement away from the church at that point in her mid-twenties. She was clear at that point in her life that she did not want to be gay. Yet, at the same time, she also knew that she no longer fit into her home denomination because of its stated antifeminist stances, its stated stances on purity before marriage, and her own remaining internalized confusion about being both a lesbian and a Christian.

> Yeah. I guess so, Yeah. Definitely as far as, the big things that were constantly, the two big sermons or Bible study topics that I heard they were all about either drinking or dating and really you shouldn't do either (chuckles) but you shouldn't drink at all and if you have today then these are the guidelines. So, yeah, I guess purity and …

Rebecca's way of processing all of this confusion was to leave the church for a decade. In September 2005, Rebecca met her future spouse at the same corporation where she was working. Through her relationship with her wife, Rebecca was able to conclude that she definitely was a lesbian during this period when she was outside of a religious identity and feeling nurtured within the spiritual identity stage.

After six months, Rebecca and her now wife moved in together and came out to their families. Within two years, they relocated to the Northeast with the same company. Her wife, a musician and actress, looks straight, according to Rebecca. Their attraction was mutual and intense. After five years of living together, they had been married ten months prior to the interview.

Hannah. As discussed earlier, Hannah's experience of "significant" homophobic and antifeminist oppression as an adolescent with a burgeoning lesbian sexual identity drove her away from the church and into a period of spiritual identity. Her experiences in the church, coupled with her family's lack of acceptance of her, drove her not only away from the church but her family as well by the time she was a twenty-year-old junior in college. Because of her experience of oppression by the church and her family, Hannah turned to alcohol to numb the pain of her rejection. Because of being so demoralized internally, Hannah shared, she attended three colleges.

> Yeah. So, there was never alcohol in my house at all, so, um, but I uh, I started drinking some, and then drugs came into the picture later. So, when I describe my college years it sounds like what the heck are you doing moving to all these places? Part of it is my life then became very scattered. You know, with what was going on with me with drugs and alcohol. So, um, I went to [college on the West Coast] the first year, I went to, uh, a school in [another college on the West Coast] up in the wine country the second year, and then the last two years I went to [name of university] University in downtown [names city]. And by the time I was a junior in high school, I wasn't speaking to my family and had no contact with them, which had something to do with the gay thing, but not entirely with the gay thing. So I wasn't talking to them anymore, um, so that was, you know, I was, and there was definitely, I mean, since we're talking about the gay thing, there was an element of the gay thing, but there was (sic) a lot of other things going on with um, my family besides that.

During and for several years after college, Hannah lacked the understanding or the life experience to inform her that religious and lesbian sexual identities could coexist. Although Hannah left the church over a period of time between her late teens and early twenties, she really did not want to leave. She simply did not know how she could be in the church and still be a lesbian. At this point in her life, leaving the church enabled Hannah's sexual identity to emerge without guilt.

> Right. So I, essentially I knew that I was really very connected to the church. Um, somewhere around late

high school, I stopped, I mean, so, when I went to college I didn't go to church anymore at all. I totally, and, um, was sad about it. Like, I really—I was very sad about it, but I felt like there wasn't a place for me, really.

As previously stated, part of Hannah's lived experience from her early teens through her midtwenties was the repression of her own sexual thoughts about being attracted to women through both substances and promiscuity. From her junior year of high school through her midtwenties, Hannah used sex with men to repress her attraction to women. She also continued to date men and women until she became sober.

So, um, I actually didn't, speaking on the like, relationship sexuality front, I really didn't date initially when I was sober. Cause I knew I was in a pretty bad, um, place emotionally. And I had been very promiscuous and also a very active dater.

In her recovery from drugs and alcohol, when Hannah's streams of sexual and religious identities merged in her mid-twenties, she was able to take the risk of being fully out. She stated she never dated men again.

It would all click, and I didn't think that I wouldn't be attracted to women but I thought that if I could meet a guy I was attracted to I would go with that because that would be more socially acceptable. Like there was definitely that still at play. Um, and let's see. So then there were several years of kind of just, um, oh let's see. Oh, no let's see, then I, then I did, I uh, moved in with someone. I started dating someone. Her name was [name of woman]. She was like nine years older than me and we, I moved in with her in the [name neighborhood in large metropolitan city] for a short period of time. And then that ended, and I, um, was, let's see, then I eventually got a job in an office doing something and that job led to another job that led to another job that led to me working um, [names city where she was working] in like a back office. Like, working, um, I was a buyer of like computers for a firm. All that to say that I had some more financial success (Sic). So I was like, you know, doing better, in terms of that. I wasn't doing anything I was excited about, [but] I was able to live, I was able to have my own apartment, and I was like, you know, having a good time I guess theoretically. But, um, let's see. So then um, things had gotten really, really bad with the—particularly with the drugs. So, um, in 1999 I, um, got sober. And that was a big turning point.

From her gay twelve-step programs, she found her way back to a church. She met her wife in an open and affirming church, where the AA meetings were held, and then they went to seminary together. In regard to her recovery and being out, Hannah spoke about becoming a more authentic person.

Like If felt at a certain point like I was being really inauthentic. Um, when I was in recovery it [promiscuity] stopped. I'm saying this is kind of like, once I was in recovery I really couldn't do that kind of, uh, it felt like, Yeah. Um, it, and there was a lot of relief in that. Like, there was a lot of relief in being more of a real person.

When she was out fully in a church environment, Hannah was also able to take the risk of being an out lesbian seminarian within a homophobic denomination, the denomination that nurtured her return to church. She is in the unique situation of being one of the few out lesbian clergy in a heteronormative denomination. Yet she reports a very strong fit as an out lesbian minister at a congregation that she and her wife co-pastor.

Leah. Like Hannah, Leah used substance abuse to repress her burgeoning lesbian identity in the wake of being conflicted about how being a homosexual fit into her religious beliefs. As stated earlier, Leah had experimented with Christian fundamentalism for a year in order to repress her growing sense of homoerotic attractions. By the time of late junior high school and the beginning of puberty, as Leah stated:

[I had] some inkling that [she] was different. Yeah. I was obsessed with my best friends. I felt like something was different or maybe even wrong at that point.

However, when her year of being "born again" did not save her from this growing lesbian identity, she turned to drinking alcohol during high school, then marijuana in college, to numb her confusion about being Catholic and possibly a lesbian. After leaving the religious identity stage and entering into a stage of spiritual identity during her college and post-college years in her twenties, in her confusion about being a lesbian, she periodically would attend mass to try to be cured of being lesbian. When "mass did not cure" her, she dated a man at college for several years, and she knew she loved him, but she "knew something was wrong."

Despite her sense that "something was wrong" with the man she dated, Leah tried but felt she did not find fit with the lesbians she met at college either. Then, after her junior year of college, Leah experienced a life-changing event when a drunk driver killed her best friend from high school. Leah said the event emotionally devastated her, so she started AA and saw a therapist. She quickly found release in coming out to her therapist.

Umm, I came out of the closet to my therapist. This is what's going on. This is why I'm' drinking heavily. Umm. I'm freaked out that my friend died. So I got sober. I—I got sober. It came out all in one shot, I started going to AA.

Leah met her first girlfriend in a gay AA meeting, and they were together for four years. She said they were young both chronologically and developmentally as lesbians, and also new in recovery. Thus, they split up amicably. On the positive side though, her first lesbian relationship and her experiences in the gay AA meetings enabled Leah to reconcile her lesbian identity with God, though at this point she still had not attended church. This relationship enabled Leah to grow into her lesbian identity from the ages of twenty-three to twenty-seven.

> Uh and I, so I met my first girlfriend in AA. She also
> was Catholic. Irish-Polish Catholic. I know. (Chuckles)
> We were a good fit. We had a lot of the same [family
> dynamics]. Yeah. And a lot of spiritual and religious
> questions. So we were together for four years and we were
> pretty young. And we umm, we never went to church,
> but um, we were really spiritual. And just um, we read
> a lot together. And um, just trying to find a way of self-
> acceptance and God acceptance. (Sic) As lesbians.

During this time, Leah was a reporter, but she began to sense a call to ministry. Almost simultaneous with her sense of call, she met her current partner, who was an openly gay journalist also. After that, Leah was ready to return to church and religious identity. She then took a year to firm up her new relationship and her finances and entered a four-year dual MSW/MDiv program. Three years into their relationship, they had a private commitment ceremony, but they have not gotten married. Still, at the time of this study, Leah had been with this same woman for sixteen years.

> [We had our] own little commitment ceremony when
> [they] climbed a mountain together in Colorado. It was
> really just us and our dogs were our witnesses. And it was
> very lovely and spiritual.

AGE OF COMING OUT INFLUENCED BY INTERPLAY OF FIT AND OPPRESSION

The above two sections related the narratives of the seven research respondents who experienced a delayed coming out due to their experiences of an early conservative religious identity. Here in this section are the narratives of the remaining six women in the sample, who reported an earlier age of coming out. Rachel, Esther, Sarah, Abigail, Deborah, and Mary came out in the age range of sixteen to twenty-six.

It is worth noting that although some of these women experienced significant homophobic oppression in their childhood churches and (or) by their families of origin, they were able to come out in their twenties.

For this group of women, coming out in their twenties seemed possible due to their unique mix of high fit and their high capacity to differentiate, which appeared to ameliorate their experiences of oppression. In order for the women to come out when they did, it was found to be most significant that they demonstrated the ability to question the authority structures of their early religious identities and then to formulate their own beliefs about the interplay of religious and sexual identities. Although all but Rachel reported significant experiences of oppression during their coming out processes, their experiences of fit seemed to be push factors for them to come out.

Deborah and Mary both experienced high homophobic oppression in multiple faith communities and in multiple denominational contexts. The homophobic events that occurred during their early years as out lesbians would foreshadow their multiple experiences of homophobic oppression in a range of ten to fifty congregations. Unfortunately, at the time of this study, neither Deborah nor Mary had experienced an ongoing sense of fit in a faith community. There is a comparative observation between Deborah and Mary. Mary appeared to be unable to find her voice within a denomination in a way that would allow her to stay in ministry, whereas Deborah appeared to find a lesbian feminist voice that enabled her to remain within a denomination that continued to oppress her.

Rachel. During the time that Rachel came out, she reported that she had had no negative experiences of oppression in the church—a highly progressive social justice–oriented congregation—she had been attending at the time. She had already differentiated from her early religious identity as an Orthodox Jew by her conversion to Christianity, and as a result, Rachel had continued to experience an emotional cutoff from her family of origin during her twenties and early thirties.

Rachel suggested that her coming out process was painless. She not only was in an open and affirming congregation and denomination during the time she came out, but she denied any difficult contemplations about coming out as other women in the sample did. Rachel stated she came out when she fell in love with her partner, who was the only woman she had dated. Prior to her wife of thirty years, she had been dating men exclusively. Thus, according to Rachel, her "only marker ... around sexual identity" was when she fell in love with her current spouse. The only oppression that she reported was from her family of origin. She chuckled when she shared a story of her brother telling her parents that she was gay, prior to her coming out to them. Apparently, her brother said to her mother one day, "You know she's gay." And then Rachel joked that her mother had wanted her to "have children and to have a house with a white picket fence."

Rachel described meeting her spouse at the age of twenty-six when her male friend had invited her but then backed out of the dinner plans. So Rachel and her now wife went to the theater and then to a little Italian restaurant by themselves. Rachel said they hung out all that summer, and although her spouse is her one and only lesbian relationship, she has never doubted the bond she has with her. Rachel's lack of hesitation to identify as a lesbian is based in her love for her spouse. She stated, "And it was like, *Wow, this is different, and it doesn't feel so bad.*" Rachel's love for her spouse is poignant in her voice poem:

> I was clearly attracted to her
> She was clearly attracted to me.
> She kissed me one night
> I never once doubted
> That my love for her was wrong.

Rachel's story of sexual identity is that she dated men in high school and in college and had a several-year relationship with a married man, until she fell in love with her current female spouse in 1979. She laughed that they had been "engaged for thirty-one years" before they could be legally married in the summer of 2011. In 1980, they privately committed themselves to each other at a friend's cabin, having their "own little reception and a little commitment."

She related that she had met her wife through a mutual friend, when they were both working in theater-related industries. Up until that point, Rachel had believed that she would not be married until she was thirty-five, but then she would have a traditional marriage. Finally, Rachel implied that, for her, there is gender fluidity in her sexual identity. She talked about never having consciously struggled as a lesbian, but her identity emerged when she started dating her now wife and began her only lesbian relationship.

If something were to ever happen to her [wife], I have no idea what I would do in terms of whether I would stay with a woman, or go back to men. I have no idea.

Esther. Esther came out at the age of nineteen and was the second youngest to come out in this sample of women. However, she perceived that her coming out as a lesbian was delayed because of her early religious identity. In other words, Esther believed that her religious role models— namely her parents and her church role models—would have believed she was a failure if she had come out. Ironically, in the end, Esther had the support of her parents in her coming out process, but she had internalized a homophobia from Christian programming and the conservative religious views that she was immersed in as a child.

According to Esther, her sexual identity began to emerge around the seventh grade, but she stated that by mid-high school she was continuing to experience an internalized homophobia because she was worried about being a failure to her parents, who were leaders in her denomination—as well as to her denomination, which she perceived to be like an extended family. Esther stated her belief at the time was that her denomination in and of itself did not make her homophobic but that there was a cultural ethos within the denomination that strongly influenced her decision to keep quiet about controversial issues. She stated that although her parents were not homophobic, her mom worried about appearances, and her mother's sense of appearances was reinforced when her father became a seminary president.

And so, so, what I can remember where, like where I got it—I think certainly growing up in the [name denomination], you know to be quiet. People have said that they are pretty amazed at the silencing ability of the [name of the denomination]. Um, that you, you learn how to conform really well. But we all knew this dynamic, especially from the time that my Dad became president of the seminary. We knew that there were going to be certain expectations placed upon us.

Esther stated it was her father, not her mother, who gave her the gift of being able to discern between traditional denominational and religious beliefs. In this regard, she stated that she is like her father in that she does not always worry about what others think. Esther believed that this trait gave her the strength during her coming out process in her home denomination to be able to assert her own ideas.

> I take after my Dad, when he is upset, he takes a deep breath and softens his voice; I don't really care.

Through the support and unconditional acceptance of her parents, Esther was able to come out to them at the age of nineteen during the summer between her freshman and sophomore years of college. It was after her freshman year at college, while working on a factory assembly line, that she came to terms with her sexual identity as a lesbian. Her parents, and especially her father, were immediately accepting of her sexual identity. In fact, she remembers her father asking her when she came out to him why she was so homophobic. In other words, Esther struggled with her own internalized homophobia until she was nineteen, when her father gave her permission to be gay. She stated that her internal struggle with her lesbian identity had been reinforced by denominational messages to comply.

> I always really liked church, I, um, never saw anything negative about it. [It did not form my homophobia.] No, no, and what's interesting is that I do remember when I came out to my Dad, my Dad said, "Why are you so, so homophobic?" And um, I could remember, um, he [Dad] said you never heard a sermon about it and you didn't get it from your parents.

In fact, Esther stated that her father, a seminary professor in the denomination, knew she was gay before she did and was instrumental in getting her to the open and affirming congregation that she attended during her college years and prior to seminary. She believed that her parents and this LGBTQ-affirming congregation, which was ironically in the heteronormative denomination of her birth, were instrumental to her successful coming out process. In this piece, Esther spoke about her positive and humorous experience of coming out at her church, which was an open and affirming church in a large metropolitan eastern city.

> [Names associate minister] was the first person I came out to at [names church] Church. He was such a queen. Like a week after I came out to him with fear and trepidation; he had no idea that he was the first person that I had come out to. He turns to the woman whom I was teaching Sunday School with and says, "So [names woman she co-taught with], [Esther] discovered she was a lesbian, um, have you ever been with a woman before?" And I am saying, "I'm teaching Sunday School with this woman [who is a Christian lesbian]."

In this voice poem, Esther's experience of being encouraged to come out to her family and to her church was encouraged by a beloved mentor, family friend, and leader in the denomination. Here, Esther's words demonstrate the gratitude she experienced during the time of coming out for being encouraged to come out to a traditionally heteronormative denomination by a progressive female leader.

> I could have figured it out a long time ago
> I had just figured out that I was gay
> I would go up and visit [name of older mentor]
> I had just come out to myself
> I would go up to visit her
> I had just come out to myself
> I burst into tears
> I am just sobbing
> 'Cause I'm gay

Sarah. Looking back on her childhood and adolescence, Sarah stated she could see in a bunch of different relationships with girls, that there had been the potential "spark of relationship," although nothing had happened. For her, as a good church girl from the Midwest, she did not have the language for being gay and did not think she even knew a gay person growing up. She said her home state was not a "safe place for [gay] people" in the seventies and eighties.

In college, she started to think about "sexuality stuff," and although she loved her denominational context at college, she found it confining. That's when she intentionally studied overseas in order to expand her thinking. She had dated men in college and in seminary but did not enter into any relationships with them. On being interviewed, Sarah expressed that she believes that if she had gotten into any heterosexual relationships, she would have realized at a younger age that she was attracted to same-sex relationships. Having had no prior sexual relationships, when she fell in love with her future wife, Sarah began to identify herself as a lesbian. She has only been in a sexual relationship with her wife and wonders if she is actually a bisexual. However, as stated by her, for all intents and purposes, she identifies as lesbian.

> I think that I'm lesbian—that's the easiest way to name it. I think there's an understanding of bi-sexuality. Probably is what it is. I love [names wife] and that's only with one person and that's who I'm with. And by certain standards you say that I'm lesbian then say that. Am I bi? Maybe. I don't know what I am exactly, but …

Abigail. Looking back, Abigail had a sense of being a lesbian while in high school. However, she speculated that her childhood and adolescent conservative theological context repressed her awareness of her lesbian identity longer than if she had been raised in a more progressive religious identity. Abigail reflected on the repressiveness of her early religious identity:

> That's ok. Um it was a [home nondenominational] church that broke off from the Presbyterian around the Angela Davis incident—That was the conservatism of, "oh we can't support …" The Presbyterian Church supported the—what—From the PCUSA. Grew up in that church. Then my parents changed churches and started going to a CMA, Christian Missionary Alliance Church

so, I had my, my teen years in a CMA Church—very conservative—no female Clergy, you know—all sorts of things. Then I went to a Free Methodist College, which is [very conservative too].

During college, prior to coming out during her seminary years, Abigail experienced an intense but nonsexual relationship with a female friend, which allowed her to entertain the idea that she may be a lesbian. During her first year of college, she also became engaged to a man in the military in what she calls that "fuzzy time apart," but she broke it off, knowing that "marrying him was the wrong thing." Although her coming out in seminary was at the age of twenty-two, Abigail reported that she did not fully come out until two decades later when she was in the current ministerial position she holds. It was there that she felt fully able to be out in a church context without fear of oppression. This occurred two years prior to the time of this study. Like Hannah, Abigail's current ministerial job is at an open and affirming congregation that is outside of her own denomination. Ironically, the congregation is in a heteronormative congregation; however, the church hired her with its board having full knowledge that she was a lesbian, for the purpose of engaging in social justice ministries.

So, yeah that was when I got here [the current church where she is associate pastor], I came fully out.

The context of seminary and her experience of its theology, which she experienced as less conservative than that of her early religious identity, provided Abigail with the freedom for the first time in her life to explore her growing lesbian identity. Here, Abigail reflected on the contrast of her early religious identity to the religious context she experienced in seminary when her sexual identity emerged.

Well, yeah and quite honestly, um I think my awakening to orientation and sexual identity set me in that direction [of social justice ministries]. [My sexual orientation] wasn't until, um, I did not fully come to an understanding of that until Seminary.

Thus, it was during her first year of seminary that Abigail acknowledged to herself that she was a lesbian. After reading Mollenkott (a lesbian feminist theologian), she said,

> I spent the whole night awake in the fetal position because
> I realized at that point what was going on.

When Abigail met and began a relationship with her current partner of twenty-two years, while at seminary, she came out to only one professor, who was also lesbian. They were pretty certain that this was the one professor who they "kind of knew" was a lesbian. In regard to her relationship with her partner, she stated that when they realized there was something between them, they both "kind of freaked out." She stated that from her "senior year of college through seminary and at least five years beyond that [she lived in fear] of being discovered by persons in authority in her denomination that she was a lesbian."

Thus, it appeared that the experience of her early religious identity, coupled with her homophobic experiences at the seminary, created so much fear that Abigail chose to remain closeted to her denomination during her seminary. In other words, Abigail was afraid of not being able to get ordained or to get work after seminary. Of that uncertain time, Abigail stated, "Um so we [she and her partner] were closeted during seminary."

Her fear of being discovered as a lesbian was reinforced late in her seminary training, when she was doing clinical pastoral education at a hospital with an unsupportive supervisor. She said at the time, she had a major depressive episode in response to these experiences of oppression. At the time, she stated that she spoke about intense fear of being outed in seminary by someone else.

> I was terrified of everything (she laughed); of death; of
> people knowing about [her] orientation; of everything.

In response to the oppression she encountered and wrestling with her fears of her true sexual orientation being discovered, she stopped eating and lost a lot of weight. Her experience of oppression during her post-seminary years, while training as a chaplain and experiencing homophobia there as well, greatly exacerbated her depression and anxiety. Specifically, she shared that she became suicidal when her chaplain supervisor discovered she was a lesbian and consequently gave her a poor evaluation.

> I stopped eating. I pretty much had a Major Depressive Episode. There's too much of me (laughs) to get anorexic but I did lose a lot of weight. I stopped eating. Yeah I ugh, I would weep every night, high anxiety, suicidal thoughts and my supervisor didn't do anything about it.

Abigail's first-person voice poem below expressed her more than twenty-year journey to fully coming out as a lesbian. Abigail continued to experience ongoing homophobic oppression in several chaplaincy jobs and in multiple denominations for several decades after her graduation from seminary.

> I didn't know what to call it
> I didn't know how to name
> I think my awakening set me in that direction [social justice]
> We were closeted during Seminary
> We finally realize there was something between us
> We both kind of freaked out
> I was not comfortable trying to get a parish with not being honest
> I pretty much had a major depressive episode
> I stopped eating
> I did lose a lot of weight
> I did CPE and fell completely apart
> I went into therapy
> I think that that [spiritual] journey made a difference in my comfort level with identity
> When I got here I came fully out

Deborah. With little internal struggle, Deborah cited that her sexual identity emerged during adolescence, while she was in college. Thus, Deborah was unique from the six women in this sample who came out young, despite significant experiences of homophobia in either their faith communities or families of origin. Deborah first remembered having awareness of homoerotic attraction at thirteen years old when "she fell in love with [her] history teacher." She was still living in the Bahamas at that point and had no context for understanding what she was experiencing. She stated that all she knew at that point was that "something was just not right." Although Deborah came fully out during her college years, she reported continuing to experience homophobic oppression at the time of this study, which was three decades after she had been in college.

Her first time coming out came out at the age of sixteen when she was a freshman in college, making her the woman who came out at the youngest age in the sample.

> Um, yeah I was actually going on seventeen. Yeah, so, like, I guess, my birthday is in August, so it was just before my birthday. So I, um. So, I knew I wasn't satisfied, that there was something more to, uh, living my life as a total person, and the first place. No clue, totally clueless, and then there's no one to even talk to about it. There isn't any LGBT organization, none of that's going on, so you're pretty much—for me I was just in this state of just knowing something was just not right. Then the way you, the way I, then came into the life. I came into the LGBT life through a friendship with one of the people who lived in the apartment complex that I, uh, where I lived when I was in [names southern city].

While she was in college, Deborah did not have a formal LGBTQ organization to support her during her coming out year in the 1980s. Rather, during the years that she was a college student, Deborah stated that the community was "so underground." Deborah described this "as a subterranean life that was fueled by the fear at that time of the as of yet unnamed gay disease."

Also during college, she fell in love with a woman, who remained her best friend still at the time of this study. In that friendship, which did not become sexual, Deborah stated that she became aware of being able to be more authentic when she came out.

Being totally free to be myself and to give love as a person-
-it was kind of outside of the scope of gender, of being
totally free to be myself and it was just realizing your total
self. So, I think the first person I actually fell in love with,
I wasn't with, we were just—I just didn't even know all of
those feelings could exist, as powerful as they were.

In speaking with her, it seemed that Deborah's positive experience
of being in touch with her lesbian identity at a young age ameliorated
her experiences of homophobic oppression in the church. Thus, Deborah
denied that her coming out process itself was painful, but she spoke
with anger about her struggle to find a goodness of fit with a Christian
congregation later. Beginning with her Roman Catholic roots, Deborah
experienced a lack of fit in church because of her race, her gender, her
sexual identity, her clothing, her style of worship, and her theology. The
following voice poem reflected Deborah's anger and hurt in response to
her multiple experiences of oppression in more than fifty congregations.

> I was wearing pants
> Just as I walked in the door, wearing pants,
> When I looked around
> I was the only, uh, woman-female-wearing pangs
> They didn't wear pant in there at all
> And then one other church I went, I didn't wear a hat
> You could just feel a gasp
> How could you walk in her without a hat?
> You could feel it
> The preacher talked about homosexuality being an abomination
> And looking right at me
> I felt like
> He was looking at me
> Maybe he wasn't
> I just move right along
> I went searching for Jesus again

In terms of her own relationship history, Deborah stated that she had been in a holy union from 1998 until 2008, when her partner left her during her recuperation from her near-fatal motor vehicle accident. Deborah stated with moist eyes that her next partner left her within a year of the interview. Thus, Deborah stated that she was unable to handle the exacerbation of her chronic health issues after another car accident. Currently, she reported that she is in a new relationship, but she declined from giving any details about it.

Mary. Like Deborah, Abigail, Sarah, Esther, and Rachel, Mary came out young despite significant experiences of homophobic oppression. Like Deborah, Mary stated at the time of the interview that she did not feel a goodness of fit in either a specific congregation or in any of the four denominations in this study. In contrast to Deborah, however, Mary's sexual identity and her religious identity have not been constant, with her sexual identity being both heterosexual and homosexual. In her adulthood, Mary's religious identity has not been a constant either like it was for Deborah.

Because of her extensive heteronormative experiences, Mary reported at the time of being interviewed that she continued to be hesitant to become a part of a church community. However, she still longed for the experience of belonging as a lesbian Christian. After her broken heterosexual relationship in her mid-twenties, and then after three broken lesbian relationships, Mary found herself drawn back to God. However, Mary has not found a goodness of fit in a Protestant denomination or congregation. Regarding her experience of the church's homophobia, Mary spoke with both sadness and anger regarding her lack of fit in multiple congregations or denominations.

> The Church really needs to change to become more accepting of people with different theological views, of people with different sexual orientations, and you know, there are people who do believe in God but are not coming to the church because the church is not really meeting their needs and the church is being really exclusivist.

Regarding the emergence of her sexual identity, Mary said that she knew around the fifth grade, around the age of ten or eleven, that she was different, and she remembers then not having a goodness of fit in her peer group. Retrospectively, Mary knew from that point on that something was different. She wasn't necessarily attracted to women or girls at that point, but she wasn't feeling what the other girls her age were feeling in terms of being attracted to boys.

> I wasn't feeling the same way as my girlfriends who started to want to play with boys. Not necessarily that I was attracted to women or girls at that point. I wasn't really feeling that. But I knew I wasn't feeling what they were feeling at that point.

When Mary came out at the age of twenty-four, she stated that she knew she was never going to date men again. She stated that she is actually bisexual because she likes men and finds them physically attractive. However, she stated that she identified as a lesbian because she had not dated men since her divorce from her husband in her mid-twenties.

> My preference is to date women, but there's just an, uh—I like women better. Let's just say that.

In regard to her sexual identity history, after Mary left her marriage to her husband of six years, she had a series of four lesbian relationships, each lasting five years. She stated that she is the one who ends each relationship, but did not elaborate on why, though it appeared that Mary's lifelong struggle to find fit stems from her poor attachment to alcoholic caregivers in her childhood. Mary has longed throughout her adult life to feel a fit in some church. As evidence to her experience of heteronormative church communities, she experienced a strong fit in church when she was still married to her husband and her daughters were young. However, in her experiences as an out lesbian, before and after seminary, she has not felt she fits in any of multiple Christian denominations she has participated in. Mary has not even found she fits in with any of the several denominations that purport to support gay and lesbian ministry. Of those experiences, she said, she found a few times in her adult life, both before and after seminary, that she did not fit into the LGBTQ community in or out of church. With pain and emotion in her voice, Mary stated the following:

> And I didn't feel like I could particularly come there in my brokenness and um, mostly by the pastor. And I just felt like I'm not even accepted in my own community. It was really, really incredibly difficult. Incredibly difficult … [her voice then became inaudible in the audio and trailed off].

For many years, Mary reported struggling with her sexual orientation as a lesbian, although she had come out to her family and friends by the age of twenty-four. She believed that her multiple experiences of church oppression reinforced her personal struggle and increasingly caused her to isolate and feel that "[I] had nowhere to really talk about [my experiences of homophobic oppression in church]."

STAGE 4: REVISED RELIGIOUS IDENTITY

All but three of the women (Rachel, Deborah, and Mary) in the sample stated they struggled tremendously with a split between having a Christian religious identity and a lesbian sexual identity. The remaining ten women (Hannah, Leah, Martha, Rebecca, Esther, Rachel, Ruth, Naomi, Abigail, and Sarah) began to heal their internal splits between their religious and sexual identities in this revised religious identity stage.

The four themes that emerged after the women came out and before they would feel ready to go to seminary were the following: (1) absence of split between religious and sexual identities; (2) the healing of the split between religious and sexual identities; (3) the extended struggle with perception of mutually exclusive identities; and (4) the intentional seeking of a faith community that was considered safe.

There was a wide age range, between the ages of twenty-one and fifty-two, of the women in this revised religious identity stage. The variation in ages of the women in this sample correlates with the ages of coming out and the ages of call to ministry. This fourth stage appeared to be a necessary developmental step after the sexual identity (stage 3) and before the clergy identity (stage 5).

Characteristically, at the beginning of this fourth stage, the women experienced a void because of their perceptions that as lesbians they could not fully be a part of a faith community. As a result of this expressed emptiness, toward the end of this fourth stage, the women sought to reengage in faith communities that were LGBTQ affirming. Thus, the major task of this developmental stage was for the women to integrate their lesbian identities into their religious identities. For the women who had formed stage 2 spiritual identities, they also needed to be integrated into their revised religious identities.

Absence of Split between Religious and Sexual Identities

Rachel, Deborah, and Mary denied having this struggle with needing to compartmentalize their Christian identities and their lesbian identities in order to remain involved in church. Rachel, a Jewish convert to Christianity, had not identified herself as a lesbian until she fell in love with her partner, and she denied any struggle to find fit in a Christian church as a gay woman. In contrast, Deborah and Mary reported having multiple spiritual and religious identities and multiple intimate relationships with women, but like Rachel, they denied having experienced confusion between their religious and sexual identities. Rachel was involved in a liberal Christian denomination after her conversion, while Deborah and Mary were involved in theologically conservative Christian denominations. However, Rachel reported a consistent fit with her denomination, whereas Deborah and Mary struggled to find fit with any denomination, including their denominations. Also unlike Rachel, Deborah and Mary continued at the time of this study to experience significant homophobic oppression in their faith communities. However, it was as if their multiple congregational and denominational allegiances, which were not all Christian, enabled them to deny their own internal splits between their spiritual and religious identities. In other words, it appeared that the function for Deborah and Mary in maintaining multiple simultaneous Christian and non-Christian allegiances was for them to continue to find genuine acceptance and community as a lesbian. However in maintaining multiple allegiances and memberships, Deborah's and Mary's internal confusion about their beliefs remained at the time of the interviews and created an ongoing sense of alienation and clinical depression.

Rachel. After her conversion from Judaism to Christianity, Rachel attended a liberal Protestant congregation where she was exposed to feminist and lesbian liberation theologies. In speaking of her current lived experience of both her religious and sexual identities, Rachel said the following:

> Yeah, I don't know if it's a fluidity [regarding her sexual identity] as much as it's openness. Openness. But it's fluidity. Either way. It's fine.

Deborah. During her long interview, Deborah spoke in a detached manner with little emotion. It was almost as if by remaining cut off from her emotions, she felt she could protect herself from the pain of years of oppression, as if her flat speech and emphasis on social justice issues, rather than her own emotions, also prevented her from having to access her real struggle as a black lesbian woman in a predominantly white denomination.

> We're all a part of the proletariat group in so many, in so many words, but, I mean, so here we are, we're all in a struggle on one level or another. Whatever our struggle is: racism, sexism, classism, you know, all of those "isms."

Mary. After coming out, Mary longed to return to a Christian community, where she would not experience any more isms. Here is a story that Mary told about knowing that this particular church group was not genuinely supporting her because they considered her to be too radical as a lesbian Christian.

> And um, I was the full moderator of PGLAS and um I sort of advocated for us to have this diversity dance which they never had before and I had someone from Soul Force come out and I arranged all this and, um, they and some of the other groups were so resistant to it because they

were so fearful. And we had this little parade around the seminary and they were so staged in fear about, about all of it. And you know, I just said, "I can't do this anymore. You guys have to do it because I'm not going to do it." They wanted me to be the co-moderator because they knew I was gay and yet I felt that the heterosexual people that were there wanted to run the show and they wanted to tell me what I needed as a member of the gay and lesbian community. And I just felt like no.

Healing of Split between Religious and Sexual Identities

Esther, Sarah, Abigail, Naomi, Hannah, Leah, Martha, Rebecca, Ruth, and Eve reported having an intense struggle with their internalized split between their religious and sexual identities. Differences between the participants centered around whether to leave the church or stay. Whereas Esther, Sarah, Abigail, and Naomi never left the church, Hannah, Leah, Martha, Rebecca, Ruth, and Eve left the institutionalized church prior to the time they were coming out (sexual identity: stage 3).

Esther, Abigail, Sarah, and Naomi, in particular, spoke about their churches of childhood emphasizing sexual purity. Through positive experiences of family members, professional colleagues, community, or ecumenical experiences, they began to do less compartmentalizing of their religious and sexual identities. Their experiences of oppression had pushed them to think outside of traditional church models to find employment with the marginalized in their communities (i.e., chaplaincy work, food pantry work). Nonetheless, they had to rework religious identities to include their lesbian identities before they were able to fully embrace their calls to ministry. Esther and Sarah had come out prior to entering into seminary; Abigail came out during her first year of seminary. Naomi was an anomaly in this study in that she went to seminary in her thirties, while still identifying as a heterosexual. However, like Esther, Sarah, and Abigail, Naomi was only to revise her religious identity to include her lesbian identity when she came out.

Esther. Esther's sense of internalized homophobia was deep, with her

197

remembering how she intuitively knew as a child and as an adolescent to keep silent in the same small homogeneous denomination in which she grew up as a young child. She did not know where she learned this strategy, just that she learned early that "growing up in the [denomination of her birth] you know to be quiet."

However, once Esther attended an open and affirming church of her home denomination during her college years, her split between her religious and sexual identities reintegrated into a revised religious identity. The scenario involved an older progressive woman in her denomination who gave her permission to come out and still remain in the church. This same woman, prominent in her home congregation and an activist from the sixties, also gave her permission to become an out lesbian minister.

> She was like that's the only image I can manage—like phew. Why are you not going to ...? phew. You are so tal ... And all of a sudden, I burst into tears and I am just sobbing—'cause I'm gay. She looks at me and said, "I kind of thought you might be, but I've never met any other lesbian." Esther chuckled. Like really, [name of woman], really, I don't think so, But um, she was so gracious and just looked at me and said, "That's not a good enough excuse." And you know that's absolutely no excuse. That's a copout. And then, you know, she just said, "I hope that you're safe and I am sorry that society is not really ready for you."

Abigail. Soon after coming out, Abigail stated that it was her engagement in social justice ministries that enabled the beginning of healing the split between her religious and sexual identities. Abigail said that she had done a yearlong internship with a battered women's program as a chaplain during seminary, which together with her coming out process led to her interest in social justice–type ministries. In her own words, she said the following:

> Um I think my awakening to orientation and sexual identity set me in that direction [of social justice ministries].

In addition, after she had come out, Abigail heard the Gospel stories in the Bible with new ears. She began to understand how the Gospel is for oppressed persons of society.

> How it's heard by oppressed people, so how it's heard by women; how it's read by LGBTQ persons, how it's heard by African Americans, how it's heard by immigrant and you know. Thus, she stated that she aims to read the scripture in the beginning, and in the end to do mission because justice and mercy is the goal.

Thus, Abigail's revising of her Christian identity to include her lesbian identity began to include a social justice component of ministry.

Sarah. Part of Sarah's self-acceptance as a Christian lesbian was aided by her experience of support of and acceptance from progressive parents. Sarah also attributed her ability to come out as a lesbian as being due to her exposure to the diversity of global Christian and spiritual ideologies through her experiences of being an exchange student during college in Europe and continuing her involvement with the World Council of Churches.

> So I was doing all this international stuff for the [name denomination]. Them knowing full well that I was gay. Very public and in some ways I think it was a positive thing. Because as we are pushing international issues such as sexuality, that was becoming more and more of a conversation.

Like Esther and Abigail, Sarah's revised religious identity converged with her lesbian identity because of her belief in social justice and advocacy efforts to ameliorate issues affecting the world and the church.

Naomi. Just prior to this interview, Naomi had interviewed for a position in the mid-Atlantic region of her denomination, in anticipation of being married and relocating. She experienced some hesitation about her disclosure of moving to marry her female partner. However, she knew at that point that she no longer was willing to remain closeted for the sake of accepting a denominational judicatory sanction against homosexuality. Naomi stated that she felt that she needed a sabbatical from congregational ministry to reflect on her identities and how she and others had worked to hide them from others and themselves. In her anticipated writing projects, Naomi hoped to communicate how integrity and authenticity emerge when one no longer hides his or her true identities.

> The number of different identities that I tried to fit into in order to please other people [and] how integrity and authenticity emerge when one no longer hides his or her true identities.

In her upcoming move to a new region, Naomi anticipated that she was going to write about her many identities as a lesbian, a mother, a wife, a minister, and more. Naomi, like Esther, Abigail, and Sarah, was able to assume a public voice as an out lesbian minister with integrated sexual and religious identities.

Leah, Martha, Rebecca, Ruth, and Eve felt able to return to church once they had integrated their lesbian identities into their religious identities. The push for these women to complete this task of this developmental stage was that this group of women seemed to grieve the community that they had experienced in church as children and adolescents. They wanted to re-experience the good parts of church without re-experiencing institutional oppression.

Rebecca. Rebecca returned to church after a decade away from the institutionalized church. During that time away from the church, she came out, and she longed to return to church but feared experiencing heteronormative and male normative oppression again in the institutional church. The caring and inclusiveness of community in the corporation that she worked for, however, allowed her to explore religious identity and return to the church. However, in her time after experiencing a spiritual community and after finding a partner, she desired to move back toward the religious identity that she had believed was unavailable to her as a gay woman. Rebecca described finding an open and affirming congregation with lesbian ministers who began to unlock her buried call to ministry.

Oh gay minister, that's great. So they just sort of took us in and I don't think it took long before she was like, "Hey you need to learn some [name of denomination] liturgy. Why don't you help me with the liturgy this week?" It was just, you know, she very quickly folded me in o what was going on and so, um I preached for the first time at [name of congregation] before I came [to seminary], which was weird to me. I'm like; I can't believe this was my first time at the pulpit except that when else would I have been invited into a pulpit?

Rebecca did not experience a long period of time in the revised religious identity period because her return to church pretty quickly revealed her repressed call to ministry (clergy identity: stage 5).

EXTENDED STRUGGLE WITH PERCEPTION OF MUTUALLY EXCLUSIVE IDENTITIES

The stories of Naomi's, Ruth's, and Martha's coming out and calls to ministry cannot be told without understanding how the three struggled well into middle age with what they thought were mutually exclusive identities of their lesbian and Christian identities. Although they came out before they acted on their calls, it seems that they had been struggling with both identity streams for decades. For them, there was no separation, and this became their foundation for pursing their clergy identities.

Naomi. Her coming out story is narrated earlier in the paper.

Ruth. Similar to Naomi, Ruth's coming out occurred while she was in seminary and in early congregational ministry. Rather than blatant oppression, what Ruth appears to have experienced was a minimization of her experiences and beliefs as a young woman growing up in a Roman Catholic tradition. Her experience of religious oppression was more about women not being in leadership than LGBTQs not being a part of ministry. For instance, when Ruth was a girl, she was told she could not serve on the altar with the priest because she was the wrong gender. When she wanted to be a priest, Ruth was told that it was not possible. When Ruth understood that becoming a priest was not possible, even after completing a master's in pastoral counseling at a Jesuit university, she got married. For Ruth, being married meant that defending against her multiple homoerotic experiences as a girl and as an adult.

Her voice poem, which is a literary device that is borrowed from the listening guide methodology, reflected Ruth's internalized belief that in that era of her life she could be neither a clergywoman nor a lesbian. The differences in font reflect the two decades of internal religious struggle that delayed both her coming out as a lesbian and her call to ministry. For her, the two are now intertwined.

> I grew up with a very strong interest in faith and in Christian religion
> *I played priest*
> I couldn't be an altar girl
> *My first sexual experiences was at age twelve with another girl*
> I have call to the priesthood
> *I fell kind of head-over-heels to a woman*
> I spent a year looking for a church
> *I started going to an Episcopal church*
> I truly fell in love with a woman
> *I joined the mainline church*
> I had a crush on the lesbian Pastor
> *In seminary, I met more lesbians than I've ever known my entire life*
> I just feel like I was living the wrong life [heterosexual marriage]
> *We ate and we talked for five hours [her first date with her partner]*
> I'm coming out to my congregation.

Once Ruth had embraced her lesbian identity, she was able to integrate it into her religious identity, which she had never left. Once she had completed this developmental task, Ruth felt as though she had more integrity in her ministry.

Martha. After much soul searching, Martha left her Franciscan Order in 1973, at the age of thirty-five. Although her Christian identity in St. Francis's Rule for Life had been nurtured in the order, Martha felt a need to leave. Her exposure to a less restrictive lifestyle, when she was living in a halfway house for mentally ill women, had opened her to additional perspectives on faith and alternative lifestyles. As previously stated, Martha had also begun to understand herself as a lesbian while living in the context of many lesbians.

> And my [Catholic] theology and my sense of who I am and who God is in my life conflicted with my being a lesbian. Yeah. And Catholicism took a different [pause] the repressiveness of Catholicism, just in some ways [pause]. The smallness of how thing of, of necessity of how we lived was not, ah, was not agreeable with m new understanding of myself. Part of that had to do with when I left [pause]. When I finally left the convent, I was 35 and I really had a breakdown. I wasn't hospitalized. I had to continue to work, but I felt like I should have been hospitalized. I went to therapy [pause] Life transition, but also when you were in the convent at that time you were, ah, you were given a number. The first book you read was "Pride: thief of the Holocaust." You were not an "I," you were a "We," every sense of ego was to be gotten out of you.

SEEKING SAFETY IN PROTESTANT MAINLINE DENOMINATIONS

With the exception of Esther and Sarah, who remained in their denominations of birth, the remaining eleven women in the sample left their faith traditions of birth. The remaining eleven (Abigail, Rebecca, Deborah, Mary, Eve, Rachel, Martha, Hannah, Leah, Ruth, and Naomi) women in the sample sought a new denomination in which they hoped they would not experience oppression. Hannah, Deborah, and Eve are exemplars in having reported the experience of entering into one of the mainline denominations through the warmth of the congregations they first encountered and unintentionally landing in a Protestant mainline denomination.

Hannah. Immediately when she got sober, Hannah wanted to return to church. Up until that point, Hannah felt that she was unworthy to go to church, but in early recovery, she felt that it was something that she needed to do in order to stay off drugs. She continued to recall what had begun to enable her to feel safe enough to return to church.

> The meeting was on like the third floor at [name of] church. And the hallway up towards, like while you're walking in the hallway. [The pastor] had all these, um, newspaper articles of various things that [name of] church did and how they were gay and lesbian affirming.

Hannah found safety in a theologically progressive congregation, which paradoxically was part of a homophobic denomination. This was the same denomination in which she ultimately sought ordination.

Deborah. Paradoxically, the open and affirming congregation, which she would later intern at, is the part of an oppressive denomination that does not endorse LGBTQ inclusion. However, from the time she went to this congregation, Deborah reported that she felt immediately welcomed. Regarding being welcomed to this congregation where she interned, she stated the following:

> I went for more than one visit, but the only church other than the church with my family that I felt like I could stay in and not want to leave was [name of congregation].

Deborah found safety in a theologically progressive congregation of a denomination. This is the same denomination in which she ultimately sought ordination.

Eve. Eve is an exemplar of a lesbian consciously seeking a denomination with which to affiliate. She had returned to her religious identity after having multiple experiences of oppression in various church settings. Fortunately for her, she has had a positive experience in her chosen denomination as she completes her seminary training.

The following story describes her welcome into her denomination, which sealed her call to ministry in that denomination as well.

> The pastor was communing everybody by name that's how small the congregation. And in that moment I thought I think I want to do this again. I want to come here. So I

went to that church like three to four weeks and actually at the end of that very first Sunday, when I told myself that I could never ever come out in church because they would kick me out. And at the end of the very first Sunday, and old woman turned around and said, "Hello and welcome. I hope to see you again." She said, "It's funny. I came to this church because my daughter and her partner came here. They don't even come here anymore but I still do." And the first words that I said anywhere to anyone is, "I don't think my partner will come because she is Catholic, but I would like to come again." And she said, "Oh honey, that would be great. Hope to see you soon." So I came out to this woman in this first statement and she was really great.

Thus, within a year of the funeral for a cast member who died in real life and who she officiated at the production studio, Eve was enrolled in a denominational seminary of her newly chosen denomination.

Leah. Leah had come out during her spiritual identity stage, while she was working as a newspaper reporter. During her reporter days, Leah stated, she was privileged to report on topics such as clinical pastoral education and LGBTQ inclusion into Christian churches. From that, she believed she felt called to ministry, but she first had to reaffiliate with an open and affirming denomination.

Yeah. And it was like a calling that came out of a calling. You know, that's the way I look at it. You know, um ... I considered journalism a calling. Yeah. Yeah. So, I applied to Yale Divinity School. Now at this point I had gotten involved in [names congregation in a New England city]. Uh, and very open and affirming. Um Hm. Yup. And while I was at United um, oh, of the ministers, one was openly gay and (sic) also still out I was a reporter. I did. I wrote an article on the opening and affirming process in the [names denomination]. God—early '90s. So I did all these things that were converging into, pushing me into ministry. There are no coincidences. Yeah.

Martha. When Martha emerged from her spiritual identity around the age of fifty, she immediately enrolled at a local progressive Protestant seminary. While at the seminary, mentors encouraged her to become involved in a large local church that was also very progressive. From an ecological theory perspective, Martha found a niche with this particular congregation because there were multiple clergy on staff who were either gay or lesbian. By default, she would also became a part of the ordination process of that particular congregation's denomination.

> Got into [names seminary]. Got hooked up with [names prominent church]. Finished [names seminary]. Uhhh, met a wonderful [names denomination] minister, not gay, but there were obviously at [names seminary] a lot of gays and lesbians who were in ministry.

STAGE 5: CLERGY IDENTITY STAGE

The completion of this integration process in revised religious identity (stage 4) allowed the women's latent calls to ministry to reemerge from early stages. Some of the women reflected that their calls to ministry came during their early religious identities (stage 1) but that they were repressed because of the conservative theological contexts that they were raised in. Other women in the sample reflected that their calls came during their spiritual identities (stage 3) or their revised religious identities (stage 4). Their calls emerged from a deeper sense of wanting to do social justice work or to embrace a life with spiritual ideals.

Six of the women (Deborah, Mary, Leah, Eve, Rebecca, and Rachel) felt called to ministry in adulthood. The remaining seven (Esther, Sarah, Hannah, Naomi, Abigail, Martha, and Ruth) women felt called to ministry at a young age but had perceived that their call and coming out were delayed due to the inculcation of their early religious identities. Only Deborah and Rachel perceived that they had not experienced delayed coming out processes due to homophobic oppression in their early religious formations.

The six themes that emerged as the women were forming their clergy identities were the following: (1) experience of enrolling in seminary before coming out; (2) the lived experience of being called in childhood; (3) the lived experience of being called in adulthood; (4) the lived experiences of ministerial oppression; (5) the lived experiences of finding a niche in ministry; and (6) the importance of being out in ministry.

There was a wide age range in this clergy identity stage (beginning at age twenty-two), due to the various ages that the women came out as lesbians and worked toward the integration of their religious and sexual identities. This fifth stage followed the revised religious identity stage (stage 4), where all thirteen women in the sample were able to successfully integrate their sexual and religious identities.

Characteristically, at the beginning of this fifth stage, the women intuited that their lives would remain unfulfilled if they did not become ministers. Thus, during this stage, the women initially contemplated calls to ministry. Some of the women allowed their latent calls to ministry to emerge. Their tasks included enrolling at a seminary and completing their ministerial training processes, which ended in ordination. This task also included the ministerial roles that women entered into toward the end of this stage.

Enrolled in Seminary before Coming Out

Abigail, Ruth, and Naomi were exemplars of women who were articulate about their calls to ministry at a young age, despite their early experiences and early religious identities (stage 1) delaying both their coming out processes and their calls. Abigail was the youngest woman in this sample to come out, as she went to seminary right after college and came out during her first year of seminary at the age of twenty-two. Ruth came out during seminary when she was in her late thirties. Although Naomi also went to seminary in her thirties, she did not come out for another fifteen years, after her second heterosexual marriage ended in divorce and she had been ordained for ten years.

Abigail. For Abigail, her coming out processes and her ministry training were almost simultaneous processes. As mentioned in stage 2, Abigail met her partner while in seminary, but they remained closeted throughout her seminary years and ordination process years. Abigail stated that in the early nineties, she did not believe she would be able to graduate from seminary or receive a call if her denomination knew she was a lesbian. Consequently, for two decades, Abigail had yet to work through her stages of lesbian identity development.

> So, I came to an understanding of sexual orientation and identity during Seminary, which wasn't a real place either at that time. Well, I am (chuckles) but not under the care anymore but yes, at that point, I was under the care of the [names denominational judicatory in a Northwest city] but then when I got my job with Women's Faiths because after I graduated I got a job as a Chaplain at the Battered Women's program. I went—In [names eastern city] I was ordained through the [names denominational judicatory in the mid-Atlantic region]. I had an advocate there named [names mentor] who was a Clergy, a [name of denomination] Clergy woman who pushed the [judicatory] on ordaining me to that position because they normally would not ordain to a non-parish position (at the same time) to the church. I was closeted—[It was '91 or '92] um so we were closeted during Seminary [voice trails off].

Ruth. Ruth credits the self-exploration and reflection regarding her sexual orientation during her seminary years with her ability to come out shortly after her graduation. She had been repressing her bisexual identity but knew she had been exhilarated by previous sexual encounters with women during her heterosexual marriage. Like Abigail, due to fears of not being able to get employment or be ordained, Ruth remained professionally closeted for a decade, in what Cass (1979) would characterize as stages of identity tolerance / identity acceptance.

> And this point the sexuality piece dies down for a couple of years until I get myself back into the ordination process.

And go to [name] Seminary. And I commute back and forth to [names large eastern city] and I meet more lesbians than I've ever known my entire life. And this begins to feel a little like Paul's thorn in the flesh for me. This begins to feel like something I can't shake. And I mean I can tell you—humph—whoa—(Begins to cry) I'm surprised that this is so emotional for me, but I can tell you that I had times driving down to the city when I was literally crying in my car saying to God, "Take this away. Take this away please."

Like Abigail, due to fears of not being able to get employment or be ordained, Ruth remained professionally closeted for a decade.

Naomi. Naomi truly is the outlier research participant in this sample in that she did not come out until she had been ordained for a decade, when she was in her forties. Although she was a minister in a progressive denomination, she still found it difficult to acknowledge her hidden lesbian identity, and it emerged finally after two failed heterosexual marriages and physical and mental health issues—with the support of a female clergy support group. She attributed part of her delays in both coming out and going to seminary to still needing to please a demanding mother. After her mother died when she was in her thirties, she felt freer to explore who she was.

Naomi's experience varied from Abigail's and Ruth's in that she had been ordained for more than a decade before coming out at all. This piece of transcript gives voice to Naomi's denial for two decades of her lesbian identity.

Yeah. I was about 35–36 [when I went to seminary and got divorced the first time]. And I spend a lot of nights just being miserable, honestly. I wasn't really—I had this notion that I was never going to be able to go back into relationships as a revolving door. Still I wasn't a person who wasn't able to even get into the revolving door because it just keeps moving. So it was a long while before I thought seriously about whether I was able to really connect with anyone ever again. Um, and I presumed if I ever did, it would be a man because that's all I had known up to that point. After that, I had met a [female] friend, and in the contact in the relationship with that friend, we began to have feelings that were really unexpected for me. Towards this friend. Yeah. And the way we would—the way we would make the next plan to see each other back in the days of paper calendars—Remember those? I just remember I always made sure I had my little book with me because I knew she would say, "When can we see each other again?" And I wanted to see her again and not wait on chance. It was—it was a relationship that never developed into anything beyond a friendship but that I reflected on a lot and never talked to anyone about it. Um, in fact I still have files on my computer that I saved from a floppy disk. I converted those files to have them on my laptop now.

Being Called When Young

Seven of the women felt called to ministry at a young age. However, despite having had the experience of a call, Esther, Sarah, Hannah, Abigail, Martha, Ruth, and Naomi each believed that their calls to ministry (and their coming out processes) were delayed by their conservative religious identity formations. Of these women, only Abigail went to seminary immediately after completing her undergraduate training. In other words, not only had they experienced the homophobic oppression in their early religious formations that delayed their coming out processes (stage 2), but they had also experienced male normative oppression in their childhood and adolescent religious contexts.

Of these women, Hannah, Ruth, and Naomi were the most articulate in describing how their early religious formations functioned to delay their call processes. Through the developmental phase in the revised religious identity stage (stage 4), these three women were introduced to more progressive theologies and social constructs than those they had originally been exposed to.

Hannah. For Hannah, her early call to ministry was evidenced in her description of wanting to be a minister's wife as a child.

> I actually felt very connected with the church, um, early on in my life. Now I'm going back no like, elementary school. It was important to me, And I actually. It's funny to think about now, but I—in the [name of childhood denomination] church, there's no really formal role for a woman, right?

Hannah experienced a call to ministry within the two denominational contexts that had oppressed her—the denomination of her birth and the denomination that she joined after her return to church (stage 4), respectively.

> There's no, uh, I remember thinking that very early on, like you know, elementary school, that I would like to be a pastor's wife, because that was the one roles I saw of women. And that women could actually, ah, the pastor's wives actually did get to do a lot. They used to run the Sunday school, and you know, all that kind of [stuff].

Second, Hannah experienced a call when she was a member of a progressive city church within the denomination that she joined after sobriety and returning to church. This congregation operated with an inclusive and affirming mission, apart from the homophobic policies of the denomination, and outside of the denomination's position statement opposing LGBTQ ordination. Early on in recovery, Hannah began to think in earnest about going to seminary. However, she continued to be very concerned about the "gay" part of going to seminary. She knew that this was a wonderful congregation but did not think there were lots of other churches as inclusive as that church.

> It was a big, it was a big, um, a big part of that journey for me. So, um, and then, so then I, I, year, I don't know, I would, you know, things progressed for a while; I started thinking maybe I want to go to seminary? Which was a

211

really weird though for me, but you know I still felt sort of the residual shame of stuff that had happened in the past. So um, and just the gay thing. I was like, there's no way I'm going to go to seminary, I'm gay. Yeah. I mean, I don't (sic) that I had been fully out to myself but I'd kind of had accepted the full reality of it. Yeah. I was really, uh, getting back into church.

At this point in her call process contemplation, Hannah had integrated her religious and sexual identities (revised religious identity); she did not know that being a minister was possible as a lesbian.

Ruth. Like Hannah, Ruth's journey toward becoming a Protestant minister was rooted in her strong religious identity as a child. As a young child, she played priest with her brother and remembers wanting to be a Benedictine nun. Ruth discovered that Roman Catholicism was very different outside of a Jesuit university. Ruth reflected on her contemplation of becoming a Roman Catholic priest during her time at the Jesuit university.

I saw I could get a degree in Pastoral Care and Counseling, so I thought Perfect. Psychology and Religion. Uh, and once I got into that program, it was not long before my interest was turned more towards ministry, which as a Roman Catholic woman, I was thinking Chaplaincy. Uh—college chaplaincy, hospital chaplaincy. And uh, I must say there were all these wonderful women chaplains at Boston College and I was attending a church in my early 20s in [names New England city] that uh—that women preached once or twice a month there because it was at [names] College. The theology faculty was preaching. So I was really hanging on to this, someday. Not-now-but-someday idea. And I was--not actually thinking that I have a call to the priesthood, but I did—that interest was always there. And that someday, was always there.

After completing her master's in pastoral ministry and relocating to a new geographic region with her husband and two young children, she was unable to find a Roman Catholic parish in which to fit.

Naomi. Naomi believed that her background as a traditional southern woman delayed her call to ministry (and her coming out as a lesbian). However, she felt called as a young child, and like Hannah, it was manifested in wanting to be a minister's wife. This was the only way in her childhood context for women to have leadership in the church.

> So I think that probably has a pretty significant impact on understanding my journey to ministry and understanding my journey to understanding myself. Um, so I grew up in settings where there was a lot of expectations, so in some ways I felt like I was ten years behind in understanding what women's roles were. I had a very old fashioned sense of what a girl's roles were supposed to be.

Looking back, Naomi realized that she was most likely called to ministry at a fairly young age but did not have that understanding yet.

BEING CALLED IN ADULTHOOD

In contrast to the seven women who experienced calls to ministry at a young age, Deborah, Mary, Leah, Eve, Rebecca, and Rachel experienced calls as an adult. However, with the exception of Naomi, each of these women, whether they were called as youth or as adults, came to their clergy identities after they had accepted their lesbian identities.

Eve. When Eve began her first lesbian relationship at the age of twenty-four, she began to struggle in earnest with the incompatibility of any denominational identity and her sexual identity. She knew that she could still maintain her Christian identity, but she recognized that she was in "a community that absolutely wanted you to believe that you could not be in a church if you were gay." She added that she did not remember homosexuality being mentioned at all in her home denomination, but she knew that she would not be accepted as an "out" lesbian.

In contrast to Esther's ability to remain within her home denomination, Eve had left the church due to multiple experiences of oppression when she first felt called to ministry. As stated previously in her narrative, Eve's call to ministry came outside of the church in a television studio. In fact, she cited several times during the interview that her biggest supporters for this ministry are not religious persons within the institutionalized church but people outside of the church. In this regard, she remarked that her "biggest supporters are not [her] Christian friends." Ironically, she continues to perceive that her call to ministry is most confirmed by those outside of the church.

> My Christian friends are supporters. But my biggest supporters are my atheist friends you are like "Oh yeah. You are in the zone. This is what you are supposed to do. This is—I love how you talk about this." It startles me weekly that people who don't believe in God are the ones who say, "Wow. You are doing what you are supposed to be doing."

EXPERIENCES OF MINISTERIAL OPPRESSION

Ten of the women (Esther, Sarah, Hannah, Deborah, Martha, Ruth, Mary, Eve, Naomi, and Abigail) had either a singular experience or multiple experiences of oppression in either a congregational or denominational context. For seven of the women (Esther, Hannah, Deborah, Martha, Mary, Eve, Sarah, and Abigail), their experiences of oppression occurred in multiple contexts.

Esther, Eve, Sarah, and Hannah are exemplars of being discriminated against by their denominations while they were in their ordination and installation processes and of being discriminated against in multiple ministerial contexts. Although each of them was considered "fit for ministry" (a term used by some denominations post seminary regarding the ordination candidate's scholarly abilities, their psychological health, and their spiritual preparedness for ministry) by their denominations, they, in spite of their strong credentials, experienced prolonged and oppressive ordination processes.

Esther and Hannah rejected their home denomination because of its homophobic ordination policies. The ordaining judicatories of their home denominations blocked their ordinations because they were lesbians who had come out publicly. Thus, it took Esther years for her to complete her ordination process after graduation from seminary and Hannah, as a result of the need to affiliate with a second denomination in order to become ordained, because her original denomination refused to ordain her in light of her out identity as a lesbian clergy woman.

In contrast to Esther and Hannah, who were rejected by their denominations during their ordination processes, Sarah and Eve accommodated to their denominational policies in order to become a part of the in-group. Sarah and Eve's denomination has not fully blocked LGBTQ persons from becoming ordained but instead has devised an alternate route that ensures they will become ordained. Eve had not yet begun her ordination process at the time of the interview. However, Sarah stated that it took her denomination ten years to ordain her post seminary graduation. Thus, being a part of a homophobic ordination process was her way of maintaining her prior in-group status. Since both Esther and Sarah strongly identify with their denominations, they are willing to remain, with the intent of becoming change agents.

During their interviews, Abigail and Mary shared experiences of being discriminated against in hospital chaplaincy positions, in addition to repeated experiences of not being hired as pastors of congregations. Due to the level of oppression they experienced at different points in their clergy development, both Abigail and Mary have coped with the employment loss by doing second master's degrees in social work or counseling and working multiple jobs simultaneously.

Esther. Esther spoke with honesty about the ethnic homogeneity of her home denomination, which, although was a fit for her as a child and adolescent, severely oppressed her when she attempted to be ordained as a lesbian. Even though she currently serves as a pastor of a congregation in her home denomination, because she is a lesbian, her judicatory will not install her either. Five years after her experience of being rejected as an ordination candidate, she has begun to experience the pull back to her denominational roots. She stated it is because of the warmth she experienced as a child and her connections. Esther has grieved because of her experiences of marginalization in the church. Esther's emotional anguish of being rejected and longing to be fully in the in-group (Tajfel and Turner 1979) of her home denomination is reflected in this voice poem.

> They had to try to contain it and not
> We were getting minimum without benefits
> We don't have retirement benefits
> We don't have insurance benefits
> I had worked two jobs and busted my ass for years and years
> Sorry, I can't help you, until, until you want to install me
> They are not going to shut us down
> I was more than happy to leave it
> As more time has gone by, it's creeping back up on me
> I had really sort of had it with the [name of denomination] in general
> We all know each other's business; it's kind of comforting
> I mean there's definitely a stigma
> I mean
> I think there are actually a lot of similarities
> I mean
> I
> I understand
> They feel so afraid of what's gonna happen
> I can see
> They don't want the hassle
> They don't want the hassle

Sarah. Like Esther, it appeared that much of Sarah's identity and self-esteem came through her denominational identity. There is a sense, however, that Sarah minimized some of her oppression. Sarah presented without bitterness, in comparison to the negative impact that Esther's experiences of oppression had on her emotional well-being. Sarah added that, compared to most LGBTQ clergy, she is fortunate in that her oppression has been minimal.

> And yet at the same time, I don't think I experienced a
> lot of the really yuck stuff. I've never been thrown out of
> a church. I've never been defrocked. I've never had to live

in the closet. I've never been personally physically hurt. I've never felt what a lot of my colleagues have felt which they tell some horrible stories about.

Abigail. For Abigail, the themes of fit and oppression were on opposite sides of the same coin. From an oppression perspective, Abigail had not been able to find a church position in three of the four formula of agreement denominations. In terms of oppression, it took more than twenty years after seminary graduation for Abigail to find a position of fit. Even then, her position as a social justice minister is at a church that is outside her denomination. Abigail stated multiple times during the interview that this position was a powerful fit for her, but unfortunately, it was part-time. She supplements her income with three other jobs: as a hospital chaplain, as a dog trainer, and as a pastoral therapist.

> Yeah. I'd always expected to Pastor a Parish but that wasn't feasible then so, I tried and applied to [names denomination] churches that publicly stated they were in support of LGBTQ ordination. Yes, a more light church. Even the more light churches, one of which was a leader in the movement wrote me back and said because you are a Lesbian, we cannot hire you (laughs), which seems so hypocritical to me.

Here was the evidence of Abigail's struggle to find acceptance in a parish setting in any of the four denominations, even after she was ordained as a chaplain soon after seminary graduation.

Mary. Mary had despaired throughout her adult life to find fit in the church, both within and outside of her home denomination. Mary described her chaplain supervisor's homophobic discrimination of her lesbian clergy identity through the use of the listening guide methodology. In her voice poem, she poignantly recorded the anger and sadness that reside inside of her currently and continue to manifest in somatic and psychiatric problems.

I was pretty devastated
Because I was depressed
I was majorly depressed
And I just feel into a major depression
Two weeks later my car was hit
I didn't have collision on it
I was without a car for a while
And um, I was poor
I had no job and no car
It just felt like my life fell apart
He basically scapegoated me
What he's doing is wrong
They are too afraid to say anything

These anguished words described Mary's experience of oppression as a chaplain resident and its aftermath on her life.

ONGOING DENOMINATIONAL OPPRESSION

Four of the women in the sample disclosed that their experiences of homophobic oppression in a congregational or denominational context were continuing at the time of the interview.

Deborah. At the time of the interview, Deborah had been the pastor in her church for only five months but had already experienced significant homophobic oppression. She stressed that she was staying for a time because she believed that part of her lesbian clergy identity was to do LGBTQ advocacy and to work with LGBTQ youth. The challenge before Deborah was that although she was installed by the local judicatory as the first out lesbian in this particular denomination, there were other parts of the denomination that were protesting this action. Deborah reaffirmed her Christian identity and call to ministry and her tolerance of ambiguity in her life. For example, regarding her call to organize a new church, Deborah again expressed her tolerance of ambiguity and sense of not being certain of her future.

It may, it may be me, I don't, [pause] I don't know, I just [pause] you know, just [pause]. God is creative, you know.

Her minimization of her oppression was evidenced in her God language. Like Sarah, Deborah learned to cope with minimizing her person discrimination as an individual in an out-group in her denomination.

Esther. Esther stated her status as an out lesbian clergywoman in an institutionally oppressive denomination against LGBTQ persons had in reality been freeing.

Oh, I'm terrifying to those, they don't want to associate with me, um, which is kind of sad, in some ways, but understandable. I mean, I kind of, represent everything awful that could happen to them.

From the beginning of her time at her current congregation, Esther boldly told them that she was gay.

Esther spoke about the freedom of being out, even within an oppressive denomination. Her perception was that she is a "really free woman." Esther's choice to remain within her judicatory, which has continued to prevent her from being installed as a minister and which is important for employment security in much the same way that a professor is tenured at a university, represents an accommodation to the denominational structure's homophobic regulations. Similarly to Deborah and Sarah, Esther had chosen to remain in the denomination as a form of resistance for the purpose of creating change. Esther had begun to reengage in the life of her home denomination. However, Esther believed that it was in fact her experiences of being outside of the mainstream of her denomination that gave her the courage to press to make changes toward LGBTQ inclusion within her home denomination. Esther states she feels psychological ready to be a change agent. In addition, she longs for her childhood affiliations that were described in the early religious identity section.

EXPERIENCES OF MICRO CONGREGATIONAL/
DENOMINATIONAL OPPRESSIONS

Hannah, Abigail, Deborah, Esther, and Mary reported significant denominational and employer oppressions during and after their ordination processes. Martha and Ruth both reported that they experienced micro oppressions in the course of their ministries. These occurred by either their denominations or congregations. Again, the minimization of their experience of oppression was their way of managing their low statuses within their denominations.

Martha. It appeared that Martha experienced some form of oppression for identifying as a lesbian minister early in her ministry, even in a progressive denomination. For instance, an older mentor had advised her not to tell her calling congregation that she was a lesbian. Martha did not disclose to her first congregation that she was a lesbian. She wondered in hindsight how much she had hindered the integrity of that ministry.

> "It might not be a good idea if you told the congregation about your sexuality."

At this time, Martha agreed with her because she did not realize how her sexual and clergy identities interplayed. Upon this experience of oppression, she reflected the following sentiments.

> She said, "This is your first congregation and they're older and it might be better if you just didn't make an issue of your sexuality." And I said, "Well, I wouldn't, because it's me and it doesn't affect how I minister and whatever." And she said, "Test the water. And don't say anything."

Ruth. An example of what she perceives to be minor oppression is that although her church board endorsed Ruth's ministry, knowing she is a lesbian, they have a policy of disallowing her to officiate same-sex marriages in the church. However, her answer to the oppression is that Ruth has taken a justice stance and has, at the time of the interview, performed two same-sex weddings but has not told her church board about it.

[What] I will tell you [pause], is that I have performed two same-sex weddings. Um, I have not told my [church board] about that. It doesn't feel great, but it feels like I'm kind of willing to go out on a limb. Um, it just feels like a justice issue for me. I mean, I'm not going to say no to somebody who wants to get married, you know.

ANTICIPATED DENOMINATIONAL OPPRESSION

Naomi. At the time of the interview, one of the women (Naomi) denied having had any homophobic oppression at the hands of a congregation or her denomination but expressed anticipatory anxiety that she was going to experience regional denominational oppression for being a lesbian when she moved to marry her fiancée six weeks after the interview. Like Martha, Naomi was in a theologically progressive denomination but still expected to be unable to get a ministry position as an out lesbian.

One of the things that I had been afraid of um, let me rephrase that. When I began to face the truth, I became terribly afraid of what that would mean for my career cause their, even though in theory the [name of denomination] is very supportive of ordinations for LGBT people, it doesn't mean that they are churches who want to call them.

EXPERIENCES OF FINDING A MINISTERIAL NICHE

Rachel, Leah, Esther, Hannah, Sarah, and Abigail verbalized multiple times in the course of the interviews their sense of gratitude for feeling such a connection to the congregations or institutions in which they are doing ministry. Rachel and Leah reported a strong sense of fit in their hospitals where they are serving as chaplains. Esther, Hannah, Sarah, and Abigail reported a strong niche within the congregations that they are serving.

However, for Esther, Hannah, Sarah, and Abigail, their strong congregational fit is somewhat of a conundrum. The congregations exist in the context of homophobic judicatories that would not install them and that required alternate routes or offered no route for ordination. Further, they will not have regional mobility within their own denominations because their experiences of congregational fit are unique to that situation and are unlikely to be replicated.

Esther. Consistent with her sense of fit in church, Esther, from the beginning of her time in her current congregation more than ten years ago, felt a sense of fit and acceptance. She attributes that to her openness from the beginning about being gay. This, however, is not without the cost of loneliness and being cut off from the rest of the local denominational judicatory that does not fully accept her ministry because she is gay. Here, Esther contrasted her unique experience of congregational fit with denomination oppression and her fatigue and isolation.

> They were
> They were
> They're really supportive
> They don't want to associate with me
> Ostracize you
> Abandon you
> They feel afraid
> They don't
> They don't have the capacity to handle it
> You know
> I mean
> So when I say it's pretty lonely
> Yeah it is really lonely
> But the lonely (inaudible), lonely

Sarah. Sarah said that it would be very difficult to find another call because she is a lesbian. Further, she knew a lot of LGBTQ clergy within her denomination and others waiting for a first call, and she felt extreme gratitude for having a position that she really loved. For now, Sarah feels settled into a unique urban, ecumenical, and LGBTQ-affirming ministry that would be hard to replicate anywhere else in her denomination. Like Esther, Sarah reported fatigue as a result of her denominational oppression, but also like Esther, her gratitude for ministry was evident.

This is life and you know, you do what you do and do what you can and I certainly have a lot of colleagues and support. We've really got a strong community around here. So I feel a lot of support and yet honestly I get tired too.

Abigail. Abigail stated that the congregation, which is outside of the denomination that holds her ordination credentials, hired her with full knowledge of her sexual identity. Thus, after being ordained for two decades, Abigail felt safe enough professionally to fully come out. Like Esther and Sarah, Abigail cited gratitude for the ministry she finally received.

So, yea that was when I got here, I came fully out. There's not going to be another church that's going to hire me. It's not going to happen. I really don't think so [voice trails off]. I'm content and yet I wish I could have more.

IMPORTANCE OF BEING OUT IN MINISTRY

Being out means more success in ministry to the women in the sample. Being out in ministry means having more integrity in ministry for all thirteen of the women in the sample. For these women, success in ministry is being able to talk about themselves in authentic and open ways. It means no longer having to hide their true selves. It means being more authentically able to counsel LGBTQ persons. It means being able to do more thorough LGBTQ advocacy in their churches and communities. Esther, Martha, Ruth, and Sarah were particularly articulate about this finding of having more success and integrity in ministry when out.

Esther. At this point in her lesbian clergy journey, Esther encouraged colleagues to mutually embrace their gay and ministerial identities. In fact, she increasingly had become angry with her colleagues in her denomination of birth who were gay and not out.

Being closeted makes you really less than capable, I mean it definitely is, like, a huge burden on your ministry,

because it doesn't allow you to be fully yourself, but and
it isn't just closeted folks who are gay, it's also liberals in
general, anyone, anyone who's afraid to speak their mind.

Abigail. Abigail stated that when she read the oppressive stories in the
Bible, she was hearing the stories with "new ears." In other words, Abigail
heard the familiar stories of individuals being healed from whatever their
oppressions were in both the Old and New Testaments of the Christian
scriptures with new meaning that brought her to new ways of doing ministry.
To promote advocacy and policy change in various denominations, Abigail
has led retreats for LGBTQ youth and healing services for LGBTQ persons
who have been oppressed by the church. Abigail said that by being out,
her understanding of the scriptures changed, particularly in messages to
the oppressed and marginalized.

How it's [the Bible] heard by oppressed people, so how its
heard by women; how it's read by GBLTQ [sic] persons,
how it's heard by African Americans, how it's heard by
immigrant and you know ...

Thus, Abigail stated that she aims to read the scripture in the
beginning, and in the end to do mission because justice and mercy is
the goal. Being out enabled Abigail to be part of the resistance necessary
within her denomination to move toward more LGBTQ inclusion.

BEING OUT DRIVES SOCIAL JUSTICE

Esther, Hannah, Rachel, Deborah, Abigail, Sarah, and Leah felt that
having the integrity to be out in ministry also drove social justice efforts
in their communities. In addition, these women perceived that being out
enhanced their ability to do ministry. For instance, being out allowed
persons struggling with same-sex attraction to have counseling assistance
by these lesbian clergy; being out meant becoming involved in multiple
social change ventures; and being out meant more honesty and integrity
in doing their own ministries. In comparison to the other women in the
sample when they were interviewed, Esther, Hannah, Deborah, Leah, and

Abigail were extremely articulate about the ways in which being out was a formula for doing social justice.

Esther. Esther was perhaps the most articulate when speaking about the importance of being out in ministry. Over time, Esther has encouraged her colleagues to mutually embrace their gay/lesbian and ministerial identities. Therefore, she has increasingly become less patient with her colleagues in her denomination of birth who are gay or lesbian and who do not have the courage to be out.

> Being closeted makes you really less than capable, I mean
> it definitely is, like, a huge burden on your ministry,
> because it doesn't allow you to be fully yourself, but and
> it isn't just closeted folks who are gay, it's also liberals in
> general … anyone who's afraid to speak their mind.

Esther's stance was slightly different from that of Hannah, Deborah, Leah, and Abigail in that she was adamant, with tinges of anger, that in order to be successful in ministry, a gay or lesbian minister has to be out. She actually derided her gay and lesbian colleagues who remained in the closet.

Hannah. Hannah spoke about the irony of doing significant social justice work in her small urban congregation. With a little bit of a competitive spirit, she stated hers was the only congregation growing in her denominational judicatory. She also added that she still cannot be installed, but her ongoing experience of denominational oppression drives her social justice, including her feeding more than eight hundred people a week through her congregation's food program. Her voice poem demonstrated her dedication to her work.

> I mean we have 800 people coming every Thursday
> I mean
> I think we're both just really grateful
> So I'm not installed here
> I think
> We're the only growing church in the [denominational judicatory]
> I mean [wife] and

We are really unprotected here
I think on some level
I try not to think about, about it
If I thought about it a lot
I didn't think
I'd be able to do this
I just do
What I'm supposed to be doing?
I think there's an understanding that, um
We don't push for installation
That's kind of where I feel like
And I don't
I don't think about it much
It bothers me if
I think about it

Deborah. Deborah brought the pain of her perceived rejections from fifty congregations and the ongoing homophobic oppression from her current denomination into her soliloquy below on the importance of advocating for LGBTQ youth.

And in the ... in this darkness, and in the shadows, you have young children—younger than me, because I didn't come into my own sexual identity till I was almost an adult, I was just not even thinking about anything like that, um, but you have these young children who going through puberty—are going through puberty in these shadows. And they're aware that there are gays and lesbians and they are growing up in the shadows and some of them have gay and lesbian parents, and are growing up in the shadows still, because their parents are also in the closet. So, you have ... so, you have these children growing up without any sense of viewing your body as a temple, any sense of recognizing the image of God in another person, so it's object-to-object interfacing in a moment.

Like Hannah, Deborah's energy for social justice, and in particular LGBTQ youth who have ongoing oppression experiences, was notable during the interviews. Her pain was palpable, but she minimized it for the sake of promoting social change within her community, church, and denomination.

Leah. Although it seems almost counterintuitive for a soft-spoken woman, Leah has become an outspoken advocate in recent years for LGBTQ inclusion in the Christian church. A by-product of Leah having integrated her spiritual, sexual, and religious identities is her sense of call to advocacy. Now that Leah has been ordained ten years as a lesbian minister, she feels strongly that her advocacy work requires her: (1) to publicly advocate for LGBTQ individuals seeking ordination in their respective denominations; and (2) to clinically facilitate the integration of the disparate voices of spirituality, religion, and sexuality in LGBTQ individuals.

> Yeah. So you know I just try to work with that as best as I can. And be there and show them different aspect of the scripture that challenge, you know, some of the other aspects of scripture that claim to condemn LGBT people and you know, I just … it just breaks my heart to see it over and over and over again. And every new generation, it just doesn't matter. You know, The Church as a whole. Yeah. [Pause] it's just [pause] I think it's [pause] think It's an all-out war. I really do.

Four separate times toward the last part of the interview, Leah spoke with emphasis about the need to be involved in both advocacy and clinical work with these individuals. From an anti-oppressive methodology perspective, Leah's words reflected her sentiments about the church needing to engage in *an all-out war* to bring about the full inclusion of LGBTQ persons in various Christian denominations.

Abigail. Abigail stated that it was her coming out process during her first year of seminary that enabled her to move toward a call to engage in social justice ministries. Abigail said that she had done a yearlong internship with a battered women's program as a chaplain during seminary, which together with her coming out process led to her interest in social justice–type ministries.

> Um I think my awakening to orientation and sexual identity set me in that direction.

Thus, Abigail's call to do social justice ministries was marked by her multiple ministry roles: in working with battered women, in becoming a social worker, in working as a hospice chaplain, in working as an associate minister of social justice in a progressive congregation.

Stage 6: Spiritual Identity Stage

A second stage of optional spiritual identity seemed to occur for the women who leave professional ministry for a period of time or permanently. Only two women (Naomi and Mary) in the sample entered into this development stage. The women in this spiritual identity stage had contemplated leaving the institutionalized church over a period of time. They had experienced prolonged homophobia as well.

This stage of spiritual identity functioned as an alternative to church involvement, while at the same time allowed these women to make meaning out of their desire to maintain a connection to God. Thus, this spiritual identity stage (stage 6) was similar to the first spiritual identity stage (stage 2) in that it was optional. It also appeared each time as a placeholder for women who desired a connection with what was sacred when a church connection no longer seemed to function for them. The significant difference in this spiritual identity stage from the first one was that, although these two women have left or anticipate leaving ministry for a time, they still articulated having a religious identity that was specifically Christian. In addition, there were differences between the two spiritual identity stages as far as placement along the developmental journey: the first occurring prior to ordination and the second occurring after ordination. Lastly, this second stage of spiritual identity was not supported by the homosexual developmental or religious developmental literatures.

At the point that the interviews were conducted, it was unclear whether Naomi and Mary would remain in this spiritual identity stage and return to professional ministry. It was also unknown if any of the other women in the sample would enter into this stage. However, at the point of the interviews, the stories of the other eleven women did not point in the direction of this stage. The ages of the women in this stage ranged from thirty-five to forty-eight and therefore could represent the terminal stage in this lesbian clergy logic model for these two women. This stage followed the clergy identity (stage 5). Thus, it appeared that Naomi and Mary might remain at this stage unless at a future point they returned to the clergy identity (stage 5).

In terms of the developmental tasks of this stage, the women may demit (i.e., give up their ordination status) from their denominations and (or) leave the institutionalized church, given their involvement in careers that perform LGBTQ advocacy (e.g., writing and counseling) outside of the church. Furthermore, these two women developed a spiritual identity (stage 6), providing an alternative to their clergy identities (stage 5). This spiritual identity stage was manifested by their utilization of a mix of Christian and alternative spiritual resources in their professional work.

Developing Spiritual Identity When Leaving Clergy Identity

The two women (Naomi and Mary) who were in this stage stated that they needed to leave professional ministry for an indefinite period of time. It appeared that a mix of chronic health, mental health, and denominational homophobic oppression experiences might have been factors in moving these two women outside the boundaries of professional ministry. Developmentally, Mary had experienced multiple periods of spiritual identity, which had functioned as placeholders in between periods of leaving her church attendance. On the other hand, Naomi has never left the church before. Unlike Mary, she denies that she had never experienced homophobic oppression from her denomination, but her experience of homophobic oppression was more internalized than Mary's, which was marked extensive congregational and denominational tension.

Like Mary, Naomi had an insight during the interview that she actually may have experienced an earlier spiritual identity, which she had not recognized during her twenties and thirties and had used to repress her lesbian identity. Like Mary, Naomi recognized that the repression of her lesbian identity for so many years was at a great expense to her health, causing depression and autoimmune issues to emerge. Finally, Naomi's experience may be similar to the experience of Mary, in which she decided to leave her clergy identity for a time. Both Naomi and Mary continued to ponder at the time of the interview if they would leave the institutionalized church for a time, in addition to their clergy identities (stage 5).

At the time of the interview, Mary was completing her master's in pastoral counseling. She appeared, like Naomi, to be ambivalent about wanting to remain in ministry. Naomi still, at the time of her interview, maintained her denominational identity, but Mary had demitted (or withdrawn officially) from her denominational identity. However, like Naomi, Mary wanted to remain connected to a religious identity but not a clergy identity.

Naomi. Naomi made little mention of having a spiritual identity during her interview, until the end when she alluded to leaving ministry in the near future. However, upon more probing, Naomi reflected that possibly she had a realization that she had utilized a spiritual identity to repress her sexual identity, until she came out as a lesbian in her forties. Toward the end of the interview, Naomi spoke about her plan to take a break from her lifelong church life, or at the least her clergy life. Within six weeks of the interview, she was planning to move to a new region of the United Stated and get married for the first time to a woman. Naomi was uncertain that she would be able to practice as a minister when she moved because that region of her denomination was quite homophobic. Thus, in talking about her transition to being married to her fiancée and her move to a new region of the country, Naomi relied more on spiritual language than religious images in this part of her interview. During her time off from ministry, she planned to author non-church articles, in addition to the church blogging and articles that she currently did.

> But, um, at this point what I am thinking, I'm going to take three months and I'm going to do some writing that isn't for church work. I do a lot of writing. I'll do some writing that isn't for church. I." Use it as a sabbatical time. It seems where God is; there the Spirit is matching mine.

Mary. In spite of and perhaps because of her mental health and self-esteem issues, Mary had resolved at the point of the interview to be open about her sexual identity with whomever she encountered professionally. Rather than identify as a clergywoman, Mary had decided that her new ministry call would be outside of the institutionalized church and focus on seeking ways to create safety in church for members of the gay and lesbian community. Mary's plan was to establish through her pastoral counseling practice a specialty in gay and lesbian issues.

Despite her new goals for ongoing LGBTQ work outside of ministry, Mary appeared to be ambivalent about leaving the institutionalized church. Here, both her anger and grief about leaving her clergy identity are evident.

> Just incredibly, incredibly depressed. It's really kind of taken a major toll on me. And you know, I've left the church for a while. And then I say, "What do I do with myself as a spiritual being?" You know, so it's a detached plan. It's a dilemma.

STAGE 7: SYNTHESIZED IDENTITY

The women who have achieved this stage of synthesized identity have maintained their foundational denominational and religious identities while at the same time transcending beyond them. There were eight women who achieved this final stage of lesbian clergy development. The youngest woman was thirty-five, and the oldest woman was sixty-two.

The majority of the women (Hannah, Esther, Abigail, Martha, Ruth, Rachel, Leah, and Deborah) appeared to have reached a synthesized identity of lesbian clergy development. Five of the women (Rebecca, Eve, Sarah, Naomi, and Mary) have not reached this synthesized identity stage. Two of the women dropped out of ministry (Naomi and Mary), and three of the women (Rebecca, Sarah, and Eve) are too new in ministry to have achieved this stage.

It appears from the interviews that the progression of the women to this synthesized identity stage was enabled by their ability to find new meaning in their homophobic oppression. Rather than be embittered by their experiences, they have found the ability to focus their ministries on the marginalized populations. They also appear to have found freedom in being in a minority position of being fully out lesbian clergy in their denominations. In the freedom, they have found the ability to more fully express controversial opinions without fear of being censored and to break the denominational policies if they believe they are unjust.

The characteristics of the women in this stage were: they gave more allegiance to their religious identities than their denominational identities; they accepted that there is truth in all the previous religious identity stages but that there was also a sense of mystery and paradox in religion and spirituality. The phases of this stage of development were to incorporate nontraditional spiritual practices into their ministerial practice (e.g., yoga, meditation) and focus on the following social justice work (i.e., hunger, racial injustices) at the congregational and (or) denominational levels: LGBTQ advocacy and inclusion in their denomination and society; and an emphasis on universal love for society, rather than on individual concerns.

Reduced Allegiance to their Denominational Identities

For Hannah, Esther, Abigail, and Deborah, their denominational identities have come to mean less than they formerly did. In contrast to these three women, Sarah and Eve, who have not yet achieved this stage of development, remain very tied to their denominational identities because they are newer in ministry. For Esther and Hannah, their experiences of the denominational rejection of their ordinations and the denominational refusal to install them has functioned to drive them towards a deeper religious identity, rather than a denominational identity. For Deborah, her experience of the judicial (denomination) appeal of her installation has also driven her toward a deeper religious identity. Unlike Esther, Hannah, and Abigail, Deborah was installed in her denomination, but then it was later appealed to a higher judicatory. Esther, Hannah, and Abigail were ordained by different denominations than the ones in which they were currently serving, therefore allowing them more latitude in making bolder statements about their experiences of homophobic oppression and about other LGBTQ congregational ministries in which they were engaged. Some examples of increased allegiance to their religious identities were as follows: putting LGBTQ issues before the denomination; defying denominational regulations in performing marriages of same-sex couples; writing articles and books on LGBTQ inclusion; leading workshops on LGBTQ inclusion; and believing in transformative justice that goes beyond any one denomination.

Esther. For Esther, the experience of being an out lesbian minister in a denomination that refused to ordain her freed her to take risks in her ministry. Here, Esther sarcastically cited her home denomination's culture of sameness that was intolerant of gays and lesbians in active church leadership. This experience of serving an open and affirming church in a denomination that refused to ordain her has enabled her to maintain a bold proclamation in her identity as a lesbian minister within her home denomination in order to push the LGBTQ issue forward. This experience of serving an open and affirming church in a denomination that refused to ordain her has enabled her to become more outspoken about making changes regarding LGBTQ and other social justice issues. In other words, Esther maintains a bold proclamation in her identity as a lesbian minister within her home denominations in order to push the LGBTQ issue forward.

Hannah. As Hannah told her story of denominational oppression by her denomination, she connected her feelings to her experiences of heteronormative oppression by her home church. Thus, Hannah has the ability to see God's transformative powers beyond her current denominational affiliations, such as the ministry of the food pantry at her church, which serves eight hundred persons per week.

> The only problem is with the—I would say the church, really just the church, fits into a one minister full-time job. But the hunger program—I mean we have 800 people coming every Thursday.

Hannah remembered that she knew in high school the difference between her religious identity and her denominational identity. However, Hannah stated that the importance of these social justice ministries trump her anger toward her denomination. In other words, Hannah has reframed her anger at her denomination for its unwillingness to ordain or install her into a righteous anger that she directs into making denominational and societal changes.

Abigail. Like Esther and Hannah, Abigail served in an open and affirming congregation in a denomination that maintains homophobic policies about ordination of clergy. Like Esther and Hannah, as well as Deborah, Abigail has found freedom in being fully out in a homophobic denomination. Here, Abigail demonstrated how this freedom has afforded her the ability to do exciting programs in her congregation around social justice, such as a healing worship for LGBTQ persons and a summer camp for LGBTQ youth. In this passage, Abigail described with emotion that joy of leading worship to victims of oppression in her congregation.

> And just doing the liturgy yesterday stirred my gut, you know, that I haven't felt in a long time. And I don't feel closeted or oppressed, but to be speaking those words in front of our community and to be hearing my brothers and sisters speak their pain.

Deborah. Deborah reaffirmed her Christian identity and call to ministry as reasons for her tolerance of oppression in her denomination. She spoke about her religious identity providing her with the ability to tolerate the ambiguity regarding the future of her current employment, given the current judicatory appeal regarding her installation and given her ability to emotionally tolerate the oppression. Here, Deborah implied that she was not worried about her future in ministry, given the fact that her religious identity was more important than her denominational affiliation.

> It may, it may be me, I don't [pause]. I don't know, I just [pause] you know, just [pause], God is creative, you know. Yeah, yeah … and I say that if God has this congregation for me then it'll happen. So I'm not even worried about it.

THE COMINGLING OF SPIRITUAL AND RELIGIOUS IDENTITIES

Three of the women in the sample have what they refer to as comingled spiritual and religious identities. These women have integrated their spiritual practice into their synthesized identity through the addition of other spiritual practices. These faith practices range from Buddhism to Franciscan Catholicism to Jewish practices, which they believe enhances their Christian faith practice. For instance, Rachel uses her Jewish faith practices in her chaplaincy work. Leah, Martha, and Ruth were all raised as Roman Catholics and have integrated the early church mystical practices into their ministries. Abigail has introduced spiritual practices from Buddhism into her Christian daily rituals.

Abigail. Abigail uses faith practices borrowed from Buddhism, such as meditation and guided imagery, in her pastoral counseling work and in her work with LGBTQ individuals both in her church and in hospital settings.

> I tried some different things and I finally decided on guided imagery with this group because you could use guided imagery in a way that was welcoming of all faiths.

Leah. Leah described her ministry as a mix of spiritual and religious identities. In addition, her religious identities included a mix of Protestant intellect and Roman Catholic contemplative practices. Here, Leah has found a way to integrate her spiritual gift of mysticism into her practice of professional ministry.

> So I feel now that I have a lot of liturgical, sacramental, and spiritual, natural, super-natural, you know, all-encompassing Spirituality. You know, when I hear people say "I'm spiritual but not religious" I understand that. And when I hear people say "I'm religious, but I think 'spiritual' is a bunch of who ha or wo-wo" or whatever, I understand where they are coming from too.

Martha. Like Abigail and Leah, Martha's lesbian clergy identity has synthesized her Franciscan and Protestant theologies. Martha consistently does not view Franciscan tenets to be divergent from her views. Martha was ordained in 2000 and continued to explore the integration of Francis's Rule of Life into her denominational theology. She stated that her belief in the Rule of Life was really more her daily spiritual practice and was compatible with her denominational beliefs.

> Really, I think really it would be a Franciscan; it would be more, more Franciscan than [name of denomination]. Although, I think they're intertwined. Cause, I still have that conservative, you know, Rule of Life, disciple in kind of stuff. It could be my age too. You know …

Rachel. Rachel's identity as a multi-faith chaplain at the hospital where she works speaks to her synthesized identity as a lesbian minister. Her understandings of the teaching of both Christianity and Judaism were important to her in her work as a chaplain. Simultaneously, Rachel maintained her pastoral work at her congregation as a minister, holding religious identities as a Jew and as a Christian. In her religious practices, she utilizes nonreligious spiritual practices such as prayer and meditation. From a Christian perspective, she uses prayer and other rituals of the church. From a Jewish perspective, she utilizes the practice of reading from the Jewish prayer book in Hebrew.

> And actually, umm … for me, and this is one thing that I have talked to the leadership of the [names denomination] about this, I do not identify myself as a [names denomination] chaplain. I define myself as a multi-faith chaplain. Umm, and … [voice trails off] …

Rachel also described the manifestation of her synthesized identity as a multi-faith chaplain in her book. Rachel's book is on pastoral care with death and dying issues in a hospital setting.

> And, and I should send you the chapter of this book I wrote about my theology. Its, it's a book for pastoral care umm, of about when I am with someone, I am really of a duel mind. And duel heart because while that person maybe Jewish I'm still; while I may be helping them, do

verbalize their own religion and their own belief system. It has not [speaking slowly and deliberately] my belief system has gotten broad enough that I can welcome that.

Emphasis on Universal Love for Community

Deborah, Ruth, Hannah, and Esther all reported a heightened spiritual health that enabled them to transcend the rules of their own denominations for the sake of healing those who are marginalized. According to these women, the importance of rising up about one's own denominational wars was necessary for the purpose of healing the denominational splits around the LGBTQ issues. Further, it was for the purpose of creating inclusivity for the LGBTQ community in the church as a whole. Unlike Deborah, Ruth, Hannah, and Esther have not been installed by their denominations due to homophobic policies that are preventing that process from occurring. However, in a similar manner to Deborah, Ruth, Hannah, and Esther believe that they have little to lose in continuing to push the LGBTQ inclusion agenda forward in their denominations. Ruth, Hannah, and Esther are out in their denominations and have continued their congregational ministries without reprisal from their denominations.

Deborah. Deborah was an exemplar in her denomination as the only out lesbian in the study who was installed into her congregational ministry. However, this is not without the price of ongoing homophobic legislative appeals from other parts of her denomination. Thus, Deborah perceives that she has little to lose but to follow her divine call to continue pushing the LGBTQ agenda forward in her denomination. During the interview, Deborah stated repeatedly that she personally struggled to understand how others within the church could stop someone else from "experiencing God's greatness." Here, Deborah spoke about her calling as a lesbian minister to bring LGBTQ youth into an understanding that they can be a part of the church.

> What I had noticed was that because the broader sys ... the broader society had this view of gays and lesbians and pushed that community into, like I call it the darkness, um, into the shadows? And in the, the in this darkness,

and in the shadows, you have young children—younger than me, because I didn't come into my own sexual identity till I was almost an adult, I was just not even thinking about anything like that, um, but you have these young children who going through puberty—are going through puberty in these shadows. Yes, and they're aware that there are gays and lesbians and they are growing up in the shadows and some of them have gay and lesbian parents, and are growing up in the shadows still, because their parents are also in the closet. So, you have, have, so, you have these children growing up without any sense of viewing your body as a temple, any sense of recognizing the image of God in another person, so it's object-to-object interfacing in a moment.

Ruth. Clergy in Ruth's denomination were disallowed to perform same-sex marriages because of the "Peace, Unity, and Purity Report." This 2011 denominational report had asked the entire denomination to enter into a season of mutual forbearance and to prevent churches to cease from prosecution. Ruth had taken a justice stance and, at the time of the interview, performed two same-sex weddings, despite the denominational legislation.

> I will tell you, um, is that I have performed two same-sex weddings. Um, I have not told my [church council] about that. It doesn't feel great, but it feels like I'm kind of willing to go out on a limb. Um, it just feels like a justice issue for me. I mean, I'm not going to say no to somebody who wants to get married, you know.

Hannah. Hannah remained a copastor in what she believes is an exciting spirit-filled and growing ministry. It appeared that Hannah had the ability to tolerate what some might consider a homophobic denomination, in order to have the opportunity to live out her call as a minister in a dynamic congregational setting that lives it life without interference from its parent denomination.

You know, one of the most vibrant, let's say. Or one of the places where things are actually happening [in the denominational judicatory]. And so I don't think they want to squash that. But at the same time, there are some people that are really, um [critical of me].

Esther. Finally, Esther spoke with anger and sarcasm about her ongoing experience of homophobic oppression in her denomination. Yet here in the beginning of the quote was the real Esther in that it reflected her call to do LGBTQ advocacy and ministry in the church, despite her experiences of oppression. For Esther, the meaning derived from her experience of oppression drove her to heal others, despite the risk of cutoff from her denominational affiliations. At this point along Esther's lesbian clergy journey, her call is to heal homophobic oppression in the church.

But even if I wasn't. Even if I wasn't safe. Even if I was in the [names denomination of birth], I'd bring it out—like you know—so they could take away my church? Ya know like, do me a favor, and shut down that soup kitchen— that would be delightful! Like oh Ill go on a vacation! You want to send me back to being a—wall streeter? Ok! That's not a problem! Just get off my back! But I mean granted, I wouldn't do that [pause].

SUMMARY

The results of this qualitative study of thirteen lesbians were descriptive of the women's respective journeys toward becoming clergy. Each of the women came from the sampling population of one of the four Protestant mainline denominations. The investigator found that the journeys of the women could best be detailed in a stage theory of lesbian clergy development. The stage theory involved seven sequential stages that were less tied to age and instead tied to developmental tasks. The exceptions were the second and sixth stages, which were spiritual identity stages, which all thirteen women did not pass through. The stages were as follows: (1) an early religious identity; (2) an optional spiritual identity; (3) an emerging lesbian identity; (4) a revised religious identity that included space for the lesbian identity; (5) clergy identity from seminary training, through ordination, through ministerial positions; (6) an optional spiritual identity; and (7) a synthesized identity that integrates the religious, sexual, and spiritual identities into the clergy identity.

Only one of the women, Mary, had been in all seven stages. Seven of the women, who had left their early religious identities due to their experiences of both heteronormative and male-normative oppression, developed spiritual identities for a minimum period of a decade. The function of this period was to provide for these women a non-religiously based community. In other words, it became a community free of judgment for these seven women to come out. The second stage of spiritual identity functioned for the two women who left either permanently or for an interim from the clergy profession. The six women who did not enter into this first stage of spiritual identity (stage 2) were able to complete their developmental tasks of differentiating from the literal religious ideas of their childhoods and were able to come out as lesbians while still maintaining their religious identities. In contrast, this second group of women who entered into the second stage of spiritual identity (stage 6) had continued to experience ongoing psychological and physical issues, which they attributed to the prolonged homophobia that they had experienced while working as ordained clergy in their respective denominations. The two women in this second group of women continued to state that they had Christian identities but that they could not serve in ministerial jobs at the time of the interview. This sixth stage became the terminal stage for these two women.

All thirteen of the women were a part of the early religious identity stage, which was both formative and oppressive for each of the women. The women experienced the oppression in varying degrees: there were two women who remained in not only their early religious identities, but the same denominational identities throughout their lives. In addition, there were seven women who, as cited above, had experienced such significant levels of homophobic oppression that they exited their religious identities to enter into the spiritual identity stage (stage 2). Finally, there were five women who exited their denominational identities to enter into new ones, but who maintained their religious identities lifelong. The two women who remained in their denominations of birth were most able to tolerate their experiences of oppression because it appeared that their strong denominational/family identities ameliorated the pain from the institutional oppression they experienced.

All thirteen of the women came out as lesbians between the ages of thirteen and forty-eight. The lesbian identity stage overlapped with the first spiritual identity stage (stage 2) for the seven women who had left their religious identities and with the early religious identity stage (stage 1) for the six women who remained, during their coming out processes. The three major findings pertaining to the sexual identity stage of development were: (1) with the exception of one woman (Naomi), no matter what age the women came out, their early religious identities preceded their sexual identities; (2) for seven of the women, they perceived that their coming out ages were delayed by their experiences of their early religious identities (Ruth, Hannah, Eve, Martha, Rebecca, Naomi, and Leah); and (3) the coming out age was influenced by the interplay of each woman's unique experiences of fit and oppression. For example, the higher age of coming out appeared to correspond to their experiences of poor fit with partners, families of origin, and (or) faith communities.

In contrast, Deborah and Mary were exemplars of not reporting a delayed coming out and came out in the spiritual identity stage (stage 2), presumably because they had multiple religious identity experiences of homophobic and male normative oppression. Further, Ruth and Naomi remained in their religious identities when they came out during seminary and after ordination, respectively. Whereas Hannah, Eve, Martha, Rebecca, and Leah came out when they were in their spiritual identity stage (stage 2).

In this sample, all thirteen women revised their religious (stage 4) beliefs to incorporate their lesbian identities before moving onto their clergy identities (stage 5). This task of revising their religious identities appeared to be true for all thirteen of the women. The revised religious identity stage functioned for the women who had not left their early religious identities (stage 1) in giving them permission to be both lesbian and Christian simultaneously, as well as those who did leave their early religious identities to enter into their spiritual identities (stage 2). In fact, this revised religious identity (stage 4) stage appeared to have a pre-contemplative function for the women exploring a future of training as ministers (stage 5).

All thirteen of the women in the sample entered into the clergy identity stage as well. However, for three (Eve, Rebecca, and Sarah) of the women in the sample, this clergy identity was the terminal stage. An interesting finding relates to the age of experiencing a call to ministry; seven of the women cited being called in childhood and that it was realized only after they came out, and six of the women cited being called in adulthood. All but two of the women (Deborah and Rachel) perceived that both their calls and coming out processes had been delayed due to their internalized early religious ideas that supported straight male leadership in churches. Another significant finding was that the multiple themes of oppression in becoming clergy and being clergy were evidenced in the narratives of the women's lived experiences. It appeared that the lesbian clergy in the discriminated out-group of their denominations that have been victimized by denominational heteronormative oppression also became change agents. The reason that the eleven women who remained clergy at the time of the interviews remained in their denominations despite institutional oppression was their stated commitment to remaining within their oppressive denominations for the purpose of creating change. These women stated that they were committed to creating LGBTQ inclusion in their denominations in the years ahead.

Finally, eight women in this terminal stage of lesbian clergy development were able to achieve a clergy identity that synthesized fully their religious, sexual, and spiritual selves. The eight women in the sample who entered into the synthesized identity stage were the women who were able for various (e.g., supportive families of origin, intact partner/spouse relationship, strong goodness of fit in congregation or organization, involvement in LGBTQ advocacy work) reasons to find new meaning in being a part of the marginalized out-group of their denominations.

What appeared to enable these women to achieve this stage was their ability to move beyond their wounds of oppression, due to their strong commitment to their clergy calls, which functioned to enable them to seek justice in an unfair and violent world. In this final stage, these women who achieved this final stage of development were able to reframe their wounds resulting from homophobic oppression into redemptive ways of healing other wounded individuals living at the margins of society.

All but five of the women in the sample achieved the seventh and final synthesized identity stage. Two of the women dropped out of ministry due to an inability to tolerate ongoing homophobic experiences by their denominations. Three of the women are too new in ministry to have achieved this level of integration of their spiritual, religious, and sexual identities in a manner that they can transcend denominational rules.

It is in this seventh stage that eight of the women, despite ongoing experiences of heteronormative oppression, remain committed to LGBTQ inclusion and justice in their denominations and the church at large. Finally, in terms of developmental progression, time will tell whether Rebecca, Eve, and Sarah will eventually reach this stage on their developmental journeys to be lesbian clergy. Eve and Sarah seemed to have the ability to move to this final stage as they matured in ministry. Like Hannah, Esther, Abigail, Martha, Ruth, Rachel, Leah, and Deborah, Eve and Sarah were denominationally anchored and had supportive congregations and partners but were involved in social justice ministries that surpassed their denominational bounds.

CHAPTER 5

DISCUSSION AND IMPLICATIONS

OVERVIEW OF STAGE FINDINGS

This study examines the perceptions that the lesbian clergy have of their many identities, providing insight into their journey toward integration of their religious, sexual, and spiritual self-identities. It explores the interplay between their experiences as lesbian clergy through the lens of ecological theory (Gitterman and Germain 2008) and homophobic oppression concepts (Dominelli 2002). Utilizing a qualitative approach, this study contributes to the social work literature through extended interviewing of eleven lesbian clergy and two seminarians from four denominations. Further, this study explores their progress in achieving an integration and reconciliation of their religious, sexual, spiritual, and clergy social identities (Tajfel and Turner 1979). It serves as an academic exercise in theoretically understanding their journey, as well as a social justice commentary on the oppression they suffered as a result of prejudice and misunderstanding within their religious institutions. As such, the study blends social theory (ecological, anti-oppressive, and social identity theory) with Christian theology, exploring the research participants' experiences of denominational and congregational heteronormative policies and beliefs within the context of their ongoing experiences of oppression and how they found or did not find ecological fit (Bronfenbrenner 1979; Gitterman and Germain 2008) within their families, congregations, and denominations.

STAGES OF THE JOURNEY

In reviewing the narratives, the author found that the women shared a similar journey in terms of the sequence of their spiritual and professional development. Each of these women moved through these various stages of identities in a sequential manner. Thus, one stage of identity gave rise to another identity, all within the context of environmental and personality factors. Movement through the continuum was driven primarily by the growing awareness of their lack of fit with the restraints of their conservative upbringing. In essence, movement from one identity stage to another identify stage was defined by the following: 1) the awareness of a lack of fit and experiences of oppression; and 2) the individual's emotional ability to individuate and to define herself during a life crisis—that is, how she was able to maintain her sense of worth and self while navigating her way through various denominational affiliations.

Seven unique stages were identified: (1) each woman began her journey having internalized the conservative religious identities born out of the homophobic policies of her individual denomination of childhood; (2) after the early religious identities, many (but not all) of the women experienced a stage of strong spiritual development in adolescence or early adulthood, adopting a sense of spiritualism that lay outside the orthodox teachings of their denominations; (3) following their self-identification as being spiritual, their sexual identity as lesbians or as bisexuals emerged; (4) after the women came out to themselves and to others as lesbians, the women went through a stage in which their religious identities became integrated with their sexual identities; (5) the women were able to recognize their calls to ministry as a religious formation process and went through their processes of seminary training, ordination, and employment; (6) for the women who left the ministry, there was an interim temporary or permanent stage in which spiritual identity became primary; and (7) after becoming ordained clergy, some of the women appear to have moved toward an integration of their spiritual, religious, and clergy identities within a context of lesbianism. While their spiritual identity remained constant, it is important to note that their denominational identities changed at various developmental stages: generally before and during the coming out process; at the point of reworking their religious identities; during seminary; during the ordination process; and (or) during the employment process after ordination.

In summary, the five major findings pertaining to this lesbian clergy identity development, which are detailed below, were: (1) with the exception of one woman (Naomi), no matter what age the women came out, their early religious identities preceded their sexual identities; (2) the first spiritual identity stage was a replacement for church for the women who had left their religious identities and a place to come out with the perception of less guilt; (3) for seven of the women, they perceived that their coming out ages were delayed by their experiences of their early religious identities (Ruth, Hannah, Eve, Martha, Rebecca, Naomi, and Leah); (4) the coming out age was influenced by the interplay of each woman's unique experiences of fit and oppression; (5) the ability to go to seminary and become ordained was preceded by a reconciliation of their religious and sexual identities; (6) the second spiritual stage was again a replacement for church for the two (Naomi and Mary) who left church due to their ongoing experiences of institutional oppression; and (7) the highest level of functioning for clergy is marked by being out to their denominations and by involvement in social justice work.

STAGE 1: IMPACT OF EARLY RELIGIOUS IDENTITIES

Each of the women had an early formative and conservative religious identity, which generally delayed their coming out as lesbians and ministerial call processes. However, despite ongoing regional antifeminist and heteronormative attitudes, and in some cases homophobic policies, all thirteen of the lesbians eventually developed clergy identities. Indeed, each of the women experienced their early religious identities as a *critical developmental task* leading to the formation of their clergy identities. Although the women in the sample experienced various levels of homophobic and male normative oppression during their childhoods or adolescence, nonetheless, they were also able to negotiate each of the developmental stages toward integration of their identities. However, the degree of oppression and lack of fit for the women did affect their rate of progress, with levels of oppression directly affecting the age of the participants when they came out as lesbians and when they were called to the ministry. In particular, those women who reported high levels of fit with their families of origin, partners, congregations, and institutional employers were best able to manage the homophobic oppressions of their denominations during their ministerial formation process and ministerial years. Conversely, those women with higher levels of homophobic oppression during their ministerial formation processes reported extraordinary struggles in becoming ordained. The scale to which the women perceived their oppression was found to correspond to their response to their early religious identities, in acceptance, accommodation, or in rejection (see Dominelli 2002).

Stage 2: Spiritual Identity

One of the important findings of the study is that not all the women went through a spiritual identity stage. Even if they did, the development of a spiritual identity came at varying times in their journey. Participants could be classified as falling in one or more of four categories: (1) those who did not experience a spiritual identity stage at all along their journeys; (2) those who experienced a spiritual identity stage before ordination (stage 2); (3) those who experienced a spiritual identity stage after ordination (stage 6); and (4) those who comingled spiritual and religious identities after ordination (stage 7).

The spiritual identity stage appeared to function as a placeholder for six of the women (Deborah, Mary, Rebecca, Eve, Hannah, Martha, and Leah). They entered into a spiritual identity stage after they had rejected their early religious identities as a result of the incongruities between their growing awareness of their sexual orientations and the policies of their birth denominations. This finding supports the research of Knight and Hoffman (2007) that showed lesbians needing a period of spiritual identity in order to "maintain a type of personalized religion without having to deal with organized religion" (p. 17). This identity stage became also an organizing theme for their later stage-specific behaviors, particularly as they returned to a revised religious identity (stage 4). At the end of this spiritual identity stage, it was interesting to note that these women reengaged in a Christian congregation.

In contrast to the six women listed above in the sample, Esther, Sarah, Naomi, Abigail, Ruth, and Rachel did not report needing a period of spiritual identity in order to come out or to heal from experiences of oppression. This group of seven women instead developed not a distinct spiritual identity but rather a set of *spiritual practices* that enhanced their denominational ministerial practices. Esther stated emphatically that it was her spiritual practices that enabled her to withstand the homophobic oppressions of her denomination. All seven women were able to remain in their Christian congregations while they came out.

Stage 3: Sexual Identity

The women during the sexual identity stage were characterized by the questioning of their literal belief structures (Fowler 1981; Park 1986) and by their struggles to adjust their religious beliefs to accommodate their emerging same-sex attractions. In addition, the women in this third stage of developing their sexual identity began to: 1) internally accept their lesbian identities; 2) engage in their first lesbian relationships; and 3) negotiate with their desire to maintain themselves within their religious or denominational communities. For the majority (seven) of the women, staying within their early religious identities was difficult during their coming out processes. There was a questioning of and differentiating from their religious authority structures, while they simultaneously became aware of their same-sex attraction during this emerging sexual identity stage.

Seven of the participants (Naomi, Ruth, Martha, Eve, Rebecca, Hannah, and Leah) were examples of women whose coming out processes were delayed because of their early religious identities. The women in this group came out in the age ranges of thirty-one to forty-eight, as compared to the remaining women in the sample who came out in the age ranges of sixteen to twenty-six. Of these seven women, Naomi, Ruth, and Martha's coming out and calls to ministry were most problematic, with each struggling into middle age with what they thought were mutually exclusive lesbian and Christian identities. Although they came out before they acted on their calls to ministry, it seems that they had been struggling with both identity streams for decades.

It is worth noting that although the remaining six women experienced significant homophobic oppression in their childhood churches and (or) by their families of origin, they were still able to come out in their twenties. For this group of women, coming out in their twenties seemed possible due to their unique mix of high fit and their high capacity to differentiate, which in turn appeared to ameliorate their experiences of oppression. In order for the women to come out when they did, it was found to be most significant that they demonstrated the ability to question the authority structures of their early religious identities and then formulate their own beliefs about the interplay of religious and sexual identities. Although all but Rachel reported significant experiences of oppression during their coming out processes, their experiences of fit seemed to push them to come out.

STAGE 4: REVISED RELIGIOUS IDENTITY

This fourth stage appeared to be a necessary developmental step after the sexual identity (stage 3) and before the clergy identity (stage 5). There was a wide age range, between the ages of twenty-one and fifty-two, of the women in this revised religious identity stage. The variation in ages of the women in this sample also correlates with the ages of coming out and the ages of call to ministry.

Characteristically, at the beginning of this fourth stage, the women were experiencing a void because of their perceptions that as lesbians they could not fully be a part of a faith community. As a result of this expressed emptiness, toward the end of this fourth stage, the women sought to reengage in faith communities that were LGBTQ affirming. Thus, the major task of this developmental stage was for the women to integrate their lesbian identities into their religious identities. For the women who had also formed stage 2 spiritual identities, they also needed to be integrated into their revised religious identities. All but three of the women (Rachel, Deborah, and Mary) in the sample stated that they struggled tremendously with a split between having a Christian religious identity and a lesbian sexual identity. The remaining nine women (Hannah, Leah, Martha, Rebecca, Esther, Rachel, Ruth, Naomi, Abigail, and Sarah) began to mend their internal splits between their religious and sexual identities during this revised religious identity stage. The four reconciliation themes that emerged between stages 3 (sexual identity) and 4 (clergy identity) included the following: (1) those women who did not experience a split between their religious and sexual identities; (2) those who were able to heal the split between religious and sexual identities; (3) those who experienced extended struggles with their continued perceptions that religious and lesbianism identities were mutually exclusive; and (4) those who intentionally sought a faith community that allowed them to achieve both identities.

A significant finding is that in order for the women in this sample to move into the clergy identity stage (stage 5), they had to successfully complete this revised religious stage. By the end of stage 4, the women no longer believe that their religious and sexual identities are mutually exclusive. The groups of women who eventually came out of the spiritual identity stage and (or) the early religious identity stage utilized the revised religious identity stage to go through a process of reconciling their religious and sexual identities. Therefore, the revised religious identities ameliorated the women's experiences of denominational oppression as lesbians. In other words, the women were able to claim the identity as lesbian Christians and consequently were more able to withstand experiences of congregational and denominational oppression. Importantly, this revised religious identity stage had a precontemplative function for the women considering professional ministry as a career.

STAGE 5: CLERGY IDENTITY STAGE

The completion of this integration process in the revised religious identity stage allowed the women's latent calls to ministry to reemerge from early stages. Some of the women reflected that their calls to ministry came during their early religious identities (stage 1) but that they were repressed because of the conservative theological contexts that they were raised in. Other women in the sample reflected that their calls came during their spiritual identities (stage 3) or their revised religious identities (stage 4). Their calls emerged from a deeper sense of wanting to do social justice work or to embrace a life with spiritual ideals. There was a wide age range in this clergy identity stage due to the various ages that the women came out as lesbians and worked toward the integration of their religious and sexual identities. This fifth stage followed the revised religious identity (stage 4) stages, where all thirteen women in the sample were able to successfully integrate their sexual and religious identities.

Characteristically at the beginning of this fifth stage, the women intuited that their lives would remain unfulfilled if they did not become ministers. Thus, during this stage, the women initially contemplated calls to ministry. Their tasks included enrolling at a seminary and completing their ministerial training processes, which ended in ordination. This task also included the ministerial roles that women lived in toward the end of this stage.

The six themes that emerged as the women were forming their clergy identities were the following: (1) experience of enrolling in seminary before coming out; (2) the lived experience of being called in childhood; (3) the lived experience of being called in adulthood; (4) the lived experiences of ministerial oppression; (5) the lived experiences of finding a niche in ministry; and (6) the importance of being out in ministry.

STAGE 6: SECOND STAGE OF SPIRITUAL IDENTITY

A second phase of spiritual identity seemed to occur for the women who left professional ministry for a period of time or permanently. Only two women (Naomi and Mary) in the sample entered into this development stage. The women in this spiritual identity stage had contemplated leaving the institutionalized church over a period of time, likely due to the experience of prolonged homophobia.

This phase of spiritual identity functioned as an alternative to church involvement, while at the same time allowing these women to make meaning out of their desire to maintain a connection to God. Thus, this spiritual identity stage (stage 6) was similar to the first spiritual identity stage (stage 2) in that it was not a mandatory step. It also appeared each time as a placeholder for women who desired to retain a connection with what was sacred to them when their connection with the church no longer seemed functional for them. The significant difference in this spiritual identity stage from the first one was that although these two women left or anticipated leaving ministry for a time, they still articulated having a religious identity, which was specifically Christian. In addition, there were differences between the two spiritual identity stages as far as placement along the developmental journey, the first occurring prior to ordination and the second occurring after ordination.

This second stage (stage 6) of spiritual identity therefore functioned for two women as the terminal stage of their lesbian clergy developmental model. Both Naomi and Mary abandoned (anti-oppressive theory, Dominelli 2002) their denominational affiliations within a decade of being ordained. Both of them no longer claim a clergy identity but do claim a mix of a Christian and general spiritual identity. The spiritual identity appeared to be a mix of Christian, Buddhist, and pagan practices.

STAGE 7: SYNTHESIZED IDENTITY

The women who have achieved this stage of synthesized identity have maintained their foundational denominational and religious identities, while at the same time transcending beyond them. There were eight women who achieved this final stage of lesbian clergy development. The youngest woman was thirty-five, and the oldest woman was sixty-two.

The majority of the women (Hannah, Esther, Abigail, Martha, Ruth, Rachel, Leah, and Deborah) appeared to have reached a synthesized identity of lesbian clergy development. Five of the women (Rebecca, Eve, Sarah, Naomi, and Mary), however, did not. Of these five women, two dropped out of ministry (Naomi and Mary), and three (Rebecca, Sarah, and Eve) were too new in ministry to have achieved this stage.

The eight women who reached the synthesized identity stage had become involved in a minimum of one social justice ministry in either their congregations or communities. These women made meaning out of their own horrific experiences of homophobic oppression, and sometime male normative oppression, by reframing them and instead focusing on the social, economic, religious/spiritual, and sexual injustices around them (e.g., food pantries, youth mentoring, institutional advocacy for LGBTQ inclusion). In contrast, the two women who left ministry reported higher levels of anger and bitterness in response to their experiences of oppression and were less able to focus on needs outside of their own needs for safety.

What appeared to enable these women to achieve this stage was their ability to move beyond their wounds of oppression and soldier on their strong clergy calls to seek justice in an unjust world. In this final stage, the eight women in the sample who achieved this final stage of development were able to reframe their wounds resulting from homophobic oppression into redemptive ways of healing other wounded individuals living at the margins of society. According to social identity (Tajfel and Turner 1979) theory, the lesbian clergy who were in the out-group of their denominations became a part of the resistance that was necessary to effect social change within their denominations (Branscombe and Ellemers 1998; Doosje et al. 1995; Ellemers, Spears, and Doosje 1997; Reicher et al. 1995; Spears et al. 1997, 1999).

THEORETICAL EXPLANATION OF FINDINGS

Alternate Explanations for Resistance to Denominational Oppression

The way in which the women were able to enact social change within their denominations, despite their history of being oppressed by these institutions, is best understood by Roger's (1990) concept of "cold anger." Cold anger is what the lesbian clergy need to make changes within their denominations that continue to uphold heteronormative policies and (or) practice. Roger's book, which integrates community organizing and faith principles, provides an explanation for the women feeling purposeful by remaining in their denominations with the purpose of bringing about LGBTQ policy inclusion changes, despite their experiences of oppression. Finally, the classic Frankl (1946) book, *Man's Search for Meaning*, which is about surviving a concentration camp experience, provides a powerful understanding of the role these women are taking in their denominations in overcoming their institutional oppression. According to Frankl, the way a prisoner imagined the future affected his longevity (having a goal for making meaning out of the reason for their endurance). The concept of making meaning out of their oppression is what these eight women have done to manage and overcome their denominational/institutional oppression. Their strength comes from their ministries with other out-group LGBTQ clergy, as well as marginalized populations both within and outside of the institutionalized church.

SYNTHESIS OF THEORETICAL CONSTRUCTS

For the purposes of this study, lesbian clergy were explored through a synthesis of ecological theory (Bronfenbrenner 1979; Gitterman and Germain 2008), anti-oppressive theory (Dominelli 2002, 2003, 2008), and social identity theory (Tajfel and Turner 1979; Hogg and Abrams 1988; Hogg and Vaughn 2002; Mol 1979; Wellman 1999; Hinrichs 2008), together with the construct of a feminist perspective in theology and in the social sciences. From a social work perspective, ecological theory explores the "fit and social timing of life issues for the lesbian clergy in their families, communities, and churches." Anti-oppressive theory, a feminist theory, also comes out of social work. Anti-oppressive theory explains the ecological context of these women in terms of their interactional patterns that may have led to oppression and helped to shape their identities. Social identity theory, a social science theory, further fleshed out the issues of these women in terms of their religious, sexual, and spiritual identities and whether they are part of an in-group or out-group in the ecological contexts.

Utilizing Bronfenbrenner's (1979) ET and Tajfel and Turner's (1979) SIT, it was argued that lesbian clergy negotiate the systems they live in, as well as the multiple social identities that exist within them, in a more heightened manner than other clergy. This is due to their struggle to define their sexual identities within the context of their already formed religious and spiritual identities. The four denominations that the lesbian PMC clergy sampled in this study live in and the effect of the denominations' theological stances on them have also been explored through social identity theory (Tajfel and Turner 1979). This is discussed below.

ECOLOGICAL THEORY

Throughout the life model of social work practice (Gitterman and Germain 2008), the ecological model (Bronfenbrenner 1979; Gitterman and Germain 2008) emerged as an appropriate foundation for understanding the issues faced by lesbian clergy. This model of human ecology attempts to explain the "level of fit" that individuals have within their various environments (Gitterman and Germain 2008). As this study demonstrated through its use of the ecological model, lesbian clergy who are able to remain within their denominations had an "adaptive level of fit" with one or more of their various environmental contexts (i.e., their families of origin, their partners, their congregations, their denominations, and their communities). Bronfenbrenner (1979) likened this type of ecological system to Russian nesting dolls with concentric circles that explain human development.

Bronfenbrenner (1979) stressed the interactions of a changing organism in a changing environment. In Bronfenbrenner's view, the environment is composed of one's immediate settings as well as the complex social cultural context in which we experience relationships across many different settings. The concentric circles include microsystems (spouses/partners, nuclear families, extended families, schools, religious organizations, congregations), mesosystems (interaction of microsystems), exosystems (local governments, work settings, school boards, denominations), and macrosystems (dominant beliefs and ideologies).

The ecological model particularly lent itself to this qualitative research method because it took into account "social time" and accounted for the "fit" of research participants' in their environment, including fit between themselves and their families of origin, with their partners, with their congregations, and with their denominations. In examining the person-environment fit within these systemic contexts or interactions of various systems on the individuals' developments (Bronfenbrenner 1979), their levels of stress (Gitterman and Germain 2008) as well as their perceptions of their social networks were explored. Among the social networks examined are the complex bureaucratic organizations that the clergy participants were a part of, their personal space boundaries, and finally their perceived status in various groups.

From an ecological perspective, the primary impact of fit was on whether the women were able to come out within the framework of their early religious stage, or because of the incongruities between experience and belief, they essentially utilized the less oppressive belief structure of the spiritual identity phase to support their psychological and spiritual needs so they could come out. Within all women, it appears that it was a lack of fit that led to internal conflict and their recognition of the incongruities between faith and sexuality, often taking years to transition from religious to spiritual identity. The higher age of coming out appeared to correspond to the degree to which they experienced poor fit with partners, families of origin, and (or) faith communities, and as such, the degree of fit served as a moderating variable that either delayed or sped up the process of coming out.

In summary, the early conservative religious identities of the women appeared to have slowed their ability to process their emotions as they moved through the later stages. In other words, some of the women appeared to have had internalized homophobia, which appeared to delay both their coming out processes (stage 3: sexual identity) and call to ministry processes (stage 5: clergy identity). Finally, some of the women appeared to have been delayed in integrating their lesbian Christian religious identities (stage 4: revised religious identity) and understanding that it is possible for them to be at once both a lesbian and a clergyperson (stage 5: clergy identity). The explanation for these slowed processes was found in the way that the women in the sample negotiated their identities through the concepts of adaptation and accommodation.

ANTI-OPPRESSIVE THEORY

The literature on stage theories (Fowler 1981; Park 1986; Troiden 1989; Hinrichs 2009) of religious and sexual development provides some explanation for the women's progression from early religious identity to sexual identity. However, it lacks the ability to demonstrate the perceived conflicts between their religious and sexual identities during coming out processes. In this study, the impact of the perceived conflicts between their religious and sexual identities were also explained by the interplay of their experiences of how well they fit within their environment and the level of oppression they experienced.

The lesbian clergy in this study, in their interactional responses to their denominational stances, can be interpreted and illuminated using a second social work theory, anti-oppressive theory (AOT) (Dominelli 2002). Specifically, AOT provided a framework for understanding the degree to which each of the participants were affected by the oppressive nature of the relationships between the individuals and organizations that they interacted with on an ongoing basis. According to AOT, individuals' identities form through their interactions between people. Thus, in applying this theory to this population, it was initially postulated that these women would have one of three responses to their denomination: (1) acceptance of its theological stance on homosexuality; (2) accommodation to living with the norms and stances of the denomination; or (3) rejection of the denomination and moving onto another denomination and (or) leaving ministry. This was borne out in the findings. It was found that the women who left their early religious identities needed to reject their religious identities in order to come out as lesbians. The age at which they did finally reject their denominations (if they did) and move to alternative churches and (or) religious practices depended a great deal on the support relationships they had in place and their individualized responses to oppression. Fowler's (1981) model of faith development and Park's (1986, 2000) model of spiritual/religious development were applicable in understanding how the women exited from the early religious or spiritual identity stage to the sexual identity stage and then eventually to the clergy identity stage. According to Park, the first stage of faith is "conventional faith," which means that each of these thirteen women were marked by an authority-bound type of faith that they did not question until they were adolescents.

- Examined from an anti-oppressive theoretical perspective, it was the degree to which each participant experienced oppression that determined their trajectory toward integration of their identities. Only two of the women accepted the status quo of their denominations in regard to the LGBTQ ordination policies by remaining within their religious identities. Four of the women failed to reconcile oppressive policies with their religious identities and left their home denominations; the remaining seven of the women rejected their denominational identities by actually shucking their religious identities for a period of time and assuming a substitute spiritual identity (stage 2) that allowed for reconciliation of their faith beliefs with their sexual orientation.

- **Acceptance of Status Quo.** The two women who remained within their childhood denominations were able to do so because of the support of their families of origin, as well as their local congregations during their coming out processes.

- **Change of Denomination.** The four women who left their childhood denominations but did not reject their early religious identities were able to accommodate to a new denominational identity, made possible by minimal family of origin support or mentors in college, seminary, or a congregation who supported them through the process of coming out while remaining in church.

- **Substitution of Religious Identity with a Spiritual Identity.** The seven women in the third group found that a stage of spiritual identity (in lieu of a religious identity) was necessary for them in order to come out as lesbians. They reported little or no family of origin or local congregational support during their coming out processes. In addition, this third group of women who left their religious identities found this lengthy (one to two decades) stage of spiritual identity to be more of placeholder for the time in between church affiliations. The implications of this for the women in this stage were mental health, somatic, and addiction issues. This delay in coming out as lesbians is consistent with Hinrichs's (2008) finding that gay and lesbian individuals who are not grounded/confined by their early formative religious identities feel less guilt during their coming out processes. The remaining six women (in groups above) who did not enter into a spiritual identity stage were able to come out while they remained in their religious identity. Thus, the women's spiritual/religious identities and lesbian identities emerged in parallel streams as indicated by the literature (Knight and Hoffman 2007).

Another important finding, however, was that the lesbian clergy experienced more integrity and success in their ministries when they came out to their congregations, institutions, and denominations. Being out in ministry thus ameliorated their ongoing experiences of denominational oppression. Indeed, the majority of the women sampled were happy in their long-term relationships and reported that this helped to smooth over their experiences of oppression. Twelve of the women were able to tolerate high levels of denominational homophobic oppression, which was consistent with the finding that the lesbian clergy in this study tend to minimize their personal discrimination in order to manage their mental health and their need to accommodate (Tajfel and Turner 1979) to their denominational structures, despite experiences of homophobic policies. This finding is supported by the literature that states that individuals in out-groups tend to minimize personal discrimination in order to manage their personal outcomes (Taylor; Olson and Hafer 2011). In addition, the experience of congregational acceptance and fit ameliorated against homophobic denominational policies.

SOCIAL IDENTITY THEORY

Tajfel and Turner (1979) originally presented social identity theory in 1979, which was then more fully delineated in 1988 by Hogg and Abrams. Hogg and Abrams (1988) stated that social identity theory is a "social psychological theory that links individuals and groups—the groups in the individual." According to this theory, individuals have several selves that correspond to widening circles of membership that extend outward from themselves in concentric circles (Tafjel and Turner 1979). In short, this theory assumes that people have multiple selves and that people's self-concepts are derived from their perceived membership in various social groups (Hogg and Vaughan 2008).

Tajfel and Turner (1979) also studied the ways in which individuals begin to identify with some social groups more than others. They identified three variables that lead to the emergence of in-group favoritism: (1) the extent to which an individual identifies with an in-group determines how much it is internalized as an aspect of self-concept; (2) the extent to which the prevailing context provides groups for comparison between each group; and (3) the perceived relevance of comparison groups by status that are either relative or absolute. Hogg and Vaughn (2008) also asserted that group membership creates in-group self-categorization and enhancement in ways that favors the in-group at the expense of the out-group. According to Tajfel and Turner (1979), the way in which individuals respond to certain groups depends upon the individuals' belief system and permeability of the group boundaries in terms of social mobility and social change factors. In other words, the permeability of group boundaries drives perceived stability and legitimacy by individuals both within and outside of the groups. Once again, this theoretical perspective was exemplary in explaining the movement and realignment of the women with differing denominations and (or) religious/spiritual practices.

Pubescent struggle with religious identity developmentally occurs just prior to Troiden's stage theory of homosexual development at the age of eighteen. In this early homosexuality identity stage, the women's confusion gives way to an "identity assumption" stage at the age of twenty-one to twenty-three (Troiden 1989). In this study, there was a wider range of years for the assumption of lesbian identity, with the range being on the high end at forty-eight years. The literature (see Troiden 1989; D'Augelli 1994; Park 1986, 2000; Knight and Hoff 2007; Hinrichs 2009) is in sharp contrast to this study's new and unique finding that some of the women in the sample who had maintained a strong religious identity were able to have their burgeoning sexual identity overlap with their religious identities. In fact, the findings of this directly contradict Knight and Hoff's earlier study that purported to show that gay and lesbian individuals did not (or could not) move simultaneously on their sexual identity and religious identity paths.

More consistent with the findings of this study, however, is literature that supports the finding that the women outside of the church who had a spiritual identity (stage 2) during their coming out process have a less difficult time in coming out (Hinrichs 2009). In addition, Hinrichs's study (2009) supports the finding that some of the women delayed their coming out processes due to their strong attachment to their religious identities. Degges-White et al. (2000), in their study of lesbian identity development, found that sexual identity is a multistage process. Through the lens of social identity theory, Hoggs and Abrams (1998) wrote about having several selves and certain identities that begin to be more important over time. This literature supports the tasks of stage 3, when the psychological task is to learn to cope with and manage social stigma while coming out. According to Troiden (1989), individuals with rising lesbian and gay identities increasingly find it important to connect with other lesbian persons in order to reduce social isolation. Thus, it appears that in order for these women to move toward having fully integrated lives as lesbian clergy, one of the first conscious tasks was to come out.

The issue of the lesbian clergy in the context of their judicatories can be best understood through the lenses of SIT since its application assists in the elucidation of various subidentities, (e.g., the religious, sexual, and spiritual identities) within each lesbian clergy participant (Tajfel and Turner 1979; Hogg and Vaughn 2002; Hogg and Abrams 2008). In addition, it can be used to demonstrate the debate within most Protestant mainline denominations between the pro-gay and antigay factions.

The "lived experiences" (Van Manen 1990) of the lesbian Protestant mainline clergy have been explored using social identity theory (Tajfel and Turner 1979; Hogg and Abrams 1988; Hogg and Vaughn 2002; Mol 1979; Wellman 1999; Herriot 2007; Miller 2005, 2007, 2008; Geisler 2006; Hinrichs 2008). Social identity theory offered a possible explanation to the place of the lesbian clergy within their denominations because it explained the in-group criteria and favoritism that creates positive self-esteem and a sense of "we," at the expense of the out-group's attributes, which, in this case, is the lesbian Protestant mainline minister.

- However, despite their out-group status, the lesbian clergy in this sample appeared to manage the toll and costs of being bullied and ostracized by their denominations. The lesbian clergy felt a strong pull to maintain their denominational affiliations because of their religious belief that they needed to stay, despite being a part of the out-group of their denominations, in order to enact policy and practice changes for other LGBTQ individuals, and in some cases for other marginalized populations. Their religious identities assumed the allegories of being a "wounded healer" (Nouwen 1979), experiencing the "cost of discipleship" (Bonhoffer 1937; Bonhoffer 1959) in order to enact changes—despite the toll to their own mental and physical well-being. This honorable ability to move beyond what most clergy are capable of doing was due to their resiliencies (Bernard 1991). The process of resiliency for these women was more possible when they achieved connectedness to persons who shared their dreams of eliminating homophobia in the church. Thus, the lesbian clergy together in their out-group (i.e., the LGBTQ denominational advocacy) ameliorated their feelings of isolation, while at the same time serving to unify and change their denominational environments through critical inquiry, dialogue, reflection, and action. Through a resiliency lens, the protective factors of these women were the following:

- their soothing and calming spiritual practices of medication and prayer;
- their religious beliefs that God had called them to be change agents and gave them meaning for their struggles as lesbian clergy; and
- their positive relationships with some or all of their families of origin, their partners, and their congregations, which became ameliorating with their challenging relationships with their denominational hierarchies.

Finally, social identity theory also offered underpinning framework for understanding the lesbian clergy. Social identity theory explained how the religious and sexual identities of the female clergy can simultaneously exist.

COMMENT ON METHODOLOGY

The author found that the listening guide (Brown et al. 1988; Brown and Gillian 1992; Raider-Roth 2002; Woodcock 2005) enhanced the interpretability of the data from the interviews but was not fundamentally necessary. When the study was designed, it was anticipated that this feminist research methodology would lend more significant data on the moods and experiences of the research participants than it did. Although the listening guide methodology demonstrated attention to some nuances in tone and affect that supported the women's words, it appears that the open coding (Miles and Huberman 1994) method for data analysis was sufficient to tell the women's stories.

The open-ended research questions for the prolonged engagement interviews were originally based on a phenomenological research methodology (Van Manen 1990; Moustakas 1994) and were premised on the three theoretical constructs utilized in this study (i.e., ecological theory, anti-oppressive theory, social identity theory). Due to the extensive data in this study and the ambitious design that was framed by three theories, the data was not analyzed with a phenomenological framework but rather through the open coding that emerged from the frameworks of the three theories used (i.e., religious, spiritual, and sexual identities).

1. Trustworthiness (Bloomberg and Volpe 2008) of the data was accomplished in the following way: thick description (Lincoln and Guba 1985); use of data analysis that compared one participant with another for each theme in each stage of development; trails of evidence that evidenced both open content coding (Miles and Huberman 1994) and voice poems (Brown et al. 1988; Brown and Gillian 1992; Raider-Roth 2002; Woodcock 2005); and the women's quotes, which adequately supported the themes that emerged for each stage of the process that these women progressed through in this logic sequence. In terms of specific types of trustworthiness, the following methods were accomplished:

2. *Credibility* (Lincoln and Guba 1985) was accomplished through prolonged engagement during the interview process and a negative case analysis.

3. *Dependability* (Bloomberg and Volpe 2008) was accomplished through reviewing the sufficiency of the participants' data to answer each of research questions.

4. *Confirmability* (Lincoln and Guba 1985) was minimally accomplished. However, the researcher's biases were noted at points in the document, and some attention was given to the participants' voice tones and affect.

Transferability of this study may not be possible as this is really an in-depth study about the experiences and identities of these women who are unique to these four denominations under consideration. It is possible, however, to use these findings to test out transferability to lesbian clergy of other Protestant denominations and gay clergy of the same four denominations.

IMPLICATIONS

The learning objectives of this study were achieved through application of the three conceptual theories to each of these research objectives in both the data collection and data analysis:

1. The lived experiences of the sampled lesbian ELCA, PCUSA, RCA, and UCC clergy were explored through the intersection of ecological (Bronfenbrenner 1979; Gitterman and Germain 2008) and anti-oppression (Dominelli 2002) theories within the context of social identity theory (Tajfel and Turner 1979). The life experiences of the women from birth to the time of the interviews were made into narratives, from which the subthemes of the study were coded.

2. In order to explore whether and how the sampled lesbian ELCA, PCUSA, RCA, and UCC clergy have experienced fit in their families, in their communities, and in their denominations, the women's narratives were coded to identify paradoxes between niche and oppression, while listening for their various identities that emerged.

3. In order to understand the meanings that the sampled lesbian ELCA, PCUSA, RCA, and UCC clergy attach to their personal histories, the women were engaged in a third interview in which they were asked to reflect on the meaning of the first two interviews and the impact that their experiences of becoming lesbian clergy in oppressive systems has had on their lives.

4. In order to understand how the lesbian ELCA, PCUSA, RCA, and UCC clergy perceive themselves regarding each of the domains of their religious, spiritual, and sexual identities, the three identities of sexual, religious, and spiritual identity were coded from the in-depth interviews and expanded into a developmental stage theory that was based on social identity literature (Fowler 1981; Miller 2005, 2007; Troiden 1989; D'Augelli 1994; Park 1986, 2000; Knight and Hoff 2007; Hinrichs 2009).

The data from this study are important in denominational policy, education, and pastoral care of the lesbian clergy. The data from this study are also important to social work policy, education, practice, and research contexts. The extraordinary women in this study were discussed at length in both the findings and discussion sections. All thirteen of the women survived extraordinary religious abuse at the hands of the very church systems that they were nurtured by early on and longed to return to and remain within. In particular, the women in stage 7 were able to not only remain in their ministry positions but were able to become involved in social justice work that brought them to a universalizing kind of love for society, including their persecutors within their denominations.

However, in moving beyond the stage theory that has been explicated here, it is extremely important to highlight that all thirteen of the women in the study are extraordinary heroines because they have had the courage to be *out in the pulpit* in denominations that have openly abused them. Each of them essentially put their lives on hold and were affected psychologically, physically, and spiritually by the religious oppression and abuse that they sustained. What has enabled them to continue in their journey toward becoming ordained out lesbian clergy is a true testament to their religious faith. Their religious beliefs that there is a cost to discipleship (Bonhoeffer 1937, 1959) and that they are called to be wounded healers (Nouwen 1979) to others who are wounded drove them forward in ways that psychological understandings are lacking in their ability to explain how they survived such adversity. What has enabled them to continue in their journey toward becoming and remaining in the ministerial profession is their high level of resiliency (Bernard 1991; Lifton 1991; Werner and Smith 1982, 1989, 1992), which is connected to their faith and positive consequences of their faith communities.

- The protective factors of the women enabled them to survive the effects of their religious abuse and institutional oppression. In sum, the study identified the following women's protective factors:
- their religious belief that they are called to make a difference in the world and to root out injustice;
- their spiritual practices, such as prayer, inspirational reading, worship, and meditation, that provide regular sustenance; and
- their relational connectedness to parents, congregations (where there is a goodness of fit), and to partners that share the same vision for social justice.

IMPLICATIONS FOR THE DENOMINATIONS

Taken together, the qualitative findings from this study have several important policy and clinical implications for lesbian ministers. Regarding policy implications, it is clear that there is a regional disparity between the perspectives toward lesbian clergy in the mainline denominations on the part of the average congregant. Women in the northeastern metropolitan areas consistently experienced less homophobia than women in other regions of the denominations in the United States. This is even true for the denominations that have policies that support LGBTQ ordination. Thus, the implication for women who have strong fit in one congregation within a denomination is that it does not guarantee they will find employment in other regions of their denominations, which thereby limits their vertical and horizontal employment mobility. The implication here is in the form of ongoing advocacy for LGBTQ inclusion and consciousness raising by each of the denominations' groups designed to promote inclusion of LGBTQ laity and clergy into church leadership.

It is hoped that this study will have the function of engaging both denominations and congregations in conversations about their involvement in institutional oppression of women. In keeping with the theme of justice and tolerance, these conversations should occur without vitriol, founded on the Christian principles found in the Bible and theological literature that guide these religious organizations. These denominational and congregational conversations are often avoided due to fears of interrupting the homeostasis of the church and the unity of congregations. Studies such as this may bring about a much-needed discussion in these institutions, so that some individuals within the political inner circles come to the realization that failure to address these difficult issues for the sake of maintaining unity within their denominational ranks will erode the very ethical fiber of their institutions.

From a social justice perspective, this work illustrates the need for denominational executives to come to a more informed understanding of the pain of their lesbian clergy and a realization that these women are not going to back down until they are given full inclusion and equality in the life of their denominations. It is the sincerest desire and prayer that even those denominational leaders who continue to believe that homosexuality practices are sinful will be sufficiently softened by the struggle of these women's stories, in order to attend to the pastoral care needs of these same women who have been so damaged by the oppression of the institutional church. It is incongruous that the very institutions that have formed the religious faith of these lesbian clergy, and the institutions that they long to be connected to, are the very ones that have harmed their faithful children psychologically and religiously, beyond comprehension, through their intolerances of their sexual orientations. In some cases, the religious trauma or abuse that they have sustained has resulted in chronic medical and psychological conditions.

Given the positive early influence of the institutional church on the founding of the social work profession in the late nineteenth century, it is ironic that the tables are now turned and that the social work profession will now target the church as being regressive in its stance on the inclusion of LGBTQ persons. In other words, it is currently social work that is more socially progressive regarding addressing the issues of oppression of LGBTQ and seeking inclusion and equality in ordination policies. Certainly, one of the policy stakeholders will be the profession of social work, which has the capacity to influence the denominational policy makers through its emphasis on equality and human rights in the various subcultures of the United States (NASW 2008).

IMPLICATIONS FOR THE SOCIAL WORK PROFESSION

Regarding clinical or direct practice implications, it is clear that the lesbian clergy have the need for ongoing support due to the multiple types of institutional oppression that they have sustained. Support for the women will be needed in the form of psychotherapies, psychiatric medications, and medical interventions. The institutional harms that these women have endured has caused the women to have psychological disorders such as posttraumatic, generalized anxiety, major depression, eating disorders, and substance abuse disorders, in addition to medical diagnoses such as asthma, fibromyalgia, and migraines.

In addition, support is needed in the education of social workers and other mental health professionals, encouraging students to acquire knowledge about lesbian clergy developmental processes. In particular, it is vitally important that clinical social workers learn about the intersections between spirituality and religion with lesbian identity development. The clinical work with this population should be founded on principles and constructs pulled from a mix of social identity (Tajfel and Turner 1979), ecological, (Gitterman and Germain 2008), and anti-oppressive (Dominelli 2002) theories. Social identity practice enables clients to create fluid identities that create well-being. Ecological or life practice assesses and creates positive environmental niches. Anti-oppressive practice enables the clients to create new non-oppressive professional relationships.

A more extensive application of anti-oppressive practice by social workers would address the needs of LGBTQ clergy and religious professionals to explore and develop new identities in a safe clinical context that is relatively free of bias and judgment. Specifically, clinical social workers must be knowledgeable about the intersections of lesbian clergy clients' religious, spiritual, and sexual identities. Clinicians need to respect, without bias, that these clients value a sense of wholeness and well-being regarding the synthesis of their religious, sexual, and spiritual identities. Clearly, the homophobic and male normative experiences of these lesbian clergy are inconsistent with NASW's code of ethics and the profession's founding principles, which are premised in social justice principles.

The current trend of spiritually sensitive social work is especially well suited for clinical work with these traumatized women. Importantly, spiritually sensitive social workers attune to the spiritual, religious, as well as emotional needs of their clients in ways that are transformative and healing (Canda 1988; Becvar 1997). In other words, clinicians need to understand that these clients cannot eliminate one of their identities in order to maintain another. Lastly, and perhaps the most important of the clinical implications, is the needs for social workers to be sensitized to the ongoing trauma that lesbian clergy continue to experience. Many of these women need to be sustained in an ongoing basis in psychotherapy for emotional support, as well as healing from the past traumatic events of emotional and religious abuse.

RESEARCH IMPLICATIONS

The framework provided by the three theories was important. However, the social identity (Tajfel and Turner 1979) theory was the most foundational in that it enabled the development of the stage theory. The concepts of fit (ecological theory, Bronfenbrenner 1979; Gitterman and Germain 2008) and oppression (anti-oppression theory, Dominelli 2002) were opposite sides of the same continuum of niche rejection for the women and were both necessary for demonstrating how the women moved through their lesbian clergy development processes.

In a future study on lesbian clergy, it would be important to design the research questions in a manner that offers definitions for the seven identities. Thus, the characteristics and tasks of the seven stages could be tested out for their theoretical soundness. And finally, the distinction between religious and spiritual identity needs to be more clearly identified, utilizing operational definitions that can be more easily tested empirically. In order to test for transferability of this study on lesbians, a larger sample from a more heterogeneous sample would be necessary.

Further, a similar study with gay clergy will be important to see if their development as clergy is similar or dissimilar to lesbian clergy, thereby testing for transferability of the stage theory of clergy development. In addition, a future research endeavor will be needed to further understand how the women have been able to manage such institutional harms and to explore in particular what their resiliency or protective factors have been.

LIMITATIONS OF THE STUDY

The exploratory study had a small heterogeneous criterion sample of thirteen women of four Protestant mainline denominations (Evangelical Lutheran Church in America; Presbyterian Church in the USA; the Reformed Church in America; and the United Church of Christ) whose demographics are primarily Caucasian. In addition, the sample was regionally limited, as the majority of the sample was concentrated in the Northeast section of the United States. It is unknown, but assumed, that women living in other regions of their denominations in the United States would have experienced significantly higher levels of homophobia on the part of their families and their denominations. Further, the racial heterogeneity of the study was limited, with only one of the research participants being an African American of Caribbean descent and the rest being Caucasian of Northern European descent.

Another important finding to consider is that all of the women interviewed were out to their families and to their denominations. It is speculated that women who were not out may have experienced higher levels of mental and physical health issues due to their internalized homophobic oppressions. It is unknown if the closeted lesbian clergy would have perceived themselves as being successful or as having integrity in their ministries.

In terms of conceptual frameworks, the interplay of the three social work theories (social identity, Tajfel and Turner 1979; ecological, Gitterman and Germain 2008; anti-oppressive, Dominelli 2002) proved to be effective in answering the research goals and objectives. In addition, the intersection of these three theories worked well to give understanding to the experiences of fit and oppression as they impacted the women's identity formations and the development of the stage theory of lesbian clergy formation.

DISSEMINATION AND UTILIZATION OF THE FINDINGS

It is anticipated that the findings of the qualitative study will benefit both the social work and ministerial communities. The themes and patterns of research on the lesbian clergy that emerged helped to create a body of social work research on a subject not receiving adequate attention. For the social work communities, this research will have application for clinicians who work with lesbian clergy struggling with the dissonance between their denominational and sexual identities. This study will enable social work and pastoral clinicians to develop niches to treat clergy who are attempting to identify their true selves while struggling with the inherent cultural, theological, and psychological contexts with which they work and live. For the denominational communities, this research could have an impact on the policy makers of the four denominations involved in this study, as well as on theological and social justice educators. And lastly, future qualitative and quantitative research designs could possibly emerge from this body of research, with researchers seeing the value of the methodology chosen in their approach to disenfranchised populations.

REFERENCES

Abramson, H. 1980. "The Historical and Cultural Spectra of Homosexuality and Their Relationship to the Fear of Being Lesbian." *Journal of Asthma Research* 17, no. 4: 177–188.

Albany Times Union. 1997. "Chastity Amendment Divides Presbyterian Church." *Albany Times Union*, February 1.

Almstrom, C. 2006. "A Three-Worldview of System Justification Theory." *Journal of Scientific Psychology* (September): 6–8.

American Psychiatric Association. 1973. *Diagnostic and Statistical Manual II*. Washington, DC: American Psychiatric Association.

American Psychiatric Association. 1994. *Diagnostic and Statistical Manual IV*. Washington, DC: American Psychiatric Association.

American Psychiatric Association. 2008. "Position Statement." *Homosexual and Sexual Orientation Disturbance: Proposed Change in DSM II*, 6th Printing. doi:730008. April 15.

American Psychiatric Association. 1994.. *Diagnostic and Statistical Manual III-R*. Washington, DC: American Psychiatric Association.

American Psychological Association Help Center, 2011. "Homosexuality and Religion." *American Psychological Association Help Center*. Retrieved from www.APAHelpCenter.org.

Ammerman, N.,2005.. *Pillars of Faith: American Congregations and their Partners.* Berkeley: University of California Press.December.

Balan, N. 2005.. "Multiple voices and methods: Listening to women who are in workplace transition." *International Journal of Qualitative Methods, 4(4).*

Banerjee, N. 2004, *United Methodist Move to Defrock Lesbian.* Retrieved from The New York times: http:www.nytimes.com/2004/12/03/national/03trial.html. December 3.

Batchelor, E. J.,1980. *Homosexuality and Ethics.* New York: Pilgrim Press.

Beck, R.,2009.."Purity and Defilement: Part 9: Purity and Justice". Retrieved from *Experimental Theology: Thoughts, Articles, and Essays Blog: experimentaltheology.*blogspot.com.September 22.

Belfast Telegraph,2009.. *TheCcan of Worms Opened by Pope's Offer to Anglicans.* Retrieved from http://www.highbeam.com/doc/1P2-2-927077.html.November 3.

Berger, K.,2014. *Invitation to Life Span* (2nd ed.). New York: Worth Publishers.

Benard, B.,1991.. *Fostering Resiliency in Kids: Protective Factors in the Family, School, and Community.* Portland, OR: Western Center for Drug-Free Schools and Communities.

Berzon, B.,2001. *Positively Gay: New Approaches to Gay and Lesbian Life* (3rd ed.). Berkeley, CA: Celestial Arts.

*Bible King James Version.,*1937. Edinburgh: William Collins Sons and Company, Ltd.

*Bible New English Version,*1961.. Oxford/Cambridge: Oxford University Press and Cambridge University Press.

Bible New Internal Version,1983. Grand Rapids: The Zondervan Corporation.

Bible New Revised Version.,1989. Nashville: Thomas Nelson, Inc.

Bible Revised Standard Version,1946. Dallas: Melton Book Company.

Bible Revised Standard Version.,1952. Dallas: Melton Book Company.

Blasius, M., and Phelan, S.,1997.). *We are Everywhere: A Historical Sourcebook in Gay and Lesbian Politics.* New York: Routledge, Inc.

Bloomberg, L., and Volpe, M.,2008. *Completing Your Qualitative Dissertation.* Los Angeles: Sage Publications.

Bocock, D. M.,2009.. *Two-and-a-half-hour interview regarding his perspectives on the homosexual ordination issue in the United Church of Christ.* (P. Pater Ennis, Interviewer) Cresskill, New Jersey. October 6.

Bonhoeffer, D.,1937, 1959.. *The Cost of Discipleship.* New York, NY: Touchstone.

Borris, K.,2003. *Same-Sex Desire in the English Renaissance: A Sourcebook of Texts.* New York: Routledge Publishers.

Boswell, J.,1980. *Christianity, Social Tolerance and Homosexuality: Gay People in Western Europe from the beginning of the Christian Era to the 14th Century.* Chicago: University of Chicago Press.

Boswell, J.,1994. *The Marriage of Likeness: Same-sex Unions in Pre-Modern Europe.* New York: Simon, Harper, and Collins.

Boswell, J.,2007.. *Homosexuality and the Church.* Retrieved from Fordham University: http://www.fordam.edu/halsall/pwh/1979boswell.html.

Bronfenbrenner, U.,1979.. *The Ecology of Human Development*. Cambridge: Harvard University Press.

Brown, L.,1988. "Project on women's Psychology and Girls' Development, Monograph No. 1." *A Guide to Reading Narratives of Conflict and Choice for Self and Moral Voice*. Cambridge, MA: Harvard University, Graduate School of Education.

Brown, L., and Gilligan, C..1992.. *Meeting at the Crossroads: Women's Psychology and Girls' Development*. Cambridge: Harvard University Press.

Brownson, J. V.,2013. *Bible, Gender, Sexuality: Reframing the Church's Debate on Same-Sex Relationships*. Grand Rapids, MI: William B. Eerdmans Publishing Company.

Buttrick, T.,1962. *The Interpreter's Dictionary of the Bible*. (T. Buttrick, Ed.) Nashville, TN: Abingdon.

Cadge, W.,2006. *Dialogues across Difference: Congregations Talk about Homosexuality*. Retrieved March 15, 2008, from Alban Institute: www.alban.org/conversations.asp.

Cadge, W., and Wildemann, C.,2005. *Dialogues across Difference: Mainline Protestant Clergy Facilitate Local Conversation about Homosexuality*. Paper presented at the annual meeting of the American Sociological Association, Marriott Hotel, Aug. 12, 2005, American Sociological Association, Philadelphia. Retrieved 4 22, 2008.

Campolo, T.,2004. *Speaking my Mind*. Nashville: W. Publishing Group.

Canda, E.,1988.. "Conceptualizing Spirituality for Social Work: Insights from Diverse Perspectives." *Social Thought, 14*(1), 30–46.

Canda, E., and Furman, L.,2010. *Spiritual Diversity in Social Work Practice* (2nd ed.). New York: Oxford University Press.

Cass, V.,1984. "Homosexual Identity: A Concept in Need of Definition." *Journal of Homosexuality, 9*, 105–126.

Chandra, A., Mosher, W., and Copen, C.,2011. *Sexual Behavior, Sexual Attraction, and Sexual Identity in the United States: Data from the 2006–2008 National Survey of Family Growth. 36*, p. 29. Retrieved from http://www.cdc.gov/nchs.

Coakley, J.,1999. *Patterns and Portraits: Women in the History of the Reformed Church in America.*Grand Rapids, MI: William B. Eerdmans Publishing.

Condon, P.,2009.*Lutherans to Allow Sexually Active Gays as Clergy.* Retrieved 2009, from http://www.highbeam.com/doc1A1-D9A7KD581.html.August 22.

Cook, J. I.,1984.. *The Church Speaks: Papers of the Commission on Theology, Reformed Church in America, 1959–1984.* (J. Cook, Ed.) Grand Rapids: W.B. Eerdmans Publishing Company.

Coser, L.,1956. *The Functions of Social Conflict.* New York: The Free Press.

Crabtree, B., and Miller, W. (1992). *Doing Qualitative Research.* New York: Safe Publications.

Creswell, J.,2007. *Qualitative Inquiry and Research Design: Choosing Among Five Approaches* (2nd ed.). Thousand Oaks, CA: Safe Publications.

Crompton, L.,2014.. "The Myth of Lesbian Purity: Capital Laws from 1270 to 1791.' *Journal of Homosexuality, 6*(1/2).

D'Augelli, A.,1994. "Identity Development and Sexual Orientation: Toward a Mode of Lesbian, Gay, and Bisexual Development." In E. Trickett, R.J. Watts, and D. Birnman, *Human Diversity: Perspective on People in Context* (pp. 312–333). San Francisco: Jossey-Bass.

Demareth, N.,2005. "The Battle Over a U.S Culture War: A Note on Inflated Rhetoric Versus Inflamed Politics. "*The Forum, 3*(2) [published online].

Derbyshire, J.,2003. *The One and the Many Christianity Today?* Retrieved June 25, 2003, from National Review: www.nationalreview.com/ derbyshire/derbyshire062503.asp.

Diamond, L.,2008. *Sexual Fluidity: Understanding Women's Love and Desire.* Cambridge, MA: Harvard University Press.

Dillenberger, J.,1962. *Martin Luther: Selections from his Writings.* New York: Anchor Books.

DiMaggio, P., Evans, J., and Bryson, B.,1996. "Have American's Social Atitudes become More Polarized?" *American Journal of Sociology, 102*(3), 690–755.

DiMaria-Kuiper, J.,1983.. *Hot Under the Collar: Self-Portrait of a Gay Pastor.* Columbia, MO: Mercury Press.

Dobson, J.,2004. "In Defending Marriage: Take the Offensive." *Dr. Dobson's Newsletter.* Retrieved from http://family.org/docstudy/ newsletters/aoo31315.cfm. April.

Dominelli, L.,2002. *Anti-Oppressive Social Work Theory and Practice.* New York: Palgrave MacMillan.

Douglas, K.,1999. *Sexuality and the Black Church: A Womanist Perspective.* Maryknoll, NY: Orbis Books.

Edwards, G.,1984. *Gay/Lesbian Liberation: A Biblical Perspective.* New York: Pilgrim.

Ellwood, R.,2000. *Crossroads of American Religious Life.* Louisville, KY: Westminster John Knox Press.

Erikson, E.,1968. *Identity: Youth and Crisis.* New York: Norton.

Evangelical Lutheran Church in America,2009. *Constitutions of the Evangelical Lutheran Church in America: Constitutions, Bylaws, and Continuing Resolutions of the Evangelical Lutheran Church in America.* Retrieved December 7. from www.elca.org.

Evangelical Lutheran Church in America.,2009. *Homosexuality and the ELCA.* Retrieved December 6, from www.ecla.org.

Faderman, L.,1981.. *Surpassing the Love of Men: Romantic Friendship and Love between Women from the Renaissance to the Present.* NY: Morrow.

Fardella, J.,2005.. Spiritual Identity and Transformation: Christian Narratives, Public Dscourse, and Critical Social Work Practice. *Critical Social Work, 6*(2), [online] retrieved from wwwq.uwindsosr. ca/criticalsocialwork/spiritualidentity [retrieved 2012 March 15].

Festinger, L.,1957. *Theory of Cognitive Dissonance.* New York: Columbia University Press.

Fortson, S.,2011, June 3. "The Road to Gay Ordination in the Presbyterian Church (U.S.A): The Denominational Battle has been Going on for Decades. The Historical Record is Much Older." *Christianity Today.*June 3.

Fortune, A., and Reid, W.,1999. *Research in Social Work* (3rd ed.). New York: Columbia University Press.

Forum, P.,2003. *Religious Beliefs Underpin Opposition to Homosexuality.* Retrieved July 9, 2007, from http://pewforum.org/docs/index.

Forum, P.,2008. *Most Mainline Protests Say Society Should Accept Homosexuality.* Retrieved April 17, 2009, from http://pewform. org/docs.

Fowler, J.,1981. *Stages of Faith*. New York: Harper Collins.

Frost, D., and Meyer, I.,2009. "Internalized Homophobia and Relationship Quality among Lesbian, Gay Men, and Bisexuals." *Journal of Counseling Psychology, 56*(1), 97–109.

Frye, B.1983. "'Homophobia' or homosexual bias reconsidered." *Archives of Sexual Behavior, 12*(6), 549–554.

Gagnon, R.,2001. *The Bible and Homosexual Practice: Texts and Hermeneutics*. Nashville: Abingdon Press.

"Gay Minister Taken off Roster, "2007, July 5. *New York Times*. Retrieved July 9, 2007, from www.nytimes.com/2007/elca.

Gecas, V.,1981. "Contexts of Socialization. "In M. Rosenberg, and R. Turner, *Sociological Perspectives*. New York: Basics Books.

Germain, C., and Gitterman, A.,1976. *The Life Model of Social Work Practice: Advances in Theory and Practice*. New York: Columbia University Press.

Giesler, M.,2006. *From Outgroup to out: Lesbian Clergy's Self-Perceptions of Leadership*.

Gilligan, C.,1982. *In a Different Voice*. Cambridge, MA: Harvard University Press.

Gilligan, C., Spencer, R., Weinberg, M., and Bertsch, T.,2003. "On the Listening Guide: A Voice-Centered Relational Method." In P. Camic, J.E. Rhodes, and L. Yardley, *Qualitative Research in Psychology: Expanding Perspectives in Methodology and Design* (pp. 157–172). Washington, DC: American Psychological Association.

Gitterman, A.,2008.." Advances in the Life Model of Social Work practice. "In F. T. (ed.), *Social Work Treatment* (pp. 389–408). New York: The Free Press.

Glaser, B., and Staus, A.,1967. *The Discovery of Grounded Theory: Strategies for Qualitative Research.* Chicago: Aldine.

Glassman, A. 2007. *"Minister is Defrocked for Being a Practicing Lesbian'."* Retrieved December 10, 2007, from Gay People's Chronicle: http://www.gaypeopleschronicle.com/stories04/december/04dec10/4dec10-st3.html.

Glynos, J.,2000. "Sexual Identity, Identification, and Difference: A Psychoanalytic Contribution to Dscourse Theory." *Philosophy & Social Criticism, 26*(6), 85–108.

Goffman, E.,1963. *Stigma: Notes of the Management of Spoiled Identity.* Englewood Cliffs, NJ: Prentice-Hall.

Goldstein, J.,1997." Presbyterians Pass Chastity Amendment aimed at Gays: Rule Mandates Celibacy of Single Church Officers." *Washington Post.* March 20.

Gonsiorek, J.,1982. "Mental Health Issues of Gay and Lesbian Adolescents." *Journal of Adolescent Health Care, 9,* 114–122.

Greil, A., and David, R.,1984. "Social Cocoons: Encapsulation and Identity of Transformation Organizations. *Sociological Inquiry,* 260–278.

Gudorf, C.,1994. *Body, Sex, and Pleasure: Reconstructing Christian Sexual Ethics.* New York: Pilgrim Press.

Guest, D., Goss, R., West, M., and Bohache, T.,2006 *The Queer Bible Commentary.* London, SCM Press.

Hall, J. H.,1998. *Remembered Voices: Reclaiming the Legacy of "Neo-Orthodoxy."* Louisville, KY: Westminster John Knox Press.

Harmon, D., and Rhodes, B.,2008. *When the Minister is a Woman.* St. Louis, MO: Chalice Press.

Hartford Institute for Religion Research,1994. *A Survey.* Retrieved July 9, 2007, from Homosexuality and Religion: http://hirr.hartsem.edu/research/homosexuality_religion.html.

Hartford Institute for Religion Research.,2008,. *A Quick Question: Who are Mainline Pastors Talking to About Homosexuality?* Retrieved February 11, 2008.

Hartsock, N.,1996. "Postmodernism and Political Change: Issues for Feminist Theory." In S. Hekman, *Feminist Interpretations of Michel Foucault.* University Park: Penn State University Press.

Helminiak, D.,(1989. "Self-esteem, Sexual Self-acceptance, and Spirituality." *Journal of Sex Education and Therapy, 15*(3), 200–210.

Helminiak, D.,2000. *What the Bible Really Says about Homosexuality.* New Mexico: Alamo Square Press.

Helminiak, D.,2006. *Sex and the Sacred: Gay Identity and Spiritual Growth.* New York: Harrington Park Press.

Herek, G.,1984. "Attitudes Toward Lesbians and Gay men: A Factor Analytic Study." *Journal of Homosexuality, 10*(1/2), 39–51.

Herek, G.,1984. "Beyond 'Homophobia': A social Psychological Perspective on Attitudes Toward Lesbians and Gay Men. *Journal of Homosexuality, 10*(1), 2–17.

Heskins, J.,2005.. *Face to Face: Gay and Lesbian Clergy on Holiness and Life Together.* London: SCM Press.

Heyward, C.,1984. *Our Passion for Justice: Images of Power, Sexuality, and Liberation.* New York: Pilgrim Press.

Heyward, C.,1989. *Speaking of Christ: A Lesbian Feminist Voice.* New York: Pilgrim Press.

Heyward, C.,1989.. *Touching our Strength: The Erotic as Power and the Love of God*. San Francisco: Harper & Row.

Heyward, C.,2000. *Staying Power: Reflections on Gender, Justice, and Compassion*. Cleveland, OH: Pilgrim Press.

Hiltner, S.,1972,. Kinsey and the Church—After Twenty Years. *Journal of Sex Research, 8*(3), 194–206.

Hinrichs, D.,2008. Comparing Spiritual Development Theory to Homosexual Identity Development Theory. Retrieved May 1, 2009.

Hinrichs, D., n.d.." Comparing Spiritual Development Theory to Homosexual Identity Development Theory." *Unpublished Master's Thesis, Kansas State University.*

Hodge, D.,2005. "Epistemological Frameworks, Homosexuality, and Religion: How People of Faith Understand the Intersection between Homosexuality and Religion." *Social Work.* 50(3):207-18, August.

Hodge, D., Johnson, B., and Luidens, D.,1994. *Vanishing Boundaries: The Religion of Protestant Mainline Baby Boomers*. Louisville, KY: Westminister John Knox Press.

Hoffman, L., Knight, S., Hoffman, J., Boscoe-Huffman, S., Galaska, S., Arms, D., ... Calvert, C.,2007. "Examining the Interplay of Religious, Spiritual, and Homosexual Psychological Health: A preliminary Investigation." *Paper presented at the 115th Annual Meeting of the American Psychological Association in San Francisco, CA in August 2007.*

Hogg, M., and Abrams, D.,2008. *Social Identifications*. New York: Taylor and Francis.

Hogg, M., and Vaughan, G.,2008. *Social Psychology* (5ᵗʰ ed.). Edinburgh, Scotland: Pearson Education Ltd.

"Homosexuality and the Clergy,"1978. *Time*. Retrieved February 10, 2008, from www.time.com/magazine/article.

Hudson, Z.,2007.. *Gay Lutheran Pastor Begins New Job Fight: Schmeling's Plight Could Mark Turning Point for Denomination*. Retrieved from Washington Blade: www.Washingtonblade.com/2007/2.

Hunter, J.,1991. *Culture Wars: The Struggle to Define America*. New York: Basic Books.

Jansen, G., and David, D.,1999. "Honoring Voice and Visibility: Sensitive-Topic Research and Feminist Interpretive Inquiry." *Affilia, 13*(3), 289–311.

Japinga, L.,1999. *Feminism and Christianity: An Essential Guide*. Nashville, TN: Abingdon Press.

Johnson, W..2001. "Protestantism and Gay and Lesbian Freedom." In B. Berzon, and B. Frank (Eds.), *Positively Gay: New Approaches to Gay and Lesbian Life*. Berkeley, CA: Celestial Arts.

Kaleem, J.,2012, "Presbyterian Church will Start ordaining Gay Clergy. *Huffington Post*. September 20.

Kaleem, J.,2014. "One-Third of mMllennials who Left their Religion Did it Because of Anti-Gay Policies: Survey. *Huffington Post*. (http://publicreligion.org/research/2014/02/2014-lgbt-survey. February 26.

Kirk, J., and Miller, M.,1996. *Reliability and Validity in Qualitative Research*. London: Sage Publications.

Klein, W., and Bloom, W.,1995. "Practice Wisdom." *Social Work, 40*(6), 799–807.

Knight, L.,2003, *Citizen*. Philadelphia: University of Pennsylvania Press.

Knight S. L. and Hoffman, L.,2007. '*Sexual Identity Development and Spiritual Identity   Development: The Impact of Multiple Llines of Development*". Paper presented at   the 115th Annual Meeting of the American Psychological Association, San Francisco, CA, August 2007, pp. 1–34 [online] Retrieved www.academia.edu [2013 June 15].

Kniss, F.,1997, "Cultural Wars: Remapping the Battleground." In H. William (Ed.), *Cultural Wars in American Politics: Critical Reviews of a Popular Myth* (pp. 259–280). New York: Aldine De Gruyter.

Kohlberg, L.,1981. *Essays of Moral Development*. San Francisco: Harper Collins.

Krondorfer, B.,1999. "Reclaiming the Spirit: Gay Men and Lesbians Come to Terms with Religion. *The Journal of Men's Studies, 7*(3), 436.

Kwon, L. (n.d.). *Opens Ordination to Noncelibate Homosexuals.* Retrieved August 22, 2009, from The Christian Post: www.thechristianpoint.com.

Latin Networks Limited Corporation. 2010. *History of Lesbianism*. Retrieved from en.lesbians.tv/history-of-the-lesbianism.html [15 May, 2015].

Lief, H., and Kaplan, H.,1986. "Ego-Dystonic Homosexuality." *Journal of Sex and Marital Therapy, Winter 12*(4), 259–266.

Lifton, R. J.,1993. *The Protean Self: Human Resilience in An Age of Transformation*. New York: Basic Books.

Luidens, D. 2009. "The Mournful Sounds of Implosion." *Perspectives: A Journal of Reformed Thought*. Retrieved November 9, 2009, from www.PMC.org/perspectives.

Luidens, D., and Nemeth, R.,1987. "'Public' and 'Private' Protestantism Reconsidered: Introducing the Loyalists. *Journal of the Scientific Study of Religions, 26,* 450–464.

Luther, M. 1522. *Luther's Works: Word and Sacrament* (Vol. 3), Minneapolis: Augsberg/Fortress Press, p. 255.

Marshall, J., and Rossman, G.,1999. *Designing Qualitative Research* (3rd ed.). Thousand Oaks, CA: Sage Publications.

May, D.,2004. *Women in Early America, Survival, and Freedom in a New World.* Santa Barbara, CA: ABC-CLIO, Inc.

May, M.,1998. "Breaking Down the Dividing Wall: Ending the Silence about Sexuality." *The Ecumenical Review, 50*(1), 41–45.

McNeil, B., Richardson, R., and Perkins, J.2004. *The Heart of Racial Justice: How Soul Change Leads to Social Change.* Downers Grove, IL: Intervarsity Press.

McNeil, J. 1960. *Calvin: Institutes of Christian Religion.* Philadelphia: The Westminster Press.

McNeil, J. 1976. *The Church and the Homosexual.* Kansas City: Sheed, Andrews, and McMeel.

McNeil, J. 1998. *Both Feet Firmly Planted in Midair.* Louisville, KY: Westminster John Knox Press.

McPhillips, K.,1999. "Theme: Feminisms, Religions, Cultures, Identities." *Australian Feminist Studies,* 14–30.

Merton, R., Fiske, M., and Kendall, P.,1990. *The Focused Interview: A Manual of Problems and Procedures.* New York: Free Press.

Miles, M., and Huberman, A.,1994. *Qualitative Data Analysis: An Expanded Sourcebook* (2nd ed.). Thousand Oaks, CA: Sage Publication.

Miller, A., and Osterhaven, M.1963. *400th Anniversary Edition of the Heidelberg Catechism*. Cleveland, OH: United Church Press.

Miller, L. 2008. "Our Mutual Joy." *Newsweek*, pp. 28–36. December 15.

Miller, P.,1985. *A Claim to New Roles*. Metuchen, NJ: Scarecrow Press.

Miller, R.,2005. "Look What God can do: African American Gay Men." *Journal of HIV/AIDS and Social Services, 3*(4), 25–46.

Miller, R.,2007. "Legacy Denied: African American, Gay Men, AIDS, and the Black Church." *Social Work, 52*(1), 51–61.

Miller, R.,2008." The Adolescent Sexual Development of African American Gay Men with AIDS: Implications for Community-Based Practice." *Journal of Community Practice, 16*(1), 97–123.

Miner, J., and Connoley, J. 2008. *The Children are Free: Re-examining the Biblical Evidence on Same-Sex Relationships*. Indianapolis, IN: Found Pearl Press.

Mol, H.,1979 "The Identity Model of Religion: How it Compares with Nine other Theories of Religion and How it Might Apply to Japan." *Japanese Journal of Religious Studies, March–June*, 11–38.

Morawski, J.,2001. "Feminist Research Methods: Bringing Culture to Science." In D. Tolman, and M. Brydon-Miller, *From Subjects to Subjectivities: A Handbook of Interpretive and Participatory Methods* (pp. 57–75). New York: New York University Press.

Morey, L. 2003. *Essentials of PAI Assessment*. Hoboken, NJ: John Wiley and Sons.

Morgan, C.,1995. *Church to let gay clergy "marry" but they must stay celibate*. Retrieved May 29, 2005, from The Sunday Times: www.timesonline.co.uk/tol/news/uk/article527686.ece.

Morrow, D., and Messinger, L.,2005. *Sexual Orientation and Gender Expression in Social Work Practice: Working with Gay, Lesbian, Bisexual, and Transgender People.* New York: Columbia University Press.

Moutakas, C.,1994. *Phenomenological Research Methods.* Thousand Oaks, CA: Sage Publication.

Myers, D.,2008. *A Friendly Letter to Skeptics and Atheists: Musing on Why God is Good and Faith Isn't Evil.* San Francisco: Jossey-Bass.

Myers, D., and Scanzoni, L.2005. *What God has Joined Together? A Christian Case for Gay Marriage.* San Francisco: Harper Collins Publishers.

National Association of Social Work. (2008). *Code of Ethics.* Retrieved May 1, 2008, from www.socialworkers.org/pubs/code/default.asp.

National LGBTQ Task Force. 2014, October 7. *Poverty in the LGBTQ community.* Retrieved on 3 May 2015 [online] www.thetaskforce.org.

Nelson, J. 1978. *Embodiment: An Approach to Sexuality and Christian Theology.* Minneapolis: Augsburg Publishing House.

Nelson, J., and Longfellow, S.,1994. *Sexuality and the Sources for Theological Reflection.* Louisville, KY: Westminster John Knox Press.

Nicely, E.,2001. "Internalized Homophobia, Stages and Processes of Change and Alcohol Use Among Gay Men. *Unpublished doctoral dissertation.* Alameda, CA: The California School of Professional Psychology.

Nouwen, H. J. M.1979. *The Wounded Healer: Ministry in Contemporary Society.* New York, NY: Bantam Doubleday Dell Publishing Group Inc.

O'Connor, P.,2002. *Oppression and Responsibility: A Wittgensteinian Approach to Social Practices and Moral Theory.* University Park, PA: The Pennsylvania State University Press.

Olson, L., and Cadge, W.,2002. "Talking About Homosexuality: The Views of Mainline Protestant Clergy. *"Journal for the Scientific Study of Religion, 41*(1), 153–167.

Ostling, R. 1989, November "The Battle over Gay Clergy." *Time.* Retrieved February 11, 2008, from www.time.com/time/printout.

Owens, S.,2009, May 1). *The Homosexual Identity was Created by Those who Fight against Them: The Irony.* Retrieved May 1, 2009, from Bloggasm: www.bloggasm.com/the-homosexual-identity-was-created-by-those-who-fight-against-them-the-irony.

Parks, S.,1986. *The Critical Years: Young Adults and the Search for Meaning, Faith, and Commitment* (1ˢᵗ ed.). San Francisco, CA: Harper.

Parks, S.,2000. *Big Questions, Worthy Dreams.* San Francisco, CA: Harper.

Pattison, S.,2000. *Some Straw for the Bricks: A Basic Introduction toTtheological Reflection.* (J. Woodward, and S. Pattison, Eds.) Malden, MA: Blackwell Publishing.

Patton, M.,1990.. *Qualitative Evaluation and Research Methods.* Newbury Park, CA: Sage Publications.

Pelinger, C.,1992. *Episcopal Women: Gender, Spirituality, and Commitment in an American Mainline Denomination (Religion in America).* New York: Oxford University Press.

Piaget, J.,1969. *Psychology of the Child.* New York: Basic Books.

Piaget, J.,1970. Piaget's Theory. In P. M. (Ed.), *Carmichael's Handbook of Child Development* (pp. 703–732). New York: Wiley.

Piaget, J.,2000. *Psychology of the Child.* New York: Basic Books.

Plante, T., n.d.. *Ethical Considerations for Psychologists Xcreening Applicants for the Priesthood in the Catholic Church: Implications of the Vatican Instruction on Homosexuality.*

Polikoff, N.,2008. *Beyond Straight and Gay Marriage: Valuing ALL Families under the Law.* Boston, MA: Beacon Press.

Presbyterian Church in the USA,2008. *Book of Order* [retrieved on line 8 June 2008]www.pcusa.org.

Presbyterian Church in the USA,2009. *Preparation for Ministry Questions Asked Frequently by Presbytery Committees on Preparation for Ministry.* Retrieved October 15, 2009, from www.pcusa.org.

Pruess, R.,1993. *Luther: Word, Doctrine, and Confession.* Retrieved October 2, 2009, from www.confessionallutherans.org/papers/drpreus.html.

Quackenbush, A.,2008. *Spiritual Identity.* Retrieved April 20, 2008, from Regina Unitarian Fellowship: www.nonprofits.accesscomm.ca/umitarian/Talk_Identity.html.

Radin, C., 2005) *Debate Over Gay Clergy is Testing Many Faiths: Vatican Expected to Announce Ban.* Retrieved February 10, 2008, from www.boston.com/new/local/articles/2005.

Raider-Roth, M.,2002. *Trusting Knowledge: Examining the Relational Complexities of Student Self-Assessment and Work.* Paper presented at the American Education Association (2002 AERA Conference) in New Orleans, Louisiana.

Ramirez, J., 2005. Reformed Church Finds Minister Broke Rules by Officiating at Gay Marriage." *New York Times.* Retrieved June 18, 2005, from www.nytimes.com.

The Refiner's Fire. *Advice For 'Gay' Clergy and Advocate of 'Gay Rights': You're Not Biblical.*,2007. Retrieved July 9, 2007, from www.therefinersfire.org/gay_agenda.html.

Reformed Church in America, 1978. *The Acts & Proceedings of the 172nd Regular Session of the General Synod. LVIII.* Grand Rapids, MI: Reformed Church Press.

Reformed Church in America., 2005.. *The Acts and Proceedings of the 199th Regular Session of the General Synod.* Grand Rapids, MI: Reformed Church Press.

Reformed Church in America., 2007. *Dialogue on Homosexuality Offers Online Survey.* Retrieved July 9, 2007, from www.rca.org/netcommunity/page.

Reformed Church in America.,2007) *Homosexuality: Seeking the Guidance of the Church.* Retrieved July 9, 2007, from www.rca.org/netcommunity/page.

Reformed Church in America., 2007. *John Stapert Named Coordinator for Dialogue on Homosexuality.* Retrieved July 9, 2007, from www.rca.org/netcommunity/page.

Reformed Church in America., 2007. *Proposal to GSC: Dialogue on Homosexuality.* Retrieved July 9, 2007, from www.rca.org/netcommunity/page.

Reformed Church in America, 2007. *Steering Committee Formed for Dialogue on Homosexuality.* Retrieved July 9, 2007, from www.rca.org/netcommunity/page.

Reformed Church in America., 2007. *Summaries of General Synod Discussion and Actions on Homosexuality and the Rights of Homosexuals.* Retrieved July 9, 2007, from www.rca.org/netcommunity/page.

Reformed Church in America., 2007) *The Acts & Proceedings of the 201ˢᵗ Regular Session of the General Synod. LXXXVII.* Grand Rapids, MI: Reformed Church Press.

Reformed Church in America., 2009,. *Book of Church Order.* New York: Reformed Church Press.

Reissman, C., 1993. *Narrative Analysis.* Newbury Park, CA: Sage Publications.

Religion News Writers., 2006. *Gay Clergy: the State of the Debate.* Retrieved February 11, 2008, from www.religionlink.org/tip_060605.

Robinson, J.,2003. "Support of Gay Clergy Growing Slowly Surely in Gallup." *Gallup.* Retrieved from www.gallup-viewofgay20clergy.webarchive.

Rogers, J., 2003.. *Jesus, the Bible, and Homosexuality: Explode the Myths, Heal the Church.* Louisville, KY: Westminster John Knox Press.

Roste, V., 2008. *Ten Reasons Why the ELCA Should Accept LGBTQ Clergy: Or All Mainline Protestants, or All Christendom, For That Matter.* Retrieved February 11, 2008, from Christian Gays: http://christiangays.com/articles/roste.shtml.

Saleeby, D., 1994. "Culture, Theory, and Narrative: The Intersection of Meanings in Practice." *Social Work, 39*(4), 296–305.

Scanzoni, L., and Mollenkott, C.,1994. *Is the Homosexual my Neighbor: A Positive Christian Response* (Revised ed.). San Francisco, CA: Harper & Row.

Schaefer, M.,2009. *The Latest: Atlanta Pastor at Center of Lutheran Debate on Gay Clergy.* Retrieved November 3, 2009, from www.sovo.com/thelatest/thelatest.cfm.

Schafer, M.,2009. "Lutherans to Allow Clergy in Same-Sex Relationships." *Southern Voice.*

Schmidt., 1994. *Reimagining Denominationalism: Interpretive Essays (Religion in America).* (R. Mullin, and R. Richey, Eds.) New York: Oxford University Press.

Schoenber, N.,2007, February 13). "Hull House Museum Poses the Question: 'Was Jane Addams a Lesbian'?" *Chicago Tribune.*

Scroggs, R., 1983. *The New Testament and Homosexuality.* Philadelphia: Fortress Press.

Seidman, I., 2006. *Interviewing as Qualitative Research: A Guide for Researchers in Education and the Social Services* (3rd ed.). New York: Teachers College Press.

Sidanus, J., and Pratto, F.,1999. *Social Dominance: An Intergroup Theory of Social Hierarchy and Oppression.* New York: Cambridge University Press.

Simonette, M. 2008, "Community Discussed 'Recovery' of Jane Addams as Lesbian." *Chicago Free Press.* May 14.

Spears, R., Jetten, J., and Doosje, B.,2001. "The Illegimitacy of Ingroup Bias: From Social Reality to Social Resistance." In J. Jost, and B. Major, *The Psychology of Legitimacy: Emerging Perspective on Ideology, Justice, and Intergroup Relations.* New York, Cambridge University Press.

Spindt, J. Bishop, M. Div.,2009. *E-mail Correspondence Regarding the Evangelical Lutheran Church in America Clergy Formation Pprocess.* November 24.

Spranca, M., Minsk, E., and Baron, J., 2003. "Omission and Commission in Judgment and Choice." *National Institutes of Health.*

Stapert, J., 2008. *Three-and-a-half-hour interview about his views of what drives the homosexual debates in North American Protestant mainline churches. Conducted in Albany.* (P. Pater-Ennis, Interviewer.)

Streib, H., 2001. "Faith Development Theory Revisited: The Religious Styles Perspective." *The International Journal for the Psychology of Religion, 11,* 143–158.

Streib, H., Hood, R., Keller, B., Csoff, R., and Silver, C., 2009. *Deconversion: Qualitative and Quantitative Results from Cross-Cultural Research in Germany and the United States of America.* Gottingen, Germany: TVandehoeck & Ruprecht.

Sumida, K.,2011, September 22. *Telephone and e-mail conversation with University at Albany Institutional Review Board regarding ethical sampling methods.*

SUMMA THEOLOGICA, n.d.. *The Natural Law (Prima Secundae Partis, Q. 94).* Retrieved April 18, 2012, from www.newadvent.org.

Tajfel, H.,1981. *Human Groups and Social Categories.* Cambridge: Cambridge University Press.

Tajfel, H., and Turner, J.,1979. *Differentiation between Social Groups: Studies in the Psychology of Intergroup Relations.* New York: Published in cooperation with European Association of Experimental Social Psychology by Academic Press.

Tajfel, H., and Turner, J.,1986. "The Social Identity Theory of Intergroup Behavior. In S. Worchel, and W. Austin, *The Psychology of Intergroup Relations* (pp. 7–24). Chicago, IL: Nelson-Hall.

Tannahill, R.,1980. *Sex in History.* New York: Stein and Day Publishers.

Tappan, M.,2001. "Interpretive Psychology: Stories, Circles, and Understanding Lived Experience." In D. Tolman, and M. Brydon-Miller, *From Subjects to Subjectivities: A Handbook of Interpretive and Participatory Methods* (pp. 45–56). New York: New York University Press.

Taylor, J., Gilligan, C., and Sullivan, A.,1995. *Between Voice and Silence: Women and Girls, Race and Relationship.* Cambridge, MA: Harvard University Press.

Thumma, S.,2001. "Echoes of Sexual Objectification: Listening For One Girl's Erotic Voice." In D. Tolman, and M. Brydon-Miller, *From Subjects to Subjectivities: A Handbook of Interpretive and Participatory Methods* (pp. 130–145). New York: New York University Press.

Tolerance, O. C.,2007. "Homosexuality and Religion: An Introduction." Retrieved from *Religious Tolerance*: www.religioustolerance.org/hom_church1.html.

Tomlinson, R.,2009, November 24). *One-and-a-half-hour interview about his views of the issue of homosexual ordination in the Presbyterian Church, U.S.A.* Conducted in Hackensack, NJ. P. Pater-Ennis, Interviewer, November 24.

Toulouse, M.,2000. "Muddling through: The Church and Sexuality/Homosexuality." In D. Balch (Ed.), *Homosexuality, Science, and the 'Plain Sense' of Scripture.* Grand Rapids: Eerdmans.

Trinder, L.,2000. "Reading the Texts: Postmodern Feminism and the 'Doing of Research'." In B. Fawcett, B. Featherstone, J. Fook, and A. Rossiter (Eds.), *Practice and Research in Social Work* (pp. 39–61). New York: Routledge.

Troiden, R.R., 1989. "The Formation of Homosexual Identities." *Journal of Homosexuality. 12*(1–2): 43–73.

Tucker, S.,1998. "The Secular Sanctuary? Bishops, Gay Clergy and Counselors: A Preliminary Survey of the Issues." *Psychodynamic Counseling, 4*(4), 505–521.

Turner, J., and Brown, R., 1978. "Social Status, Cognitive Alternatives, and Intergroup Relations." In H. Tajfel (Ed.), *Differentiation between Social Groups* (pp. 201–234). London: Academic Press.

United Church of Christ, 2005. *Constitution and By-Laws of the United Church of Christ.* Retrieved October 15, 2009, from www.ucc.org.

United Church of Christ, 2009. *LBGT Ministries: Whoever YouAare, Where Eever You Are on Life's Journey, You Are Welcome Here!* Retrieved December 8, 2009, from United Church of Christ: www.ucc.org.

Utah Pride Organization, 2009. *Coming Out: A Journey.* Retrieved June 24, 2009, from www.Utahpridecenter.org.

Van Maanen, J., 1979. "The Fact of Fiction in Organization Ethnography." In J. V. Maanen (Ed.), *Qualitative Methodology.* Newbury Park, CA: Sage Publication.

Van Manen, M., 1990. *Researching Lived Experience: Human Science for an Action Sensitive Pedagogy.* Albany, NY: State of New York Press.

Via, D., 1990. *Self-Deception and Wholeness in Paul and Matthew.* Minneapolis: Fortress Press.

Via, D., and Gagnon, R., 2003. *Homosexuality and the Bible: Two Views.* Minneapolis, MN: Fortress Press.

Wellman, J., 1999." Introduction: The Debate Over Homosexual Ordination: Subcultural Identity Theory in American Religious Organizations." *Review of Religious Research, 41,* 184–206.

Werner, E. and Smith, R., 1982. *Vulnerable but Invincible: A Longitudinal Study of Resilient Children and Youth.* New York: Adams, Bannister, and Cox.

Werner, E. and Smith, R.,1989. *Vulnerable but Invincible: A Longitudinal Study of Resilient Children and Youth.* New York: Adams, Bannister, and Cox.

Werner, E. and Smith, R.,1992. *Overcoming the Odds: High-Risk Children from Birth to Adulthood.* New York: Cornell University Press.

Whitehead, A., 2011. "Religious Organizations and Homosexuality: The Acceptance of Gays and Lesbians in American Congregations." *Review of Religious Research, 2013:55,* 297–317.

Williams, R.,1997. *Cultural Wars in American Politics: Critical Review of a Popular Myth.* (R. Williams, Ed.) New York: Aldine de Gruyter.

Woodcock, C.,2005. "The Silenced Voice in Literacy: Listening Beyond Words to a 'Struggling' Adolescent Girl." *Journal of Authentic Learning, 2*(1), 47–60.

Wright, J.,2004. *The Inherent Dignity and Worth of All People.* Retrieved April 20, 2010, from www.sksm.edu/research/papers/inherentworth.pdf.

Young, M.,2007. *Christianity, Homosexuality, and the E.L.C.A.* Retrieved July 9, 2007, from www.mjyoung.net/bible/homo.html.

Zeira, A., and Rosen, A.,2000. "Unraveling Tacit Knowledge of What Workers Do and Why They Do It." *Social Service Review, 74,* 103–123.

Zikmund, B.,2003. *UCC Celebrates an Anniversary: 150 Years of Women Clergy.* Retrieved from http://www.ucc.org/ucnews/sep03/ucc-celebrates-an.html.

Zikmund, B., and Lummis, A. C. (1994). *Female Clergy in the United States.* Retrieved from Hartford Institute for Religious Research: http://hirr.hartsem.edu/research.

APPENDICES

APPENDIX 1:
LEARNING OBJECTIVES AND METHODS MATRIX (ADAPTED FROM LE COMPTE AND PREISSLE 1993 IN MAXWELL 2005, 100–101)

What do I need to know?	Why do I need to know this?	What kind of data will answer the questions?	Where can I find the data?	Whom do I contact for access?
What are the lived experiences of the lesbian PMC clergy?	For the purpose of designing support groups for lesbian PMC clergy and training materials for educating/ promoting inclusivity among denominational members.	Interview probes, based on phenomenological principles with detailed descriptions of their personal histories and their professional experiences.	Through the listening guide analysis of the three interviews.	Several lesbian clergy in the PMC, who are known to the principal investigator, who in turn will provide names of other potential research participants to interview.

How do the lesbian PMC clergy perceive themselves regarding their religious identities?	To understand the lesbian PMC clergy religious journey.	Interview probes, based on social identity theory, as applied to religious identity formation.	Through open coding, the religious identities of the participants will emerge in the data.	Several lesbian clergy in the PMC, who are known to the principal investigator, who in turn will provide names of other potential research participants to interview.
How do the lesbian PMC clergy perceive themselves regarding their spiritual identities?	To understand the lesbian PMC clergy spiritual journey.	Interview probes, based on social identity theory, as applied to spiritual identity formation.	Through open coding, the spiritual identities of the participants will emerge in the data.	Several lesbian clergy in the PMC, who are known to the principal investigator, who in turn will provide names of other potential research participants to interview.
How do the lesbian PMC clergy perceive themselves regarding their sexual identities?	To understand the lesbian PMC clergy sexual journey.	Interview probes, based on social identity theory, as applied to homosexual identity formation.	Through open coding, the religious identities of the participants will emerge in the data.	Several lesbian clergy in the PMC, who are known to the principal investigator, who in turn will provide names of other potential research participants to interview.

Whether and how the lesbian PMC clergy fit into their families.	To more fully understand the experiences of family in the past and present.	Interview probes based on ecological theory that explores the participants' sense of fit into their families.	Through the open coding of the listening guide, the participants' fit in their families will emerge.	Several lesbian clergy in the, PMC, who are known to the principal investigator, who in turn will provide names of other potential research participants to interview.
Whether and how the lesbian PMC clergy fit into in their communities.	To more fully understand the experiences of community in the past and present.	Interview probes based on ecological theory that explores the participants' sense of fit into their communities.	Through the open coding of the listening guide, the participants' fit in their communities will emerge.	Several lesbian clergy in the PMC, who are known to the principal investigator, who in turn will provide names of other potential research participants to interview.
Whether and how the lesbian PMC clergy fit into their denominations.	To more fully understand the experiences of living / not living within their denominations in the past and present.	Interview probes based on ecological theory (and critical conversation method) that explores the participants' sense of fit into their denominations.	Through the open coding of the listening guide, the participants' fit in their denominations will emerge.	Several lesbian clergy in the PMC, who are known to the principal investigator, who in turn will provide names of other potential research participants to interview.

What are the meanings that the lesbian PMC clergy attach to their personal histories?	To provide a reflective and possibly transformative event for the women to reflect on their experiences of family, community, and history at the conclusion of the interview process.	Interview probes designed with phenomenological method in mind.	Through the open coding of the listening guide, the meanings of their personal histories will emerge.	Several lesbian clergy in the, PMC, who are known to the principal investigator, who in turn will provide names of other potential research participants to interview.

APPENDIX 2:
A CHRONOLOGY OF
THE "HOMOSEXUAL
ORIENTATION" CONSTRUCT

Author/Thinker	Date
Plato in his *Symposium* identifies three sexual orientations: gay, lesbian, heterosexual (Gagnon 2001, 385).	385 BC / Greece
Aristotle distinguishes from the "effeminate" who desire penetration by other males and those who by "habit" prefer male penetration due to molestation as children (Gagnon 2001, 384).	181 BC / Greece
Philostratus complained that a youth who failed to respond to his advances was "opposing the commands of nature" (Gagnon 2001, 385).	Third century CE / Roman
Jerome coined the term "sodoman."	Fifth century CE / Roman province of Dalmatia
Parliament passed the Buggery Act.	1533/England
Sodomy laws	Seventeenth and eighteenth centuries / New England colonies in North America
King uses the term "lesbian loves" in toast.	1732/England
Numa Mumantius (pen name for Ulrichs, who wrote about "urnings") (www.gayhistory.com 2008)	Prior to 1868 / Germany
Ulrichs wrote openly about "urnings" for female souls in a male body (www.gayshistory.com 2008)	1868/Germany
Kertbeny uses the term "homosexual" in Germany.	1869/Hungary
Westphal used the terms "effeminate male and masculine female" as contrary sexual sensations.	1869/Germany

Tamassia—"inversion of sexual instinct"	1878/Italy
Charcot—"inversion of genital sense"	1882/France
Von Krafft-Ebing—"homosexuality" popularized in Psychopathai Sexualis.	1886/Germany
Ellis—"homosexuality" is a congenital variation of sexuality and not a disease	1897/England
Hirschfeld lobbied for decriminalization of homosexual acts.	19897/Germany
Freud developed concept of "invert" (www.gayhistory.com 2009). His concepts of homosexuality as "perversion" contributed to the mental illness criteria in the psychoanalytic community around the world.	1905/Austria
Freud developed four developmental theories of homosexuality.	1930s/Austria
Kinsey talked about two types of homosexuality: homosexual "perversion" and homosexual "inversion."	1948 / United States
American Psychiatric Association-DSM I included category of "homosexuality" as a category mental illness—sociopathic personality disturbance.	1952 / United States
Anglican clergy using term "homophile" to avoid clinical implications of sexual pathology.	1950s–1960s / England and United States
RCA/PCUSA theologians inserted "homosexual perversion" into the (1562) Heidelberg Catechism, Question 87 (Rogers 2006, 115).	1962 / United States
Bieber—Homosexuality: A Psychoanalytic Study on Male Homosexuality	1962 / United States
American Psychiatric Association- DSM II removed "homosexuality" as a category of mental illness—"sexual orientation disturbance" for those in conflict with sexual orientation within themselves.	1973 / United States
Lief and Kaplan publish article of treating "ego-dystonic homosexuality."	1986 / United States
American Psychiatric Association- DSM III-R—"ego-dystonic homosexuality" removed	1987 / United States
American Psychiatric Association- DSM IV—"Sexual Disorder NOS" remains (critics view this as another way of maintaining the "ego-dystonic homosexuality" category (Via 2003).	1994 / United States
Antigay groups of Christian churches—"homogenital"	Late twentieth century / United States

APPENDIX 3:
ON BECOMING A REFLECTIVE
PRACTITIONER

From an academic stance, I approach this research with an attempt to integrate my two disciplines: professional ministry and clinical social work. From a social work point of view, to ignore the issue of lesbian clergy would be to dismiss the social justice principle of the social work profession. From a ministerial point of view, to ignore the issue of homosexual clergy would be to ignore the pastoral care of these clergy, as well as the gay and lesbian laity of the churches and the homosexuals in society who feel that they do not have a place in the church. To ignore this issue of homosexual clergy being labeled as "sinners" by their denominations would be to ignore my prophetic call to be a change agent with the Protestant mainline denominations.

As a clergy / social worker practitioner, I have had a practice for almost twenty years with gays and lesbians, most of who have perceived that the church has rejected them but who are seeking significant spiritual connections at the same time. Thus, it follows that I have found gay and lesbian persons to be some of the most profoundly spiritual and committed clergy that I have known. Yet these same individuals have often been denied ordination and a place for ministry within their denominations.

During these same years, I have garnered tacit (Zeira and Rosen 2000) knowledge around the facets of the homosexual clergy issue. I have worked extensively with homosexuals and in understanding the pain that comes from individuals in churches interpreting the Bible to be against their lifestyles and therefore functioned to exclude them from life in a church community. I have dialogued with congregations that are honestly exploring the issue of homosexuality through theological, psychological, and biblical lenses. I have struggled with colleagues within my own denomination who have been denied ordination because of their outed lifestyle. My husband and I have been vehemently criticized for having what we felt what was a prophetic voice in promoting the inclusivity of gays and lesbians in local congregations. I suppose I empathize with my homosexual brothers and sisters, as I too fought to gain credibility and acceptance as an ordained woman in the Reformed Church in America. Women were finally allowed to become ordained in 1979 (RCA 1979). Finally, I have the least practice wisdom (Klein and Bloom 1995) in understanding the psychosocial contexts that have operated to maintain denominational structures against this homosexual lifestyle.

The Judeo-Christian value of social justice (Micah 6:8; Luke 4:16–20) is reflected in the NASW Code of Ethics (1996), which states that social justice is a fundamental ethical principal. From a clergy perspective, studying the issues surrounding homosexual clergy reminds me that all humans have a capacity to judge others, particularly when they feel religiously righteous, such as the Pharisees did (Abbott 2004), who were critical of Jesus because of his prophetic stances. From a social work perspective, studying the issues around lesbian clergy relates to the profession's core value of human dignity and the perspective that each individual whom we encounter has strengths (Saleeby 1996).

From both clergy and social work perspectives, I have come to see that interviewing the female clergy research participants may be at once a healing and a liberating intervention for them. The intervention may be healing in being able to synthesize various split-off parts of their lives and in processing the internal and external rejections that they may have experienced. This intervention may be liberating for some in being able to make decisions to move toward or away from their denominations, which hold their ordinations. In the process of interviewing the female clergy, I will utilize my insider (Kirk and Miller 1986; Van Maanan 1979) clergy knowledge to interview them. Finally, I will utilize my social work skills to transform my clinical interviewing skills into researcher interviewing skills, to gain access to the life stories and lived experiences (Van Manen 1990) of the lesbian clergy research participants.

APPENDIX 4:
RESEARCH PROBES /
DATA COLLECTION
PHASES I-III

Interview One: Personal Storying

Tell me about your childhood and your adolescence. Was there anything that you remember as being remarkable about them? Do you remember experiencing any type of oppression?

Tell me about your spiritual/religious development, embedded in your life cycle.

Tell me about dating and meeting your spouse. Your partner?

Would you please describe your current relationship with your spouse/partner?

Tell me about the significant areas of your personal history that you believe led to your call as a minister.

Would you please describe your religious identity then and now?

Would you please describe your spiritual identity then and now?

Tell me about your experience of call to ministry. What was your experience in seminary? Tell me about your experience of being ordained.

Tell me about your ministry. What areas of ministry have been difficult and what areas have been meaningful? Have you experienced oppression as a minister?

Would you mind telling me about your early sexual history?

When did you have your first lesbian experience? What events led up to your first sexual relationship?

Have you taken on a lesbian or bisexual identity? Were you out at the time of your ordination? Are you out to your congregation, to the denomination?

Do you have a sense of the order that your identities developed (i.e., your religious, spiritual, and sexual identities)? And in what order did they become apparent to you?

Interview Two: Denominational Storying

As a clergyperson, how do you perceive your ministry experiences?

What have your roles in the professional ministry been? What type of ministry have you done? What offices have you held?

Would you be willing to describe the dynamics and details of your relationships with your ministerial colleagues, your place of ministry, and your denomination?

Would you please describe the fit between you and your place of ministry?

Would you please tell me about outing yourself to your congregation? Would you please tell me about outing yourself to your denomination?

How have you experienced oppression, if any, as a minister?

What are the biblical perspectives on homosexuality? What are your biblical perspectives on homosexual clergy?

What are your theological perspectives on homosexuality?

How would you describe your relationship with your denomination? For instance, is it one of acceptance in regard to its stances on homosexuality? Is it one of accommodation in regard to your role within the denomination? Or is it one of rejection, in terms of your relationship with your denomination?

Interview Three: Lived Experience as a Lesbian Minister

What has been your lived experience of being a lesbian minister your denomination?

How does your personal experience/story fit with the denomination's story? Does your personal experience/story not fit with the denomination's story? Tell me about your experience of either fitting or not fitting.

Currently, describe your various relationships. With your spouse/partner? With your family? With your denomination? With friends?

What are the ameliorating factors that keep you in the denomination? The factor that may push you from the denomination?

How has acknowledging your homosexuality impacted your ministry? How has acknowledging your homosexuality impacted your interpersonal relationships? How has acknowledging your homosexuality impacted your sexual relationships?

What is the relationship between your religious, spiritual, and sexual identities? Is there a certain logic model to these identities for you?

What is your current stance with your denomination's theological stance on homosexuality? Has it changed in any way since you have been in ministry?

What oppression stories, if any, impacted your faith journey?

What do you think your future ministry will look like?

Do you have any other reflections that we have not covered in either this third interview or the prior two interviews?

APPENDIX 5:
DATA ANALYSIS TEMPLATE

Phase 1: Use listening guide to analyze the data that relate to learning objectives 1, 2, and 3.

Learning objective 1: Explore the lived experiences of the PMC (utilizing all four stages of listening guide).

Learning objective 2: Explore the experience of fit in denominations for the lesbian PMC (utilizing all four stages of listening guide).

Learning objective 3: Explore the meaning that the lesbian PMC attach to their personal histories (utilizing all four stages of listening guide).

The three interviews will be synthesized into a life story/plot for each of the research participants in the first stage.

A worksheet of the trail of evidence of the research participant's voice and silence, as well as evidence of the primary investigator's voice and the relationship between the two.

Listen for the narrator voice of the research participant.

The first-person voice of each research participant will be made into a transcript, showing how she is speaking for herself in the second stage.

During the third stage, the alternate and additional voices of each research participant will be made in hand-coded color, providing evidence of contrapuntal voices between psychological health and psychological distress.

Possible internalized voices may come from those of the following:

- Bible
- denomination
- family
- partner
- congregation

The third stage will possibly provide evidence of psychological health.

Possible resiliency to disconnection from one's self and a feminist identity.

The third stage will possibly provide evidence of psychological distress or loss.

Possible dissociation or separation of one's self from their lived experiences.

Write an investigator response to each participant, based on her emotional responses and bracketed material.

Phase 2: Use of open coding for evidence of a religious, sexual, and spiritual identities that relate to learning objective 4.

Research objective 4: Explore the perception of the research participant's religious, sexual, and spiritual identities (important to understanding the ministerial formation of the research participants).

Evidence of religious identity of each research participant.

Evidence of sexual identity of each research participant.

Evidence of spiritual identity of each research participant.

Phase 3: An interpretive case summary of each research participant, synthesizing all of her data.

Phase 4: A synthesized analysis that compares the data from each of the participants.

Aims of the Study:	Do I Qualify?	The Research Question:
(1) To explore the lived experiences of the sample of lesbian RCA clergy;	• If you identify as a lesbian	*How do the lived experiences of lesbian Reformed Church in America (RCA) clergy impact upon their religious, spiritual, and sexual identities?*
(2) to explore whether and how the sampled lesbian RCA clergy have experienced "fit" in their families, in their communities, and in their denominations;	• If you are currently in Seminary or a Seminary graduate	
(3) to understand the meanings that the sampled lesbian clergy attach to their personal histories; and	• If you hold a RCA, ELCA, UCC, PCUSA ordination and/or have an active ministry in the RCA, ELCA, UCC, PCUSA	Contact: Pamela Pater-Ennis at 201-962-6443 (cell) or clergyresearch@ yahoo.com
(4) to understand how the lesbian clergy perceive themselves regarding each of the domains of their religious, spiritual, and sexual identities.	• If you are willing to consent to being digitally recorded in a three (3) 90 minute interviews over a period of two to three days	

315

9 781489 726018